W9-CND-458

Ronald Reagan
THE POLITICS OF
SYMBOLISM

Robert Dallek

Harvard University Press
Cambridge, Massachusetts
London, England   1984

This book is printed on acid-free paper, and its binding materials have been chosen
for strength and durability.

Library of Congress Cataloging in Publication Data

Dallek, Robert.
  Ronald Reagan, the politics of symbolism.

  Includes index.
  1. Reagan, Ronald. 2. United States—Politics and
government—1981–   . I. Title.
E877.D34 1984   973.927′092′4   83-18351
ISBN 0-674-77940-1

Quotations from *Where's the Rest of Me,* by Ronald Reagan and Richard G. Hubler,
copyright © 1965 by Ronald Reagan and Richard G. Hubler, are reprinted by permission of E. P. Dutton, Inc., and of Sidgwick and Jackson, Ltd., London. Quotations from *Reagan,* by Lou Cannon, copyright © 1982 by Lou Cannon, are
reprinted by permission of G. P. Putnam's Sons.

For Geri, who honors the tradition
of "a government that lives
in a spirit of charity"

Preface

The historian working on a contemporary subject is bound to be met with raised eyebrows. Early in 1982, when I told a group of scholars that I was writing a book on Ronald Reagan, one of them exclaimed, "But it's too soon!" "Oh no," another replied, "it's too late!" I hope it is neither too soon nor too late. In the third year of Reagan's term we have sufficient evidence to begin explaining and evaluating the man and his administration. Even though we do not yet have access to private documents, the richness of the present public record allows us to describe the broad range of forces shaping Reagan and Reaganism. And with Reagan apparently running for a second term, it is not too late to do so. This assessment of the man and his presidency forms a contribution to the national dialogue on whether the electorate wants to extend his stay in the White House. Even if he were not running, a book of this kind would still be in order: Reaganism is not merely an aberration that will disappear with the end of the Reagan presidency, it is an important force in the nation's life that cries out for explanation. Reaganism in one form or another will persist for years to come, and it seems essential for Americans to begin thinking about what the Reagan experience means.

In some respects the meaning is already clear: Reaganism is a return to old-fashioned Republicanism—large tax cuts for the rich, less government help for the poor, weaker enforcement of civil rights, fewer controls on industry, less protection for the environment, and emotional rhetoric on the virtues of hard work, family, religion, individualism, and patriotism. Although Reagan has tried to blunt the "fairness" issue, as it is being called, by public declarations of concern for the needy, minorities, and women, and by avowing his commitment to a more just society, better public education, and a cleaner, safer environment, many Americans are not persuaded. The record of his administration on each of these issues is at odds with his rhetoric. The same holds true for foreign affairs; despite Reagan's continual talk of arms control and better international relations, his presidency has witnessed an unprecedented peacetime buildup of American military power, increased Soviet-American tensions, worsened relations with China, and little or no progress toward peace and stability in the Middle East and Latin America.

If Reaganism is partly an exercise in traditional interest politics, it is also a way of looking at the world, an ideology expressing strong feelings about how Americans should order their lives. To understand Reaganism we must not only look at Reagan's substantive impact on domestic and foreign affairs but also explore why Reaganites think and act as they do. Why is Ronald Reagan, a man whose life and career have been shaped principally by the values of the modern consumer culture, so devoted to old shibboleths about freedom, self-reliance, and frugality? Why do Reaganites, most of whom have enjoyed some of the benefits of government largesse, stand so opposed to a major role for government in economic and social affairs? Why are Reaganites so evangelistic about building up American military power? Why do they overstate the Soviet threat, seeing Soviet communism behind every difficulty abroad?

In my view some of the most significant forces influencing the Reagan movement are nonrational. While Reaganites may be seen in part as practitioners of traditional politics, pragmatists of the right operating out of rational self-interest, they should also be viewed as caught up in symbolic politics: their public goals satisfy psychological needs as much as material ends. Stated another way, Reagan's policies are less a response to actual problems at home and abroad than a means of restoring traditional values to the center of American life and boosting the self-esteem of Reaganites. Supply-side economics and anti-Sovietism are not so much substantive devices for overcoming domestic and foreign difficulties as ways of reasserting the importance of conservative beliefs and making Reaganites feel that they are once more in control of national affairs.

These nonrational impulses have received less attention from commentators than the more rational, self-serving ones. But the former deserve as much consideration as the latter, and this book is partly an attempt to right the balance. An administration led by a president who sees the world mainly as a contest between good and evil, with a former secretary of the interior who claims to have heard the voice of God, must be discussed in other than conventional political terms. I hope the following pages will broaden and deepen our understanding of the Reagan phenomenon in American life.

A number of people have helped me in this work. Most of all, I wish to thank my wife, Geraldine Dallek, who gave me the benefit of her extensive knowledge of the impact of Reaganism on federal social programs. My colleague Richard Weiss helped improve my prose and tighten my argument. William E. Leuchtenburg, who graciously took the time to comment on several chapters, raised some important questions and forced me to rethink some of my conclusions. My colleague Peter Loewenberg provided valuable insights into Reagan's personality. My friend Edward A. Goldstein, who urged me to write the book, brought to my attention a number of articles and essays and helped me understand the complex economic issues of which he has so firm a grasp. Rose Fromm-Kirsten, M.D., contributed useful comments on Reagan's personality. Aida D. Donald, executive editor of Harvard University Press, played a central role in shaping this work from start to finish. Her conviction that this is the right book at the right time was indispensable to making it a reality. Peg Anderson, an editor at the Press, made both substantive and stylistic improvements in the manuscript, for which I heartily thank her. I am indebted to David O. Levine for reading page proof. Finally, I am grateful to Timothy Seldes of Russell & Volkening for saving me valuable time by arranging the details of publication.

August 1983

Contents

Part I
THE MAKING
OF A PRESIDENT

CHAPTER ONE

Origins

FEW AMERICANS in this century have enjoyed greater popularity than Ronald Reagan. Humor, charm, good looks, an intuitive feel for national concerns, and an extraordinary ability to speak persuasively to millions of people partly explain Reagan's popularity as governor of California and president. But his attraction goes deeper: a blend of Catholic and Protestant, small-town boy and famous entertainer, Horatio Alger and P. T. Barnum, traditional moralist and modern media celebrity, Reagan speaks for old values in current accents. Like the nation, of which he is such a representative figure, he is a contradiction in terms—a hero of the consumer culture preaching the Protestant ethic.

Both facets of his personality are the products of his early years. Born in 1911 and reared in a series of small northern Illinois towns, he expresses the values of the time and place in which he grew up. "I have heard more than one psychiatrist say that we imbibe our ideals from our mother's milk," Reagan records in his autobiography, *Where's the Rest of Me?* "Then, I must say, my breast feeding was the home of the brave baby and the free bosom."

The president remembers his small-town beginnings as "one of those rare Huck Finn–Tom Sawyer idylls. There were woods and mysteries, life and death among the small creatures, hunting and fishing; those were the days when I learned the real riches of rags." Tampico, Galesburg, Monmouth, and Dixon, Illinois, with their "big green trees" and "dark red brick streets" formed "a picture of bright-colored peace" that Reagan still treasures. "There was the life that shaped my body and mind for all the years to come after," he believes. "Waiting and hoping for the winter freeze without snow so that we could go skating on the Rock River—a rink two hundred yards wide and endlessly long, as clear and smooth as glass ... Swimming and picnics in the summer, the long thoughts of spring, the pain with the coloring of the falling leaves in the autumn. It was a good life. I have never asked for anything more, then or now."[1]

Reagan's memories are not unique. Others, like the novelist and poet August Derleth and the science fiction writer Ray Bradbury, share similar recollections of small-town life in the twenties. Sac Prairie, Wisconsin, where Derleth grew up, "marked the seasons not by greeting cards displayed in store windows but by the coming and going of plants and birds: a world of farming and gossip and fishing, of men conversing in harness shops, of dam building on rain-freshened brooks, of wild crabapples and woodchucks and harvest moons." And for Ray Bradbury, Waukegan, Illinois, was "this little town deep far away from everything, kept to itself by a river and a forest and a meadow and a lake." It was "an oasis of tree-shaded streets, Victorian frame houses, and ice-cream parlors, surrounded by a green ocean of ... unpolluted prairie."[2]

This sense of traditional place went hand in hand with traditional values. From his father Reagan learned that "energy and hard work were the only ingredients needed for success." At home and in school he learned that education would give him "habits of industry" and taught him "the great ideals of our nation." Character building, pride in country, and the work ethic were the essentials of the president's early schooling. Undoubtedly, like the great majority of students questioned in a 1924 survey of a typical midwestern high school, Reagan would have agreed that "the United States is unquestionably the best country in the world" and "the white race is the best race on earth." He no doubt would also have sided with two-thirds of the students who did not think that concentrated wealth shows "there is an unjust condition in this country which ought to be changed."

Reagan's attendance at Eureka College for four years beginning in 1928 reinforced these beliefs. In the president's memory Eureka, a small-town Christian Church school located in central Illinois twenty miles from Peoria, "had a special spirit . . . that bound us all together, much as a poverty-stricken family is bound." Although "it was a small town, a small school, with small doings," it provided "pleasant thoughts of the past to balance fears of the uncertain future . . . It somehow provided the charm and enchantment which alone can make a memory of a school something to cherish. Those were the nights when we spent all of twenty cents on a date: two big cherry phosphates at the drug counter . . . and a walk home. Or when we danced in somebody's house or in the fraternity living rooms under the dimmest of lights, while the chaperones—always old Eureka grads who had met each other this way themselves—took a turn around outside or just dozed."

For Reagan, the purpose of college was not to gain an academic education; it was a vehicle for personal advancement. Reagan's older brother, Neil, thought college was "a waste of time" until he got the message from "an elderly immigrant" with whom he worked in a cement plant. The old man, who repeatedly asked Neil why he wasn't in college, said one day, " 'Look at me—ve'll always vork together, chust you and me, and zomeday you'll be chust like me—isn't that nize?' The old man never mentioned it again—he didn't have to."[3]

Reagan's attachment to old-style American virtues was not simply the product of his small-town beginnings and schooling. It was also part of a national upsurge during the 1920s of uncritical allegiance to familiar verities. Calvin Coolidge, one of Reagan's two favorite presidents in the twentieth century, was the national symbol of this mood. "Coolidge came along at a fortuitous time," the historian William E. Leuchtenburg writes, "just when the democratic creed was in need of a new version of an old symbol; he suggested the rugged honesty of the New England hills, rural virtues, clean living, religious faith, public probity." A model in some respects of what Reagan hopes to achieve as president, Coolidge worked to balance the budget and to reduce the size and role of government. "We have got so many regulatory laws already," he said, "that in general I feel that we would be just as well off if we didn't have any more." Coolidge, who perceived the country in pastoral terms, believed that "the great bulk of citizens" were "mainly responsible for keeping their houses, farms and shops in repair and maintaining them as a going concern."

Mass-circulation periodicals of the twenties reflected similar ideas. *American Magazine,* which was the most popular of these journals in a typical midwestern town in that era, regularly featured interviews with successful business leaders who offered inspirational examples of how determination and hard work could raise a man from rags to riches. George Washington Goethals, who had been born poor and who had emerged from obscurity to build the Panama Canal, counseled that "nothing is ever as hard as it seems to be." The president of the Pittsburgh Plate Glass Company, who described his hard times as a boy on a sailing ship, credited the experience with teaching him "to act on his own responsibility, to handle men, and to make advantageous business trades." "From testimonies like these," the historian Paul A. Carter concludes, "we may infer that in the twenties the spirit we usually associate with Horatio Alger was alive and well." "The only person a self-respecting man can work for," Carter quotes another 1920s businessman as saying, "is himself."[4]

It is sixty years since Coolidge served in the White House and business tycoons preached rugged individualism, but Reagan's rhetoric and ideas sound like throwbacks to that era. "I suggest to you," he declared in a typical speech in the sixties, that "there is no left or right, only an up or down. Up to the maximum of individual freedom consistent with law and order, or down to the ant heap of totalitarianism, and regardless of their humanitarian purpose, those who would sacrifice freedom for security have, whether they know it or not, chosen this downward path. Plutarch warned, 'The real destroyer of the liberties of the people is he who spreads among them bounties, donations and benefits.' " "I honestly believe it's better to create jobs by restoring the economy than to provide handouts," the president said in a meeting with black clergymen in March 1982. "Some well-meaning [government] programs robbed recipients of their dignity, trapped them into a dependency that left them with idle time, less self-respect, and little prospect of a better future."[5]

Reagan describes his own life and times as having been shaped by the traditional values he wishes to bring back for all Americans. "Reagan is like a Knight of the Age of Chivalry," Frank Van Der Linden asserts in a sympathetic biography, "scarred by many battles but holding high his sword for one more charge. He was a Lone Crusader for years as the White Knight of the Right, while he was being criticized as being far out of the mainstream of American life." Like Winston Churchill, who endured years of disdain for his views, Reagan, says Van Der Linden, has also been called to power at an advanced age to save his country.

His presidency has been a celebration of old values. Autonomy, self-help, free enterprise, individualism, liberty, hard work, production, morality, religion, and patriotism are as much the identifying symbols of Reagan's administration as the New Deal alphabet agencies were of Franklin Roosevelt's time in the White House. "Certainly, he is old-fashioned. He clings to the traditions of courtesy, civility, and gentle manners. To the total disgust of sophisticates, he embodies all twelve traits of the Boy Scout Law: He is trustworthy, loyal, helpful, friendly, courteous, kind, obedient, cheerful, thrifty, brave, clean, and reverent."[6]

Without question, Reagan's life and career have been shaped by traditional ideas about freedom, hard work, and morality. But this is only part of the story; the modern consumer culture was even more important in molding what he thought and did. He took his cue from the old Horatio Alger vision of the twenties, but his identity was also shaped by a postindustrial society where leisure and play held more appeal than work and where conformity and personal charm were more likely paths to success than personal initiative. In the twenties the country shifted from what sociologist David Riesman later called an "inner-directed" character to an "other-directed" character, and this shift was reflected in the society's new heroes. While scientists, businessmen, and statesmen, the "idols of production," were the most prominent Americans at the turn of the century, professional athletes and entertainers, the "idols of consumption," were the most admired public figures of the twenties. The newspapers of the era "began to view American life not so much as a political and economic struggle but as a hilarious merry-go-round of sport, crime, and sex." The shift was "from a Protestant ethic to a social ethic, or a fun morality; from a society based on an economics of scarcity to an affluent society."[7]

For all of Reagan's later rhetoric about the importance of traditional precepts in his early years, it was the new ethos of entertainment and pleasure that had the greatest impact on his life. Encouraged by his mother, who "gave regular readings for ladies' societies with the zest of a frustrated actress," Reagan shared the stage with her. He particularly enjoyed reading the "funny ones . . . because I sure did love to hear them laugh!" The marvelous, flickering antics of Tom Mix and William S. Hart in the Dixon Family Theatre are also prized memories of his childhood. In high school and college he took drama classes and starred in several plays, including a production at Eureka of Edna St. Vincent Millay's antiwar drama, *Aria da Capo,* presented in a one-act play contest at Northwestern University. Reagan received an award for his performance "in stunned ecstasy." Encouraged by the director of Northwestern's School of Speech to pursue an acting career, the young Reagan returned to Eureka "a little star-struck . . . For the first time, really in any adult way, I knew that I wouldn't be happy just getting a job behind a counter." In his high school senior yearbook, he described his view of life as "just one grand sweet song, so start the music."

By the time he graduated from Eureka, Reagan knew that he "wanted some form of show business" as a career. Since Broadway and Hollywood seemed "as inaccessible as outer space," he chose

radio, and sports announcing in particular. An ardent football fan
who had played the game in high school and college, he wanted
to follow the example of broadcasters Graham MacNamee, Ted
Husing, and Pat Flanagan, the "little band of pioneers" who had
become "as famous as the great teams and athletes they described." Applying first at stations in radio's "big-time center,"
Chicago, Reagan learned from a nice lady at NBC—"one of the
anonymous benefactors in my saga"—that he must start in the
sticks. At WOC in Davenport, Iowa, he got the break he sought.
Peter MacArthur, the manager of the station, a Scotsman with "a
vocabulary that could crackle and scorch," needed an announcer
for the University of Iowa football games. When Reagan mentioned that he wanted to do sports announcing, MacArthur gave
him an audition for the job. "Ye did great, ye big S.O.B.!" Mac-
Arthur exclaimed after the tryout. "Ye be here a week from Saturday and I'll give ye five dollars and bus fare."[8]

In the winter of 1932–33 a series of fateful steps, as the president remembers them, launched him on a five-year career with
WHO in Des Moines. He was available when a staff announcer
left WOC, was fired and then rehired when his replacement quit,
and was on the spot when the Des Moines station needed a sports
broadcaster. Reagan describes his success as the result of being in
the right place at the right time and of having had "the advantage
of getting into a new industry and riding it to the top." In contrast to earlier American heroes, who supposedly succeeded because of their strength of character, Reagan believes that he
gained fame through forces beyond his control. "A miracle happened," Reagan says at one point in his account of how he made
an initial advance in broadcasting, and in saying this, he places
himself squarely in the tradition of other recent celebrities, all of
whom are popularly viewed as making their way as much by good
fortune as by personal initiative. In his initial rise to stardom Reagan was the consummate example not of the self-made man but of
the "idol of consumption," with whom millions of Americans
could identify.[9]

Reagan's Hollywood career followed a similar pattern of ini-

tiative combined with lucky breaks. His success as a radio announcer encouraged his hopes of becoming an actor. When Gene
Autry hired a hillbilly band that was working at WHO to appear
in one of his western movies, Reagan dreamed of following in
their footsteps. In the spring of 1937, having persuaded the station to let him accompany the Chicago Cubs to their spring
training camp on Catalina Island off Los Angeles, he used the trip
to explore the possibility of a movie career. With the help of a former WHO singer who had had parts in pictures, Reagan made
contact with an agent named Bill Meiklejohn. When the agent
asked about his experience, Reagan decided that "a little lying in a
good cause wouldn't hurt, so the Eureka Dramatic Club became a
professional stock company," where he said he had earned twice
what he had actually been paid. The agent was impressed enough
to call Max Arnow, the casting director at Warner Brothers' studio. "Max, I have another Robert Taylor sitting in my office,"
Meiklejohn said. "I decided I didn't have a monopoly on little
white lies," Reagan recalls. "Bob at that time was the biggest sen-
sation in pictures." After a screen test a few days later, Reagan was
advised to stay around until Jack Warner could see the film. But
he replied that the next day he would be returning home on the
train with the Cubs. "I had done, through ignorance," the president later recalled, "the smartest thing it was possible to do. Hollywood just loves people who don't need Hollywood." On his
first day back in Des Moines, Meiklejohn wired an offer from
Warner's of a seven-year contract starting at $200 a week. "Sign
before they change their minds," Reagan replied. Some time later
he discovered that he had won the contract because his voice was
similar to that of a promising young actor who, on the verge of
stardom, had committed suicide. By Reagan's own account, the
combination of bluster, dumb chance, and some talent had
opened the door to Hollywood fame.[10]

Reagan forged a career as a mainstay in a series of grade B
movies. His natural, down-home quality on the screen made him
believable in any role. "That's my boy," his mother cried when
seeing him in his first film. "That's my Dutch. That's the way he

is at home. He's no Robert Taylor. He's just himself." A couple of lucky breaks, however, made him something of a star. When he got the chance to play George Gipp in the *The Knute Rockne Story,* he gained lasting notoriety as "the Gipper." Yet at the time Reagan realized that Hollywood stardom can be fleeting. After his success in the Rockne film he was assigned to replace another actor in a major role, and he reflected on the possibility "that it would be just as easy someday to throw my clothes in the corner and hang some other actor's in their place."

Reagan feels that he did not actually become a star until his performance in *King's Row* in 1941, the "finest" picture he ever made. Playing a small-town gay blade who loses both his legs after an accident, he struggled for days over how to play the scene in which the character discovers that his legs have been amputated. Fearing that he had "neither the experience nor the talent to fake it," he rehearsed the scene "before mirrors, in corners of the studio, while driving home, in the men's rooms of restaurants, before selected friends." But to no apparent avail. On the day of the shooting he was as uncertain as ever about how to play the part. Then, "in some weird way" he entered into the mood of the character and spoke the lines which made him a star. "Randy!" he screamed upon recovering consciousness from his operation. Ann Sheridan, playing Randy, rushed to his bedside. "Where's the rest of me?" he asked in a strangled voice, identifying in some vital way with the crippled character he portrayed. Reagan won acclaim for his role and a new seven-year contract worth one million dollars.

In spite of his success, Reagan was not comfortable with his acting career. "So much of our profession is taken up with pretending, with the interpretation of never-never roles, that an actor must spend at least half of his waking hours in fantasy, in rehearsal or shooting. If he is only an actor, I feel, he is much like I was in *King's Row,* only half a man—no matter how great his talents." Reagan felt that as an actor he "had become a semi-automaton 'creating' a character another had written, doing what still another person told me to do on the set." His desire was to gain the sense of space and freedom, the feeling of independence and autonomy he has celebrated throughout his life. Indeed, Reagan's present-day prescription for the nation of a return to the old habits of self-reliance, hard work, and moral constraint has a ring of personal urgency which makes one feel that he is pressing on the country what he would like to gain for himself.[11]

Yet for all Reagan's celebration of traditional American virtues, however powerful his impulse to reverse the modern currents which he sees undermining freedom and turning people into semiautomatons, he himself remains the consummate expression of the organization man, the other-directed personality who lacks genuine autonomy. John P. Sears, his former campaign manager, asserts that as governor of California, Reagan "seldom came up with an original idea, and often, like a performer waiting for a writer to feed him his lines and for a director to show him how to say them, he waited for others to advise him what to do." Reagan, a *Washington Post* columnist argues, is America's first television president, or "the first true Prop President, one whose real self is the image on the TV screen and whose shadow self is the man in the White House."[12]

Further, Reagan's advocacy of the work ethic and productive labor is little more than rhetoric. In his own life he achieved wealth and high station largely through the manipulation of an image rather than traditional productive enterprise. For all his talk of hard work and material output, he is a man of limited drive. Anecdotes abound about his small capacity for work as president. "He probably spends two or three hours a day on real work," one aide confided to a news magazine. "All he wants to do is tell stories about his movie days." "More disquieting than Reagan's performance or prospects on any specific issue," the *Washington Post* reported early in his term, "is a growing suspicion that the president has only a passing acquaintance with some of the most important decisions of his administration." The *Los Angeles Times* confirmed this picture of a detached and uninformed president during the second year of his term. Describing a bitter White House power struggle that could significantly alter his administration, the article depicted a man so removed "from the day-to-day workings of the White House . . . that he is unaware of the dimensions of the problem or of its possible consequences." One well-placed official called the infighting "a disaster, an absolute disaster, . . . out of control," with everybody having his own agenda. The president's aloofness, the *Los Angeles Times* reported on August 15, 1982, has often left him embarrassingly ignorant of the actions of his top advisers, who do not keep him fully informed of what is going on. But Reagan apparently wants it that way. He avoids press conferences because they require too much preparation, and the conferences he does hold are marred by glaring factual errors.[13]

It is a peculiar facet of Reagan's personality that a man who is so much the product of a consumer culture should be so strong a proponent of rugged individualism and other traditional values. This is an expression not of conscious hypocrisy but of genuine attachment to the small-town ethos of his childhood and, more important, of inner tensions that he himself only dimly understands. Judging from his autobiography and from what he later told Van Der Linden, in his early years he vacillated between feelings of dependence on others and longings for independence, a struggle which has played a significant part in his actions as a politician. It would be a form of reductionist nonsense to suggest that this struggle was the only major theme shaping the president's political life, but it would be as simplistic to deny that politics has been a projective arena for personal feelings that are related only marginally to the external issues.

According to Reagan's description, his parents were tied to each other partly through exaggerated bonds of dependence. This is not to deny that they had a loving marriage that gave the president and his older brother the emotional health to pursue successful and constructive lives. Nevertheless, there were other crosscurrents at work in his parents' relationship that registered on Reagan in important ways. John Edward Reagan, the president's father, orphaned at the age of three, was raised by an aunt in Fulton, Illinois. As an adult he was a rebellious, bluff, first-gen-

eration "black Irishman" with a penchant for drink. "He lived in
a time—and with a weakness—that made him a frustrated man."
He led a life of "almost permanent anger and frustration," never
earning more than fifty-five dollars a week as a shoe salesman. His
wife, Nelle Wilson Reagan, "was a natural practical do-gooder"
who devoted herself to rescuing disadvantaged people, especially
her husband, whose alcoholism made him dependent on her for
managing most of the family's affairs. "With all the tragedy that
was hers because of his occasional bouts with the dark demon in
the bottle," Reagan recalls, "she told Neil and myself over and
over that alcoholism was a sickness—that we should love and help
our father and never condemn him for something that was beyond his control." His mother "had the conviction that everyone
loved her," Reagan remembers, "just because she loved them."
"Goodwill trips" and "charitable duties," weekly visits to prison-
ers in jail or hospital patients were regular features of her life.[14]

[Reagan's childhood implanted in him powerful feelings
about dependence and independence, loss of control, and self-possession. He finds great appeal in self-reliance, and he strongly dis-
likes dependency, partly, current psychological understanding
suggests, out of unrecognized fears that he is like his father. Indeed, what is striking in the president's life is his idealization of
freedom, autonomy, and self-mastery and his antipathy toward, or
belief in the need to overcome, totalitarianism, external control,
and dependence on forces outside oneself. He has played out these
feelings in both his private and public lives.]

Many of his recollections of his early years are of rescues, vi-
gnettes in which one person saves someone else or of dependent
people in need of aid. "My mother was always finding people to
help. I can see her now with a dish, and a towel over the dish,
taking food to a family that didn't have anything to eat." At the
age of three his mother saved him from danger by "larruping"
him for crawling under a train to reach an ice wagon on the other
side of the railroad tracks. Not long after, he had to be pulled
from under an old Ford touring car which had tipped over as they
were riding. That incident left him, he believes, with a fear of

being smothered. As a boy, in wild amateur football games, he would make sure that he was not the one on the bottom of the heap. Years later, when making a war movie aboard a submarine, he felt imprisoned and claustrophobic. One Saturday night in Chicago, where he lived between the ages of five and seven, he and his brother wandered the streets in search of their parents, who had left the boys alone while they shopped. The parents found the boys just as they were being lectured by a drunk on how dangerous it was for youngsters to be out on the streets at night. Jack Reagan gave them "a good spanking to make sure they never did such a foolish thing again. My other vivid memory of Chicago," the President recalls, "was a fire. Down the street came those matched horses, pulling the fire engines, and the bells clanging. Oh, I lived for years with the desire to be a fireman!"[15]

For Reagan it was better to be the rescuer than the rescued. During World War I he remembers being taken to the railroad station to see doughboys on troop trains bound for transports sailing to France. After giving a young soldier a penny, he "often wondered who he was, and where he went, and if the penny did bring him luck." In yet another incident when he was eight years old, he remembers playing on the Monmouth College campus, where he "found [that] a nest had spilled out of a tree and young birds were scattered in the street. I gathered up the birds, put them in the nest, and shinnied up the tree and put the nest back where I thought the mother could find it." That same year he learned "a very good lesson" when, at the insistence of his mother, he confronted a bully who had been beating him up every afternoon on the way home from school. He waded in against his tormentor with a couple of punches, and the bully ran off. In Dixon, when he was ten, he loved watching silent films of cowboys "as they foiled robbers and villains and escorted the beautiful girls to safety, waving back from their horses as they cantered into the sunset."

In the most poignant of these memories, he recalled coming home one night in winter to find his father dead drunk, lying on his back on the front porch, and no one there to lend a hand but me . . . I stood over him for a minute or two. I wanted to let myself in the house and go to bed and pretend he wasn't there. Oh, I wasn't ignorant of his weakness. I don't know at what age I knew what the occasional absences or the loud voices in the night meant, but up till now my mother, Nelle, or my brother handled the situation and I was a child in bed with the privilege of pretending sleep.

But someplace along the line to each of us, I suppose, must come that first moment of accepting responsibility. If we don't accept it (and some don't), then we must just grow older without quite growing up. I felt myself fill with grief for my father at the same time I was feeling sorry for myself. Seeing his arms spread out as if he were crucified—as indeed he was—his hair soaked with melting snow, snoring as he breathed, I could feel no resentment against him.[16]

The episode must have reinforced Reagan's horror of being in a helpless condition, beholden to someone else for survival. Further, it probably encouraged him to see all human relations in extremes—one is either entirely dependent or fully free. So charged an issue as an alcoholic father who had severe difficulties controlling his impulses left Reagan little room for moderate feelings about self-possession or control over his own fate. Another anecdote about his father in his autobiography is revealing on this point. When the premiere of the Rockne film was to be shown at Notre Dame University, Reagan's mother pressed him to take his father with him to South Bend. "I felt a chilling fear that made me hesitate," Reagan writes. "We had all lived too long in fear of the black curse." An all-night escapade by his father and the actor Pat O'Brien heightened his concern. At luncheon the next day at St. Mary's College, where his father was seated next to the mother superior, Reagan had little appetite for his food. Even after the meal, when it was clear that his father had been on his best behavior, Reagan could not relax "completely." "We were still two thousand miles from home," and only on the "homeward trek" did Reagan finally feel at ease. The point is that Reagan lived in fear of his father's uncontrolled behavior and understandably places an exaggerated premium on self-mastery in his own life and in the life of the nation.

There is further evidence of his concern with self-control in a description of his experience between the ages of fifteen and twenty-two as a lifeguard each summer at Lowell Park on the Rock River. It was a fine vantage point, he believes, for learning about people. Although every one of the seventy-seven people he saved were in genuine danger of drowning, almost all of them "felt insulted . . . I got to recognize that people hate to be saved: almost every one of them later sought me out and angrily denounced me for dragging them to shore. 'I would have been fine if you'd let me alone,' was their theme. 'You made a fool out of me trying to make a hero out of yourself.' " Their response confirmed his conviction that any kind of dependency or loss of self-possession leaves people feeling angry, demoralized, and foolish. He determined early on that this would not be his fate, and as a kind of guarantee or a way to check his deep-seated fears of being as dependent as his father, he has, like his mother, devoted himself to rescuing others, both in real life and on the screen, and to idealizing self-reliance. In this, of course, there is an unintended contradiction: for a man who puts independence high on his list of virtues, it is ironic that he is so preoccupied with performing rescue missions and so in need of people who require saving.[17]

In and of themselves these memories are not remarkable. Other adults could surely recall experiences similar to the ones Reagan describes. What makes them telling, however, is that Reagan sees them as central to his early years, that he himself makes so much of them. When considered in the context of his later preoccupation in both his acting and political careers with issues of dependence and independence, servants and masters, needy victims and heroic rescuers, these recollections suggest that matters of self-possession are at the core of Reagan's inner life and are the driving force behind his evangelical commitment to individual freedom or personal self-control. Again, the important point is not that Reagan is for personal liberty; most Americans also support this, but they do not see it as so sharply under attack from big government in the United States and from communism overseas, as Reagan does. In a word, they love freedom and independence no less than Reagan, but they do not share his exaggerated fears that only fundamental change at home and abroad will preserve liberty as an American way of life.

His earliest taste of the satisfactions of being a hero in public came at Eureka College. During his freshman year the school ran out of funds to pay its faculty. To save the college, the school's president proposed a drastic reduction in the teaching staff, a plan that threatened to leave juniors and seniors without the courses they needed for graduation. Reagan and 142 of the 250 students on campus signed a petition asking the president to resign. When the president and trustees rejected the request, Reagan and other members of the strike committee, which was proposing a boycott of classes, convened a meeting of students and faculty. "This was my moment to come off the bench," Reagan recalls. Presenting the strike plan to the gathering, he "discovered that night that an audience has a feel to it and, in the parlance of the theater, that audience and I were together. When I came to actually presenting the motion there was no need for parliamentary procedure: they came to their feet with a roar . . . It was heady wine. Hell, with two more lines I could have had them riding through 'every Middlesex village and farm'—without horses yet." After a week-long strike the college president resigned, and "Eureka got back into the business of education." Campus spirit rose, a close bond developed between students and faculty, and the students received "an education in human nature and the rights of man to universal education that nothing could erase from our psyches." The analogy with the Declaration of Independence is too obvious to miss. Like some latter-day American revolutionary, Reagan saw himself as having struck a blow for freedom. Whatever the truth of that conclusion, his part in the strike satisfied a powerful longing in his nature.[18]

He found further ways to play the rescuing hero after college. As a radio announcer in the Midwest, he became a popular speaker at high school father-and-son banquets and club meetings. He loved to make these speeches, which he invariably ended with

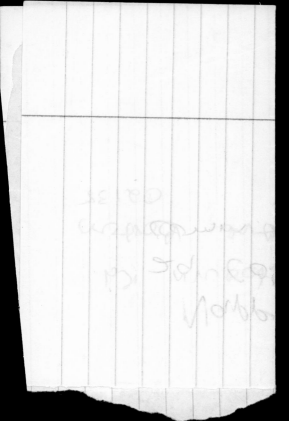

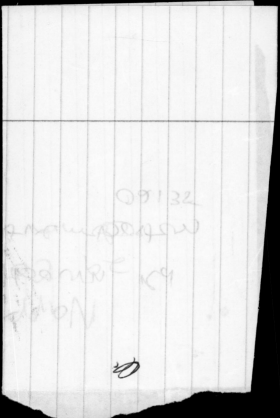

"a strong morality plea . . . urging his audiences to stay away from drink, cigarettes and cheating." Along with encouraging young men to stay on the straight and narrow path to a clean life, he remembers rescuing a damsel in distress. One night, outside the window of his Des Moines apartment he heard the voice of a girl on the sidewalk, who was being robbed at gunpoint. He pointed an empty gun at the robber—he had three at the time—who ran away when Reagan warned that he was going to let him have it with a forty-five.[19]

The image of the rugged hero rescuing others was a central feature of his movie career. Most of the early pictures in which he excelled were of "the kind in which you count on me rushing into the room, hat on the back of my head, grabbing a phone, and yelling, 'Give me the city desk—I've got a story that will crack this town wide open!' " According to his own account, he "became the Errol Flynn of the B's. I was as brave as Errol, but in a low-budget fashion." He had a flair for parts in action movies in which he fought villains in airplanes, in the cavalry, in a submarine, and even in a dirigible. Once during a rehearsal he knocked out a stuntman with an unintended punch to the jaw. He felt terrible about the accident but also found it "kind of nice knowing I could do it."

It was extraordinarily important to Reagan that in most of his films he played the part of the successful hero. In a 1968 interview with Lou Cannon, a *Washington Post* journalist and one of his biographers, Reagan strongly objected to the view that he "never got the girl" in his movies. Reagan raised this issue without being asked, revealing, in Cannon's words, an "exposed nerve." Ticking off a list of the film heroines he had "gotten," he complained that many critics of his movies had never seen them. For Reagan, one suspects, the matter runs deeper than whether he won the leading lady's heart in each of his pictures. Indeed, it is probably more a question of his self-image, of whether he is seen as a winner or a loser—a successful good guy, as he wished to see himself in real life, or an unhappy failure like his father. In each of

Reagan's fifty-three films, Cannon points out, he played the part of a villain only once. He has repeatedly expressed regret that he ever made that picture.

Nothing gave Reagan greater satisfaction as an actor than to play the part of an inspirational figure who rose from obscurity to fame, which he then used to further a good cause. This was the essence of George Gipp, whom he portrayed in *The Knute Rockne Story*. Reagan initiated the idea of doing the film, and when Warner Brothers went ahead with the proposal, he successfully pressed his case for playing the role of Gipp. He didn't have to learn any lines, Reagan recalled, because he was already thoroughly familiar with Gipp's story, which he had read in Knute Rockne's diary. Although the part occupied only one reel of the film, "it was nearly a perfect part from an actor's standpoint. A great entrance, an action middle, and a death scene to finish up." At the close of the movie the audience is reminded of Gipp when Rockne asks the Notre Dame football team to honor Gipp's deathbed request by winning one for the Gipper.

To Reagan, the great significance of this real-life episode was that Rockne used the story of Gipp's death not just to win a game but "to inspire a team that was losing mainly because of bickering and jealousy. For at least one half he gave this team, torn with dissension, the knowledge of what it was like to play together, and to sacrifice their individual quarrels for a common goal." "Reagan played the Gipper as if he were Dutch Reagan at Eureka," one biographer explains. "Although George Gipp in real life was an undisciplined athlete who ignored the lessons of Reagan's Y.M.C.A. lecture, Reagan portrayed him as a courteous, soft-spoken young man. In the film Gipper visited Rockne's home and talked over his troubles with the coach and his wife, just as Dutch Reagan used to visit faculty members' homes on cold Eureka evenings." He was so convincing in the role that he was chosen in a poll as one of the five likely stars of the future.[20]

His fame brought him chances for starring roles, but he still preferred action pictures. In 1941, for example, the studio gave him the choice of a "so-so comedy" in which he would be the lead, or a film of "adventure and action" in which he would have a lesser part than Errol Flynn. He left the decision to the studio, which chose the "escape and rescue" saga for him, and he was pleased. Indeed, throughout his career he longed to make westerns, "cavalry and Indian" epics like those starring John Wayne. In the late forties, when Warner's did not give him these parts, his agent negotiated another contract which allowed him to free-lance and star in *The Last Outpost*, a film about a Confederate cavalry captain intercepting Union gold shipments in the Southwest. But most of his films at this time were comedies like *The Girl from Jones Beach* and *Bedtime for Bonzo* and films adapted from stage plays, like *The Voice of the Turtle* and *The Hasty Heart*. These roles simply could not satisfy his inner need to play the independent hero. "You go to the rushes," he writes, "and somebody has stolen that heroic figure, and there you are—just plain old everyday you—up on the screen. It's one hell of a letdown."[21]

Participation in public advocacy groups and in the Screen Actors Guild (SAG) in the late forties helped relieve this frustration. During the thirties and forties Reagan was a Democrat, a warm supporter of Franklin Roosevelt, and a member of Americans for Democratic Action. He took this political direction partly because his father had been a Democrat and had served as head of the Dixon, Illinois, Works Progress Administration. In the immediate postwar years, "in his zeal to assure a peaceful future," Van Der Linden writes, Reagan "blindly" joined "every organization that would guarantee to save the world." Reagan says he was "hell-bent on saving the world from neo-Fascism." He became a member of the liberal American Veterans Committee, the United World Federalists, which urged world government, and the staunchly antifascist Hollywood Independent Citizens Committee of the Arts, Sciences, and Professions. He loved making speeches before these groups. When he discovered, however, that these organizations were either "Communist controlled" or sympathetic to the Communists, he broke with them and appeared as a friendly witness before the House Un-American Activities Committee investigating Communist influence in Hollywood. Although he was restrained in his appearance before the committee, telling it that the Communists had not been able to use the motion picture industry to advance their philosophy or ideology, he did describe a "small clique" in the Guild as "more or less following the tactics that we associate with the Communist Party." He also later tacitly supported the decision of the Motion Picture Association of America to blacklist ten witnesses whom the committee had cited for contempt of Congress. When the committee asked the actor Sterling Hayden to name the person who had stopped the Communists from taking over Hollywood, Hayden replied, according to Reagan's autobiography, "We ran into a one-man battalion named Ronnie Reagan." Although this was a gross overstatement of Reagan's influence, it demonstrates that his passion for heroics, for playing the independent leader rescuing people in danger of losing their freedom, had found some outlet in anticommunism.[22]

The Screen Actors Guild became the principal focus for this energy. In the postwar period, one biographer points out, Reagan became better known as a union leader than as an actor. After he became an elected member of the Guild's board in 1938, Reagan recalls, "I knew then I was beginning to find the rest of me." This self-discovery took fuller form after he returned from the Air Force in 1945. During the next two years he became highly involved in SAG's activities and served as its president for a time. In the summer of 1946, when SAG found itself in the middle of a jurisdictional dispute between two rival unions vying for control of the studio workers, Reagan led the way in arranging a quick settlement. His efforts temporarily saved the industry from a production slowdown and numerous actors from unemployment. But the agreement did not hold, and when SAG failed to arrange a new settlement, it sided with the union that was eager to keep the studios going.

Reagan was warned by an anonymous caller that "a squad was ready to take care of me and fix my face so I would never be in pictures again," but he and SAG refused to give ground. Reagan's heroics now included carrying a gun provided by the police. The danger was unquestionably real. Just before he and other actors were to climb aboard a bus that would carry them across the picket lines, the bus was bombed and burned. At first, Reagan saw the whole thing as a "ten-cent melodrama," but when a policeman showed up to guard his house, he no longer saw it as a practical joke. "Thereafter, I mounted the holstered gun religiously every morning and took it off the last thing at night. I learned how much a person gets to lean on hardware like that. After ten months of wearing it, it took a real effort of will to discard it." The sense of doing good work, despite the dangers, gave Reagan a satisfaction he was not then getting from his acting.[23]

His leadership of SAG also led him to believe that he had personally helped prevent a Communist takeover of the movie industry. "The Communist plan for Hollywood," Reagan recalls in his memoirs, "was remarkably simple. It was merely to take over the motion picture business. Not only for its profit, as the hoodlums had tried—but also for a grand world-wide propaganda base." At the time American films had a weekly international audience of about half a billion people, and Reagan believed that Communist control of the movie industry "would have been a magnificent coup for our enemies." Reagan's belief in this exaggerated danger rested on statements by the FBI and investigating committees of Congress and the California state legislature. He also pointed to a direct link between international communism and labor organizer Gerhard Eisler, "the commander-in-chief of Operation Hollywood," and at one time, "the top Communist agent in the United States." When Eisler was exposed, Reagan says, he fled to East Germany, where he engaged in "a violent radio campaign of vituperation" against the United States.

Reagan's convictions about this conspiracy were encouraged also by his sense of a personal struggle against evil. Just as the sports heroes and cavalry officers he loved to play in films gave him a sense of inner strength, so his battle to preserve Hollywood's independence from Communist control echoed in his mind as a triumph over his own fears of dependence. For him the struggle was a deeply personal one. One day in the late forties, three government agents visited him at his home. "We have some information which might be useful to you; we thought you might have some information helpful to us," they said. "I don't go in for Red-baiting," Reagan replied. "We don't either," they explained—this was a matter of national security. "We thought someone the Communists hated as much as they hate you might be willing to help us." "That got me," Reagan remembers. He wanted to know exactly what they had said about him. " 'What are we going to do about that sonofabitching bastard Reagan?' " the agents reported. This apparently convinced him that he was up against Communist agents: "The whole interview was an eye-opener."[24]

The intensity of Reagan's involvement in this anti-Communist crusade affected his family life. His marriage of eight years to actress Jane Wyman fell apart. At the divorce hearing she complained that her husband had become "obsessed with the Screen Actors Guild and political activities." Reagan had insisted that she attend union meetings, although her ideas "were never considered important," and she had little interest in their discussions. "There was nothing in common between us, nothing to sustain our marriage," she recalls. The divorce in 1948–49 shocked Reagan. "I suppose there had been warning signs," he writes, "if only I hadn't been so busy. But small-town boys grow up thinking only other people get divorced. Such a thing was so far from even being imagined by me that I had no resources to call upon." "Perhaps I should have let someone else save the world and have saved my own home," he said later. The marriage fell apart when Jane Wyman found she could not continue to bolster her husband's heroic self-image or his personal sense of independence through political activism in Hollywood.[25]

After his divorce, Reagan struggled with loneliness, which he remembers denying was there. In retrospect, however, he recalls being lonely, not because he was unloved but because he had no one to love. All this changed in 1951 when he met Nancy Davis, a young actress at MGM, whom he rescued from possible black-listing. When she saw her name listed on left-wing petitions and began receiving mail from these groups, she asked the president of SAG for help. After convincing himself of her loyalty and establishing that her name was being confused with that of another woman, Reagan gave her the good news over dinner. After a brief courtship, they were married on March 4, 1952.[26]

Nancy Reagan was the stepdaughter of a politically conservative Chicago neurosurgeon who had married Nancy's mother after her father had abandoned the family. Given her early experience of a broken family and the need to depend on relatives for support, it is not surprising that like her husband, Nancy Reagan made independence and old-style values into sacred articles of faith. She supported her husband's desire to speak out for traditional American values of family, home, free enterprise, and rugged individualism.

Encouraged by his wife and influenced by setbacks in his movie career, Reagan increasingly made national politics the focus of his zeal for autonomy and personal freedom from dependence. While he was working as a free-lance actor between 1948 and 1954, Reagan's career fell into the doldrums. He starred in a series of films that received poor reviews and failed at the box office. "In politics Reagan would often talk about personal freedom," Bill Boyarsky, a journalist and Reagan biographer writes. "But he was lost and unhappy when he was given his own freedom by Warner's." Increasingly consigned to roles in B movies, Reagan tried his hand at nightclub acting in Las Vegas. He was successful as master of ceremonies for a variety act, but he was uncomfortable doing this kind of work, especially in a city that thrived on gambling. Hence, when the General Electric Corporation offered him a contract to be a host of a half-hour television series, a promoter of G.E.'s image, and a morale booster for G.E. employees, whom he was to visit all over the country, he accepted.[27]

Between 1954 and 1962 Reagan honed his skills as a politician in talks before live audiences. He calculates that during this time he spent two years traveling and about 250,000 minutes before microphones. He visited 135 G.E. plants, where he met some 250,000 employees, whom he describes as a cross section of America who were concerned with truth and their personal liberties, "not with security as some would have us believe." During these years his speeches evolved into an attack on collectivism and centralization of power in Washington, "with subsequent loss of freedom at the local level." The speeches were meant as a "service" to people who were unaware of the danger to freedom in a vast permanent government structure, to remind them that "the individual was, and should be forever, the master of his destiny." "There is no point in saving souls in heaven," Reagan wrote in 1965. "If my speaking is to serve any purpose, then I must appear before listeners who don't share my viewpoint." It was these Americans whom Reagan wanted to bring back to an earlier faith, to a belief in the idea that "freedom . . . belongs to the individual by divine right." In his talks, Reagan questioned most of the social programs enacted in the twentieth century, declaring the progressive income tax a Marxist tool for creating a socialist state and calling mandatory Social Security an unfair restraint on those who could make better provisions for themselves.[28]

This was a long way from Reagan's earlier identification with Franklin Roosevelt and the Democratic party. True, he had become a wealthy man who resented paying high taxes, and he worked for and with corporate chiefs at G.E. who resented government interference in business affairs, influences that no doubt helped convert him into a conservative Republican. But his principal reasons for being attracted to Roosevelt's liberal leadership in the thirties and forties and for being hostile to New Deal programs in the fifties were much the same—his inner affinity for rescuing others from dependence and defeat. He had been "a very emotional New Dealer," Reagan later said. In Reagan's eyes FDR was fighting for each person's freedom from want and dependence; he was battling to restore the dignity of the individual.

FDR made everyone feel "I count," Reagan approvingly quoted a Roosevelt admirer on the hundredth anniversary of the former president's birth. "For Reagan and for millions of his fellow Americans," Cannon writes, "Roosevelt's message in the darkest days of the Depression was less an economic one than a call for renewed self-confidence and courage."

Although Reagan abandoned his New Deal liberalism for conservative Republicanism in the fifties and sixties, he refused to acknowledge that he had changed. He claimed, unpersuasively, that the Democrats had gone off in new directions and that he was still fighting for the same values—personal liberty and the dignity of the individual. Where he had seen Roosevelt as making a case for "the forgotten man at the bottom of the economic pyramid" in the thirties, Reagan now viewed himself as the champion of "the forgotten American, the man in the suburbs working sixty hours a week to support his family and being taxed heavily for the benefit of someone else." Further, in the forties Reagan attacked greedy corporations which inflated the economy and undermined the independence of workers by taking excess profits. By the fifties the culprit was big government rather than big business. But the problem was the same in Reagan's eyes—loss of individual freedom through concentration of wealth and power.

Roosevelt himself remains an inspirational figure in Reagan's mind. "His self-identification with Roosevelt served him in several ways," William E. Leuchtenburg points out. "It associated him with the last president historians have placed in the 'great' category. It permitted him to leap over comparison to more recent predecessors such as Nixon or to ideologues such as Goldwater which would have been awkward. It suggested that, like F.D.R., Reagan would inaugurate a new era, construct an enduring political coalition, contribute an imaginative domestic agenda, and originate a foreign policy that would reshape the world. And it reassured those of his Democratic followers who continued to have warm memories of the Roosevelt of their youth."

But the attachment was as much emotional as political.

When the journalist David McCullough interviewed Reagan on the occasion of the FDR centenary in 1982, "he found Reagan so chockful of enthusiasm that in the midst of a busy White House schedule he went on talking about FDR beyond the allotted time and 'with the most obvious fondness.'" FDR's flair for the dramatic, his ability to move people, his enduring image as an American hero, a great American president who rescued the country in time of dire need—all strike close to Reagan's own ideal picture of himself. Hence, as Cannon perceptively notes, Reagan's "style has remained frankly and fervently Rooseveltian throughout his life. His cadences are Roosevelt's cadences, his metaphors are the offspring of FDR's." Even though Reagan no longer sees Roosevelt's programs as promising the personal self-control and individual freedom to which Reagan is so devoted, Reagan is still attracted to Roosevelt as the successful hero he himself wishes to be. The accomplished, courageous man who overcame a crippling personal dependency and helped the nation reclaim its self-regard is the father Reagan never had.[29]

By 1964, in spite of his continuing admiration for Roosevelt, Reagan had become a prominent spokesman for the conservative cause. In the final days of Barry Goldwater's losing campaign for the presidency, he delivered a nationally televised address, "A Time for Choosing," in which he forcefully urged the case for Goldwater's conservative program. The theme, as so often in his life, was freedom, independence, and self-control. "So we have come to a time for choosing," he said. "Either we accept the responsibility for our own destiny, or we abandon the American Revolution and confess that an intellectual belief in a far-distant capital can plan our lives for us better than we can plan them ourselves." Using Franklin Roosevelt's language, he told the nation that "you and I have a rendezvous with destiny. We can preserve for our children this the last best hope of man on earth or we can sentence them to take the first step into a thousand years of darkness." With this speech and with his rise to prominence as a conservative Republican, Reagan believed that he had "found the rest of me." His life-long struggle against inner fears of crippling dependence, his idealization of the autonomy that his father never enjoyed and that he himself relentlessly pursued, were now translated into a campaign to rescue America from alien influences that he believed were about to bring the country to its knees.[30]

CHAPTER TWO

The Ideologue as Politician

B Y ANY REASONABLE measure Barry Goldwater's run for the presidency in 1964 was a political disaster for conservative Republicans. After Goldwater lost the election to Lyndon Johnson by a record-breaking popular majority, and the Republicans lost control of both congressional houses by huge margins, the conservatives seemed hopelessly defeated and incapable of gaining national control. As a prominent spokesman for the conservative cause, Reagan was a man without an apparent future. A staunch proponent of seemingly outdated ideas, Reagan in 1964 was dismissed as a more amiable but even less informed reactionary than Goldwater.

Yet circumstances and personality favored Reagan in ways his opponents did not foresee. Although Goldwater was severely beaten, he had nonetheless won over twenty-seven million votes, suggesting that the moral concerns he had voiced in his campaign were matters of some importance to a substantial part of the electorate. To be sure, no major party candidate is likely to fall below that number of votes; but even if Goldwater's support was coming from party diehards, it seems reasonable to assume that many of them were attracted to his ideas. Indeed, as the historian Richard Hofstadter observed in 1965, the decade of the sixties, like that of the twenties, was a time of relative prosperity when "issues of status politics—issues of religion, morals, personal style, and culture" came to the fore. "Ascetic Protestantism remains a significant undercurrent in contemporary America, and . . . its followers have found newfangled ways of reaffirming some of their convictions. They cannot bring back Prohibition or keep evolution entirely out of the schools. They have been unable even to defend school prayer or prevent *Life* magazine from featuring the topless bathing suit. But they can recriminate against and [try to] punish the new America that outrages them, and they have found powerful leaders to echo their views."[1]

In California, where the modern consumer culture was strikingly evident, upwardly mobile middle-class suburbanites, who had migrated from the South and Midwest, objected to high taxes, wasteful government spending, unbalanced budgets, special help to minorities at the expense of the majority, and "indecent" demonstrations on college campuses, where students showed little deference for established authority. As social scientists David O. Sears and Jack Citrin explain in a study of the California tax revolt, these people opposed "both the unrestrained right to personal self-expression and the idea that government should strive to perfect society and regulate all aspects of human affairs . . . This ideology has appealed most strongly to the predominantly Protestant, frequently fundamentalist white middle class with origins in the South or Midwest. Once in straitened circumstances but now comfortable, if not prosperous, its adherents are highly protective of home and property, and they blame government and the courts for fostering permissiveness and secularization." They were proponents of "a crusade to restore the cultural hegemony of threatened values and to reverse the onward march of government spending that only favors the grantsmen, social engineers, and malingerers."[2]

The attitudes of these Californians could be summed up as antigovernment, antiminority, and conformist. Realistically perceiving that federal, state, and local governments were appropriating some of their hard-won material gains to aid less advantaged citizens, many of these people unrealistically saw public officials as undermining their freedom of choice or independence and made government the butt of their angry personal feelings about arbitrary authority. As psychologists and sociologists have suggested, these middle-class Americans were probably docile children who unquestioningly satisfied their parents' insistence on achievement and conformity. Behind this docility, however, were unexpressed feelings of resistance and hostility to what was seen as "exorbitantly demanding authority." Ultimately viewing "authority only as something that aims to manipulate and deprive" them, these people saw their own government as "engaged in a more or less continuous conspiracy" against them. At the same time these Californians took bitter exception to the nonconformity of student radicals, who seemed to be thumbing their noses at conventionally ambitious middle-class citizens working to improve their lives and establish themselves as thoroughly assimilated Americans. They considered any kind of nonconformity as a challenge to "the whole order of things they are trying to become a part of."

The majority of middle-class Californians, however, had other concerns as well. Despite Barry Goldwater's emphasis on moral and symbolic questions in the 1964 election, he lost the state by a million votes. His militant determination to overturn the insurance and "safety net" programs of the New Deal and his apparent willingness to risk nuclear war with the Soviet Union blunted his ability to win widespread support.[3]

Reagan did not make the same mistake, and time was on his side. Although he was as fully committed to the ideas and assumptions that animated Goldwater, he was a more flexible, accommodating, and ingratiating personality with whom great numbers of middle-class citizens could identify. In his movie career he had been less the matinee idol than the boy next door, the conventional, homespun, thoroughly likeable, ordinary American. His conformity and personal charm, the same attributes that had made him a successful entertainer, made him a formidable candidate for public office. Unlike Goldwater, he was a "soft sell" spokesman for the conservative ideology. Reagan, one political opponent observed, exploited "resentments and emotions not by being a loud and threatening figure but by making wisecracks or poking fun at his enemies." Reagan managed to "get away with being a thundering conservative" by not thundering. And by the time he ran for office, he did not need to thunder. Where the targets of Goldwater's unsuccessful attack were Roosevelt's sacrosanct New Deal programs, Reagan was able to challenge the less popular, more vulnerable Great Society measures of the Johnson years.

Reagan's compulsive need to succeed—or to be seen as a winner—also served him well. If Goldwater was ready to stand or fall on principle, Reagan, in his determination to be liked and to gain his personal goals, will compromise. He is a pragmatist of the Right. Indeed, foremost in his mind is the portrait of a flexible, heroic FDR rather than that of a failed father.[4]

California conservative leaders, who understood Reagan's appeal and wished to avoid another Goldwater debacle, pressed the former movie star to run for governor in 1966. Three self-made millionaires—Holmes Tuttle, an auto dealer, Henry Salvatori, an oil developer, and A. C. (Cy) Rubel, a former president of Union Oil Company—led the campaign to put Reagan in the race. Encouraged by the fact that George Murphy, another former movie actor, had won a Senate seat in 1964, and interested in a possible bid for the presidency, Reagan agreed to run. Although he had no intention of abandoning the ideas he had expressed in earlier speeches, he readily agreed to avoid ultraconservative positions, especially on unemployment insurance and Social Security benefits, which would have alienated moderate Republicans and would have lost Democratic votes in the final campaign. To this end, he seized the chance to have his campaign managed by the political consulting firm of Spencer-Roberts, which was identified with Nelson Rockefeller, Goldwater's Republican opponent. To promote Republican party unity, in the spring of 1965 he encouraged the creation of a group called the Friends of Ronald Reagan; and he began courting Republicans from both sides of the party with speeches at functions all over the state. By the fall Reagan had already made substantial progress in selling himself to Republicans of every stripe. In speeches and during question-and-answer sessions, an observer reported, he "handled himself very well and made a very favorable impression on some liberal Republicans who had previously viewed his candidacy with considerable coolness."[5]

Reagan's goal of building party unity for the contest with incumbent Democratic Governor Pat Brown faced a serious challenge from former Mayor George Christopher of San Francisco, his Republican primary opponent. A moderate who hoped to pin a right-wing label on Reagan, Christopher identified him with Goldwater's opposition to the Civil Rights Act of 1964, saying that "a candidate who opposes civil rights is a losing candidate." Christopher managed to give some credence to these assertions in March 1966 when the two candidates appeared before the state convention of the National Negro Republican Assembly. Asked by a delegate how black Republicans could urge other blacks to vote for him after he had spoken in opposition to the civil rights bill, Reagan defended himself by saying that the bill was a well-intentioned but badly drawn piece of legislation. Furthermore, despite Goldwater's voting against the measure, Reagan said, the senator was "the very opposite of a racist." Given a chance to comment on Reagan's answer, Christopher declared his support of the bill and denounced Goldwater's vote as doing "more harm than any other thing to the Republican Party . . . Unless we cast out this image," he warned, "we're going to suffer defeat." In his reply to Christopher, Reagan lost his temper: "I resent the implication that there is any bigotry in my nature," he shouted. "Don't anyone ever imply that—in this or any other group." Unable to bear being considered an unreasoning bigot, he fled the meeting. He appeared to have tears in his eyes and was heard saying, "I'll get that S.O.B." Under prodding from his aides, however, Reagan shortly returned to the hall, where he displayed his usual good temper. When asked by a reporter whether he was emotionally fit for the coming campaign, he jokingly declared that Hollywood columnists had called him a "Boy Scout and a square." "You can't have it both ways," he said. "You can't be a wild-eyed kook and a square." By pointing out that journalists were calling him a thoroughly conventional American, he effectively blunted suggestions that he lacked the stability to serve in high office.

This episode was the only serious misstep in an otherwise well-run primary campaign in which Reagan behaved more like a flexible, consensus politician than an uncompromising ideologue. From the start he essentially ignored Christopher and focused his attention on Brown's shortcomings as governor. The state GOP chairman, Dr. Gaylord Parkinson, supported Reagan's strategy by issuing what he called the Eleventh Commandment, "Thou Shalt Not Speak Ill of Other Republicans." The injunction, which received enthusiastic support from the party organization, inhibited Christopher from aggressively attacking Reagan as an inexperienced ultraconservative who could not win the general election. Christopher's appearance and manner of speaking on television compared unfavorably to Reagan's, and his candidacy was further weakened when Brown's aides publicized his conviction in 1939 for violating milk price stabilization laws. In contrast with Reagan, who won an enthusiastic response when he described himself as a citizen politician eager to clean up the mess in Sacramento and around the state, Christopher gained little interest and support. In the primary over 1.4 million Republicans cast their ballots for Reagan, who received 65 percent of the total Republican vote.[6]

In the subsequent campaign against Brown, Reagan proved even more adept at focusing on moral or symbolic issues without being seen as a right-wing ideologue. The themes of his speeches were as much a plea for freedom, individual autonomy, and traditional values as ever. Big government on all levels, which had become the master instead of remaining the servant, was the enemy. It gobbled up the hard-earned wages of working men and women; it strangled free enterprise with regulations and red tape; it indulged welfare cheats, lazy people who could take care of themselves but preferred freeloading at the expense of more conscientious citizens; it threatened individual liberty by intruding into people's private lives, telling them, for example, to whom they had to rent or sell their homes. Our problems, Reagan emphasized, stemmed from a lack of will, from morally lax leaders who allowed criminals to go free and did little to forestall crime in the streets or to punish the "neurotic vulgarities" of university students who were running wild on campuses. He pictured California as heading toward a kind of moral collapse unless someone restored the old verities and brought decent, hard-working, God-fearing people back to the center of the state's life.

His rhetoric appealed to people across the state, but particularly to those in southern California, middle-class and lower-middle-class suburbanites who resented high taxes and government aid to minorities. Although many of these people had jobs that were dependent on government expenditures, they shared Reagan's feeling about excessive government spending and intrusions into their lives. In San Diego, for example, which relied heavily on defense spending by the federal government for its livelihood, Goldwater defeated Johnson in 1964 and Brown lost to Reagan in 1966. Taking their prosperity for granted, San Diegans voted more on symbolic or status issues than on substantive ones. Instead of voting their pocketbooks, they voted their consciences or, more to the point, they sided with the candidates who, by speaking for their values, vented their authoritarian feelings and bolstered their self-esteem. Yet while they favored less government and lower taxes they opposed the reduction or elimination of Social Security and unemployment benefits. In short, they wanted the advantages of government largesse without the high taxes, red tape, and personal limitations it seemed to foster. Because he was sensitive to this contradiction, Reagan qualified his denunciations of big government with promises not to withdraw people's hard-won benefits.[7]

Because Reagan's ideas were so much an echo of what other conservatives, including Goldwater, had been saying, Brown and his supporters tried to make Reagan's ideology a centerpiece of the campaign. Much of what Reagan said during the election contest had the quality of programmed or memorized answers by an unthinking reactionary, and this encouraged the Brown people to go after him as a right-winger who was outside of the American political mainstream. The state Democratic chairman issued a report titled "Ronald Reagan, Extremist Collaborator—An Exposé" that described Reagan as a "front man" for the John Birch Society, which the report called a supersecret group of bigots. Brown also tried to counter Reagan's celebration of himself as an amateur by portraying him as a know-nothing actor. In a television documentary, "Man vs. Actor," and in one-minute spots during the last week of the campaign, Brown was shown telling a group of schoolchildren that he was "running against an actor, and you know who shot Lincoln, don'tcha?"

But Reagan, ever skillful at playing the "good guy" and seeming less doctrinaire than he was, managed to turn aside most of these attacks. He made a systematic effort to exclude extremists or well-known ultraconservatives from frontline positions in his campaign, and liberals ultimately had to concede that Reagan was not connected with the Birch Society. Further, he successfully identified himself as a "citizen politician" who, unlike the professional politicians, wished to apply some common-sense thinking to the state's problems. Relying on a team of behavioral scientists who supplied him with information and position papers on major state issues, Reagan showed enough knowledge about most questions to remain a credible candidate. More important, he did not come across to people as an inflexible ideologue, but as a sensible, sincere man with a good sense of humor and a friendly interest in other people's concerns. In short, he had a warm, human quality that defied the stereotype of the evangelist or extremist set on an unrealistic return to the past.

In contrast, voters saw Brown as a familiar face who emphasized his past achievements but lacked plans for overcoming present and future problems. Indeed, Reagan managed to portray Brown as part of the problem, identifying him with high taxes, inflated state budgets, black riots in the Watts district of Los Angeles and the Hunter's Point section of San Francisco, the student rebellion at Berkeley, and the unpopular Rumford Act, California's fair housing law. Brown's associations with President Lyndon Johnson, who was under fire for the Vietnam war, weakened his support from liberals, and his sharp differences with Sam Yorty, the conservative mayor of Los Angeles, whom he had defeated by a narrow margin in the Democratic primary, made Brown unacceptable to many right-of-center Democrats.

On election day, voters answered Reagan's repeated campaign query, "Ya basta?" ("Had enough?") with a resounding yes. Winning with nearly 58 percent of the vote, almost a million more votes than Brown, Reagan and the Republicans won control of the executive branch of state government by a landslide and reduced the Democratic majority in the state senate to two members and in the assembly to four seats.[8]

Having won the gubernatorial election by playing on resentments against Brown and the Democrats, Reagan confronted the question of how to turn a set of attitudes or felt values into a political program. Like other conservatives in the sixties, who thought mainly in terms of negatives—reducing the size of government, curbing its hold on the individual, preventing its indulgence of welfare cheats and radical students—Reagan had no positive substantive plans for solving economic and social problems. After almost three months in office, when asked by reporters what his legislative program was, the new governor indicated that he didn't know: "I could take some coaching from the sidelines," he said to his aides, "if anyone can recall my legislative program."

His self-made millionaire friends who had helped put him in office were no help. Henry Salvatori, for example, was interested only in seeing Reagan move on to the presidency. "People criticize Ronnie for having no political experience," he told a reporter. "But he has a great image, a way to get through to people . . . Look at John F. Kennedy. He didn't have much of a record as a senator. But he made a great appearance—and he had a beautiful wife. So does the governor. Nancy Reagan doesn't have to take a back seat to anyone. And the governor has plenty of time between now and the [1968] nomination to make a record as an administrator. But I don't believe people in other states really care much about what's happening in California anyway."

Reagan's staff did not have much idea of what to do either. Philip Battaglia, his campaign manager, who became his executive secretary, and Lyn Nofziger, his press secretary, who soon took the title "communications director," were essentially manipulators of symbols, rhetoricians without a clear idea of what constituted a program. Reagan, Nofziger acknowledged, had "no political background, no political cronies, and no political machine. He didn't even run his own campaign." It "was run by hired people who then walked away and left it. Therefore, when he was elected, the big question was 'My God, what do we do now?' " Reagan and his young staff came to Sacramento, Bill Boyarsky points out, "with the attitude of men who would quickly clean up the mess . . . and move on to something else." They gave the impression of self-righteous reformers who were the "sole repository of goodness in the world," ready to rid the government of accumulated evils. But they were so ignorant of the workings of the state government that Robert Monagan, the assembly's Republican minority leader, gave Reagan and his aides a guidebook to the governor's office, outlining the historical development of the governor's role and summarizing the legal requirements of Reagan's relations with the legislature. "We weren't just amateurs," Nofziger said later, "we were novice amateurs."[9]

None of this deterred Reagan from sounding the same themes he had voiced during the campaign. When he learned after his election that the Brown administration was leaving him a fiscal crisis highlighted by deficits in the current and succeeding fiscal years, Reagan denounced the Democrats for looting the treasury and promised to meet the difficulties head on. "For many years now, you and I have been . . . told there are no simple answers to the complex problems which are beyond our comprehension," he said in his inaugural speech on January 5, 1967. "Well, the truth is, there are simple answers—there just are not easy ones. The time has come for us to decide whether collectively we can afford everything and anything we think of simply because we think of it. The time has come to run a check to see if all the services government provides were in answer to demands or were just goodies dreamed up for our supposed betterment." Expressing his determination to match outgo to income, he announced his intention "to squeeze and cut and trim until we reduce the cost of government."[10]

To achieve this goal, Reagan arbitrarily proposed a 10 percent budget cut for all departments of the state government. With the help of his finance director, Gordon Paul Smith, a management consultant who had no more knowledge of state government than Reagan and his other aides, the governor submitted a budget for fiscal 1967–68 of $4.62 billion. That sum was significantly lower than Brown's final request of the previous year and helped create the impression that Reagan meant to follow through on what he said. Coupled with a series of other economy measures—a freeze on state hiring, reductions in out-of-state travel, a halt in purchases of state cars, the cancellation of plans for new buildings—the budget helped Reagan create an image of himself as a great economizer. Dramatic cuts in the mental hygiene department added to this impression. Pointing to the fact that the number of patients in the state's mental hospitals had fallen almost 40 percent as a consequence of the use of new drugs in treatment, Reagan eliminated 3,700 hospital jobs, thus reducing the mental hygiene budget by the proposed 10 percent.

Despite the good publicity for his administration resulting from claims that he had made the largest cut ever in a state budget, Reagan's savings were more symbolic than real. Knowledgeable officials understood that Reagan could not make "immediate substantial reductions in the cost of California government." Welfare payments, for example, which Reagan had said were going to undeserving cheats, did not succumb to his quick fix. Most welfare recipients, in fact, were genuinely needy people living in poverty: an unwed mother with three children received $184 a month. It was not humane considerations that stymied Reagan but the federal government, which supplied almost half of the money paid to Californians on welfare in 1966; federal rules did not allow the state to arbitrarily reduce payments. Moreover, under state law, local education, the largest item in the state budget, could not be cut without evidence that school populations had decreased. Under the legal formula the Reagan administration actually had to increase school outlays by $40 million in 1967.

As Reagan and his aides quickly learned, a fixed 10 percent cut across the board simply could not work. Such a plan, the highly respected legislative analyst A. Alan Post pointed out, offered no guidelines for achieving real economies. Cutting special departments that operated on budgets separate from the state's general fund would not balance the budget. A 10 percent cut in the highway department, for example, which received its funds from gasoline taxes, would not bring more money into the general fund. Further, although Reagan's cuts in the mental hygiene department resulted in some short-term savings, they did little to reduce the overall costs of state government in succeeding years. When urged to make more considered, farther-reaching institutional changes in state operations which would produce no dramatic results immediately but meaningful ones later on, Reagan refused.

As a consequence, during his first term, he did not achieve significant economies. Within two months of submitting his initial financial plan, Reagan had to increase his projected budget by some $440 million to a total of $5.06 billion, the first $5 billion budget in California's history. Despite this increase, Reagan continued to act as if his first proposed budget had been put into effect. He put on this false face for at least two reasons. First, he was eager to run for president and wanted to promote the idea that he was a realistic and successful governor achieving what he had set out to do. And second, he could not accept a picture of himself as less than a strong leader who was rescuing the state from its fiscal woes and freeing people from the consequences of bad government. He refused to accept assertions that his mental health cuts had reduced the quality of care in state hospitals, and he rejected suggestions that he see the conditions for himself. Instead he blindly defended his policy by citing changes in patient-staff ratios as sufficient justification. To some observers in Sacramento, Reagan seemed like the star of a soap opera called "Citizen Governor." He unwittingly confirmed this view in a letter to a former agent of his in Hollywood in July 1967: he joked about not being able to pay the agent a commission for "this new part" of governor and complained that the job had its drawbacks, including the fact that he was having a difficult time "trying to play the 'Good guy.' "[11]

Reagan's support of the largest tax increase in the history of any state forced him into some additional playacting to bridge the gap between rhetoric and action. A centerpiece of Reagan's conservative gospel was lower taxes and less government. But from the outset of his governorship, he recognized that to meet the costs of mandated programs and satisfy California's constitutional requirement of a balanced budget, he would have to raise taxes. In addition to the legal constraints, there were major political considerations: without a tax increase the state's finances would be in serious disarray, and Reagan's bid for the presidency, which required that he build an image as an effective administrator, would receive a serious setback. Consequently, during the first six months of his term he negotiated successfully with Jesse Unruh, the powerful Democratic speaker of the assembly, for a tax bill.

The issue for Reagan was not only how to maintain his credibility with the many voters who wanted a reduction in taxes but also how to persuade himself that he was defending conservative principles that would lead to greater individual freedom. Although the bill he and Unruh pushed through the legislature increased taxes by nearly $1 billion, Reagan was able to square it with his constituents and his conscience. The law raised bank and corporation taxes and the sales tax and increased the maximum personal income tax from 7 percent to 11 percent, thus pushing more people into the higher brackets, but it also set aside money to lower local property taxes. Property taxes, which had been growing at a rapid pace to meet the costs of local government, had become the principal tax irritant to large numbers of middle-class homeowners across the state. By making it possible to reduce the property tax, which cost most Californians more than even their increased income taxes, Reagan was able to hold on to his image as a proponent of lower taxes. He made much of the fact that he resisted the method of having income taxes withheld from paychecks, insisting instead that Californians make lump sum payments after calculating their deductions. His reasoning was that "taxes should hurt" and that weekly payroll deductions appeared less painful; larger occasional or annual payments, therefore, were manifest evils. In this twisting of reality and perception, he added to his image as an opponent of higher taxes and a larger state government.

The tax bill freed Reagan from worries about balancing budgets for the next two years and even made the California tax system less regressive by putting more of the burden on those who were better able to pay. That aspect of the budget did not sit well with ultraconservatives like State Senator John Schmitz from Orange County. Attacking Reagan for failing to ease the tax burden and build the "Creative Society" he had promised in his campaign, Schmitz denounced the governor as a turncoat. Schmitz's opposition, however, helped to separate Reagan in the public mind from cranky right-wingers and boosted his presidential prospects. To Reagan himself, the passage of the tax law did not mean that his conservative hopes for lower taxes and less government were unrealistic or that his struggle to free the individual from government constraints would fail. Rather, he saw it as a chance to advance his political standing and do further battle for the principles in which he still firmly believed, as he would when he became president. He told his aides they were not responsible for the tax increase; it was an inheritance from Brown's mismanagement of state affairs. In sum, although the tax law ran counter to much that Reagan had preached in his campaign, he found persuasive ways to rationalize his turnabout. It demonstrated not that he was a hypocrite but that he was an extraordinary politician who could turn a difficult situation to good account. It also showed that he lacked a positive program for dealing with major state problems and had to rely on tortured logic and distortion to put across something sensible and realistic.[12]

Reagan actions on other major issues during his first term were equally contradictory. Shortly after becoming governor he had to decide how to respond to abortion legislation that was being pushed in the state senate. The existing law allowed abortions only for women whose lives were jeopardized by their pregnancy. In 1967, however, after nine San Francisco physicians were indicted for performing abortions on women with German measles, a disease which can cause birth defects, pressure mounted for more liberal legislation. Demands for reform from the women's movement and numerous physicians, including conservatives like his father-in-law, gave Reagan reason to accept changes in the law. Personally opposed to abortion, but sensitive to the political damage he might suffer from outright antagonism to reform of the abortion law, Reagan accepted the provision for abortions in pregnancies resulting from rape or incest and in cases where a panel of physicians concluded that the child's birth would gravely impair the mental or physical health of the mother. He refused, however, to endorse a provision that would allow abortions for women who had had German measles and who might give birth to a deformed child. He expressed moral revulsion at taking an "unborn life simply on the supposition that it is going to be less than a perfect human being." He believed it was a short step from that to "deciding after birth that we will sort out those people who should be allowed to live or not, and I don't see any difference between that and what Hitler tried to do." His opposition to the German measles article in the bill, however, was probably a way to dramatize his continuing opposition to abortion and maintain his credibility with those who were against changes in the law.

Accepting his objection, the state senate passed a bill without the German measles section. But Reagan now voiced new doubts. Taking his lead from Francis Cardinal McIntyre of Los Angeles, Reagan expressed fears that the mental health provision, allowing abortions for women who would suffer emotional deterioration after bearing a child, could become a loophole permitting abortions for almost any reason. When the assembly approved the law in spite of his objection, Reagan, after much soul searching, signed the bill. He wanted to veto the measure, but when Nofziger pointed out that a veto would antagonize Republican legislators who had voted for the law, would raise questions about Reagan's credibility, and would simply spark another round of debate about the issue in the next legislative session, the governor gave in. As Reagan had foreseen, the law did result in a high increase in legal abortions in the state, and he complained that psychiatrists were taking advantage of a weakness in the act he had not anticipated. But this complaint was blatantly false because he had raised the question of the mental health loophole at a press conference before signing the measure into law. By dissembling, however, he was able to have matters both ways: he avoided a political struggle with proponents of the bill, and he retained much of his credibility with conservative opponents of abortion.

He may also have taken real comfort from this rationalization. As with the tax increase, his impulse was to deny responsibility for the abortion law. In 1968 he focused on the fact that he had prevented authorization of abortions for mothers with potentially deformed babies, saying that "crippled persons have contributed greatly to our society." He later urged people to think carefully about who they might be doing away with and asked whether such decisions weren't a case of playing God. The issue clearly touched deep feelings in him about control over one's own life and excited long-standing concerns about freedom from dependency and external control. By 1979, after further reflection on the matter, he concluded that abortion was wrong, that it was tantamount to taking a human life and could be justified only when the mother's life was at stake. As with the tax bill, he went along with legislative change not because he agreed with it in a positive way but because he felt that the matter was beyond his control. This, of course, is typical of most state governors, but what made it remarkable in Reagan's case was the extent to which higher taxes and abortions were matters of principle on which he had indicated he could not be budged. Afterward, predictably, he emphasized his detachment from what had been done and avowed his commitment to the conservative position more forcefully than ever.[13]

On issues relating to higher education as well, Reagan practiced the politics of symbolism. From the start of his campaign for the governorship he had recognized that student demonstrations, particularly the Free Speech Movement at Berkeley opposing restrictions on campus political activities, troubled great numbers of people around the state. Having run hard on this issue, Reagan believed that his image as an effective governor partly depended on his ability to follow through strongly in his dealings with the university. In addition to being good politics, such a policy would satisfy the antielitist antagonism he shared with other self-made Californians, who saw college students and faculty as self-indulgent snobs who were contemptuous of middle-class values. Adopting the slogan, "Observe the rules or get out," Reagan did not hesitate to confront demonstrators personally and to quell riots with force. He called in the Highway Patrol and the National Guard to ensure order on campuses, proclaiming that those who wanted to learn and teach "should be protected in that at the point of a bayonet." At the start of his term his finance director announced a 10 percent cut in the university and college budgets and a plan to inaugurate tuition in both systems. Further, he took advantage of a request for a vote of confidence from Clark Kerr, the university's president, as an excuse to fire him and symbolically punish the university for its misdeeds.

Yet even though he publicly attacked the university, he had no intention of forcing himself into a position that would undermine his standing with constituents who took some pride in the state's systems of higher education. For example, he wanted students to pay tuition or at least assume a greater share of the cost of their college education, but he recognized that the catch phrase "free tuition" was one that even some conservatives did not wish to abandon. Hence, when the university's Regents rejected his call for tuition, he agreed to the idea of a student "charge" which would not necessarily support the instructional budget of the university as tuition normally does. His budgets for higher education turned out to be more generous than his public pronouncements suggested they would be. During his eight years as governor he increased spending in the state universities and colleges by 136 percent, 36 percent more than his increase in total state spending. If these larger budgets for higher education were partly a product of political calculation, they were also the consequence of symbolic victories—the firing of Kerr and the presence of law enforcement authorities on campuses. Although Kerr's departure and the presence of armed men did not bring the full measure of "law and order" Reagan promised, they did give the governor and many of his supporters a sufficient sense of control over campus radicalism to permit state support of higher education to continue much as before.[14]

On a number of other issues Reagan acted out of a concern with symbols more than with content. During his campaign he had pointed to the fact that no murderers had been executed in the state for four years. Tying Brown's reluctance to have men die in the gas chamber to a rise in crime, Reagan indicated that he would not allow criminals to go unpunished. Consequently, in April 1967, when he confronted an appeal for clemency in the case of Aaron Mitchell, a black man convicted of killing a white policeman during a robbery, he decided "to execute the sentence of the courts." "If we are going to ask men to engage in an occupation in which they protect us at the risk of their lives," Reagan told reporters, "we of society have an obligation to them to let them know that society will do whatever it can to minimize the danger of their occupation." Although Reagan had some difficult moments sticking to his decision, he refused to budge, recognizing that his credibility as an upholder of "law and order" was on the line. The execution, Boyarsky points out, "was a symbolic act to the voters, an indication that Brown's grudging acceptance of the death penalty would be replaced by a willingness to use it as a direct answer to crime in the streets." When the administration later compiled a list of its achievements, it included the Mitchell execution, emphasizing that the governor "refused to interfere with court decisions on capital punishment except in those cases . . . where clemency appeared appropriate." While he in fact granted clemency and a temporary reprieve in the only other capital punishment cases that came before him, Reagan's record as governor was firmly associated with Mitchell's execution.[15]

In yet another expression of his concern with striking the right moral chord and standing up for traditional values, Reagan refused to acknowledge that members of his staff had been dismissed for alleged homosexual activities. In September 1967, after learning from aides that a homosexual clique apparently existed in his administration, the governor demanded that the suspected staff members resign quietly at once or face dismissal with an announcement of why they were being asked to leave. When rumors of the story shortly began appearing in the press, Nofziger tried to head off exaggerated accounts by leaking the facts to several journalists. But this did not reduce interest in the story. By the end of October the matter gained national attention when Drew Pearson published a syndicated column questioning whether Reagan's political career could survive the revelation. Answering that Pearson was "stooping to destroy human beings, innocent people," Reagan denied Pearson's account and said that no one in his administration had given such a story to the press. When Pearson countered that "the facts in this case are incontrovertible," Reagan called him a liar and repeated his denial to the press: "I have never had and do not have any evidence that would warrant an accusation. No accusation or any charge has been made."

Although Reagan was undoubtedly concerned not to injure the accused individuals and their families, and although he did not actually know that Nofziger had leaked the story, he clearly lied about the whole episode for self-serving reasons. Not only did he fear that acknowledging the existence of homosexuals in his administration might ruin his chances for the presidency, but also he found the situation repugnant to his self-image as the exemplar of an upright, moral America. In his own mind, no doubt, it was better to lie and preserve the hope that traditional standards remained alive in some corner of the United States, where, as he liked to say, they could become a prairie fire that would sweep across the nation. "My God," he asked, when told of the homosexual group in Sacramento, "has government failed?" As long as the portrait of him as a morally untainted government leader remained intact, he could maintain hope that government had not failed.[16]

By the close of his first term in 1969 Reagan had largely managed to sustain the picture of himself as a citizen politician doing unrelenting battle against social and political evils. Although he had made no significant headway in reducing the size and cost of government, that did not deter him from once more making it his campaign theme in the 1970 gubernatorial election. Even though he had been governor for four years, he campaigned "as if he were going to Sacramento to clean up a mess someone else had left behind." The tone was set in a confidential cabinet memo in which Reagan called for an "all-out war on the tax-taker. If we fail, no one ever again will be able to try. We must succeed." The focus of this attack was to be welfare, which he described during the election as "the greatest domestic problem facing the nation today and the reason for the high cost of government." "Public assistance should go to the needy and not to the greedy," he declared in a speech on the "welfare mess." Also playing on the resentment of the middle class toward anti-Vietnam war activists attacking the American system, Reagan declared his faith in the decency, generosity, and fairness of the nation's treatment of disadvantaged peoples at home and abroad. "It is time we ended our obsession with what is wrong and realize how much is right, how great is our power and how little we really have to fear." Paraphrasing FDR's appeal of 1933, Reagan saw himself rekindling national hope as Roosevelt had in the Great Depression.

Although four years in office with an undistinguished record had diluted some of his appeal, these symbolic pronouncements, combined with an inept campaign by former Assembly Speaker

Jesse Unruh, gave Reagan a second term. Unruh, unable to shed the "Big Daddy" image he had suffered from in the legislature, where he had run the lower house with an iron hand, lost to Reagan by half a million votes. This was half of Reagan's winning margin in 1966, but he still commanded 53 percent of the total vote and saw good reason to continue pushing for the cuts in government and social programs he had not yet achieved.[17]

It was clear to Reagan that if he was to make an effective run for the presidency, his second term would have to be more productive substantively than his first. But his conservative philosophy of cutting, trimming, and limiting government growth and power was no more successful as a formula for change in 1971 than it had been during his previous four years as governor. Consequently, as in his first term, his actions and rhetoric followed separate paths which only occasionally converged.

The most pressing problems of his second term were increasing welfare and Medi-Cal costs and a lack of tax funds to pay for them. During Reagan's first four years in office, Aid to Families with Dependent Children (AFDC), the heart of the California welfare program, had doubled in size to some 1.5 million people. Under the weight of a national recession in 1970, the AFDC caseload in California at the end of that year was growing by 40,000 a month. To meet the problem, Reagan entered into personal negotiations with the new Democratic speaker of the assembly, Bob Moretti, who shared Reagan's eagerness for a record of accomplishment on which he could run for higher office. With the help of aides and a fair amount of political horse trading in the legislature, they hammered out a welfare reform law. Although the revised welfare program, in the judgment of one analyst, "was reoriented toward fiscal considerations and away from clients," more recipients were apparently helped than were hurt by the changes, with those who remained on the rolls receiving as much as a 43 percent increase in benefits. To Reagan's satisfaction, in the three years after the law passed in 1971, California's welfare population decreased by almost 300,000 people. Although this was partly the result of an upswing in the economy, an increase in abortions, and demographic factors beyond Reagan's control, his reforms nevertheless reduced the welfare rolls by an additional 6 percent. It was a significant achievement, but not as large as Reagan later made it seem on the campaign trail, where he took full credit for all the people leaving the program and for a substantial shift that never occurred of welfare recipients to the work force.[18]

Other actions taken in Reagan's second term were more like those of a liberal—and in recent California history this meant Democratic—than a conservative governor, although it would not appear that way to anyone hearing his later rhetoric. To meet threatened budget deficits, he accepted the need for state income tax withholding, added one cent to the state sales tax, and relied on federal revenue-sharing funds to balance budgets and provide an additional $1 billion in property-tax relief. By the end of his governorship he had returned $5.7 billion to taxpayers, including a whopping $4 billion reduction in property taxes. While he missed no opportunity to advertise these facts nationally, he never spoke of the huge tax increases he signed into law, the largest in California's history up to that time, which produced billions in new revenues. Nor did he focus on the fact that in his eight years in Sacramento the annual state budget jumped from $4.6 billion to $10.2 billion, while the operations part of the budget, over which he had most control, increased more than 50 percent, from $2.2 billion to $3.5 billion. As he justifiably emphasized later, during his governorship the growth of state government was slower than in other states and substantially less than what had occurred under Brown.[19]

Still, his overall record as governor was noteworthy not for its striking differences from Brown's or other state governors' but for its similarities to Brown's and other Democrats'. Recognizing that he could not make a successful bid for the presidency if he achieved little as governor of California, Reagan bent to the realities of a legislature controlled by Democrats and of a modern state charged with heavy responsibilities for promoting a more humane society. But he was never comfortable with this view of government, which continued to challenge his personal insistence on the greatest possible independence for the individual and freedom from external control. Unable to purge himself of an identification with the emotionally crippled father he wished to "pretend . . . wasn't there," Reagan lived in constant fear of dependency or diminished self-control. His struggle, however, was no longer between himself and some inner bogeyman, but between the individual and powerful big government which, in his view, had reversed the proper order of things, making itself the master and the people the servant.

Reagan's experience as governor had little impact on his thinking about public affairs. During the closing months of his governorship, for example, he spoke as if his term in Sacramento were a conservative model for what needed to be done in Washington. "You can have faith in the Republican philosophy of fiscal common sense, limited government, and individual freedom," he told a partisan audience. "Let me offer the experience of the past seven and one-half years in California to support that assurance." Moreover, after he left the governorship in January 1975, he began lecturing all over the country in behalf of conservative principles. Although the rhetoric of his speeches was nothing more than a 1975 version of his 1964 appeal for Goldwater, the difference, Lou Cannon points out, "was that Reagan could now present himself not as some idle conservative theorist preaching about how government could be made to work, but as a successful California governor who had translated his theories into practice. California reporters accompanying Reagan on his tours," Cannon adds, "marveled at the former governor's stirring accounts of how fiscal solvency and welfare reform had been achieved in California. There was a mythic quality to the governor's version of his own achievements, which of course made no mention of Moretti's cooperation on welfare reform or the massive Reagan tax increases. It was a selective version of reality," but one with enormous potency because he seemed to add substance to symbols. "It was highly effective in convincing Republican audiences that Reagan had the practical experience needed for the presidency."

This was shrewd politics on Reagan's part. Intuitively sensing that the antigovernment feelings he had so effectively played on in California were a viable national issue, especially when focused on Great Society programs, he continued to make them the centerpiece of his talks. But over and above the political impulse shaping his rhetoric was the fact that Reagan remained warmly committed to the free-enterprise ideology he preached, and he sincerely believed that he had never actually strayed from it. Reagan "spoke to his friends in private as if he were giving a speech to the multitudes," one of them said: "Same stories, same one-liners." If there were higher taxes, larger budgets, more government in California after he had run the state for eight years, he acted as if he had little or no responsibility for these developments. But this was not simply an act on Reagan's part; he believed it. Indeed, one of the most striking features of Reagan's political career is the extent to which he has rationalized contradictory actions or denied responsibility for them. Reporters who have followed him for some time point to his casualness about facts and statistics. Anecdotes of dubious origin and accuracy often make their way into his conversations, press conferences, and speeches. The accomplishments of his time in office are all his; the failings are the consequences of what predecessors did.[20]

In all this there are echoes of his alcoholic father, who, like most people unable to control their impulses, denied or refused to confront his overt behavior. Like the father he largely rejected but understandably could not detach himself from, Reagan plays fast and loose with the facts. Every good politician does this to some extent, but usually with a cynical recognition that this is part of the political game. While Reagan accepts the idea that politics requires some measure of insincerity, he cannot carry this very far. When his actions make a shambles of his ideology, as they repeatedly did in California, he finds ways to divorce himself from what was done. Or, when he feels pressed on an issue or when he fears he is being made to look bad, he sometimes exaggerates and distorts the facts. During the 1980 presidential campaign, for example, he "vociferously denied . . . that he sought [and lost] the 1968 nomination," which, of course, he had.[21]

Reagan began running for the presidency almost from the day he was first elected governor. In 1967–68, when he had been governor for only a year, he made a tentative, halting bid for the nomination. Fearing that his limited experience in government would not make him a creditable candidate and reluctant to split conservatives by battling Nixon and possibly throwing the nomination to Rockefeller, he hung back from making an all-out effort. When he did allow himself to be put forward openly at the Republican convention, it was too late to stop Nixon. In 1972, when Nixon ran for reelection, Reagan saw no point in challenging a Republican incumbent.[22]

Reagan felt differently four years later. In 1976 Gerald Ford was an appointed rather than an elected incumbent. More important, Reagan was now sixty-five years old and running out of time to present himself as a man still young enough to hold the office. Consequently, he went ahead, despite the ill will that it seemed certain he would generate among Republicans by challenging Ford. His campaign at once became a repeat of what he had done successfully in California—attacking big government and centralized authority as forces that undermined freedom and the quality of American life. To give his presidential bid a fresh feel and a positive program, Reagan offered a proposal for "a systematic transfer of authority and resources to the states—a program of creative federalism for America's third century." In a speech titled "Let the People Rule," he predicted that such a step would save the federal government $90 billion, produce a balanced budget, and cut individual income taxes by an average of 23 percent. Recognizing that Reagan had handed them an issue on which to defeat him, the Ford campaign pressed him to explain how the federal programs would be transferred to the states and how the states would find the $90 billion to pay for them. When Reagan implicitly replied that it would have to be done with state income or sales taxes, he demonstrated his superficiality and unrealism, which reminded people of Goldwater.

To strengthen his campaign Reagan shifted his focus from domestic to foreign affairs. Attacking Ford and Kissinger for détente and weak defense policies, as well as for proposing to give away the Panama Canal, he recouped some of the lost ground and won primary victories in several southern, midwestern, and western states. But the price of his success was a strong identification with the most conservative elements in the party and the alienation of moderate delegates he needed to defeat Ford. To attract them, Reagan followed the advice of John P. Sears, his campaign manager, that he break tradition by announcing his vice-presidential running mate in advance and that he choose Senator Richard Schweiker of Pennsylvania, a liberal Republican with a voting record praised by organized labor and the Americans for Democratic Action. But that maneuver backfired, winning Reagan no demonstrable support among moderates and antagonizing some of his conservative backers.

In the judgment of journalists Rowland Evans and Robert Novak, Reagan would have done better to preserve his ideological purity. They believe that in a convention where the rank and file were ideologically closer to him than to Ford, he might have won the nomination if he had avoided the Schweiker ploy and further pressed the case for conservative ideas. But then he almost certainly would have lost the general election to Jimmy Carter, who was also playing on antigovernment sentiment, but without the ultraconservative image Reagan had created for himself during the primary campaign. Reagan demonstrated his understanding that he had identified himself too strongly with the political right when he made his alliance with Schweiker. Later, when he renewed his bid for the presidency in 1980, he again kept his distance from the right. To gain the White House he knew he would have to yield some ideological ground—not out of faithlessness to his principles but in the service of making himself a winner and a president of the United States.[23]

In 1980 circumstances and skillful manipulation gave Reagan the White House. With Gerald Ford unwilling to make a definite commitment to run again, Reagan became the front-runner for the Republican nomination. Although he stumbled momentarily in Iowa, where George Bush won, and he fueled concerns about his advanced age by failing to mount a vigorous campaign, he recouped in New Hampshire, where he worked hard and trounced Bush, now his leading opponent, in a debate. By late March he had largely won the nomination. Aside from a series of misstatements which forced some attention on his casualness with facts and his questionable capacity for the job, he entered the Republican convention in a position to clinch the nomination and launch a successful challenge to Carter. However, when he indicated that he would make Ford his running mate, people questioned his commitment and his ability to become a full-time president in command of the job. Reagan countered this by selecting Bush for the vice-presidency and thus became the nominee of a unified party capable of appealing to a cross section of the electorate.[24]

Reagan further demonstrated his personal vitality and broad appeal in his acceptance speech before the Republican convention. In a talk characterized by the effective delivery which had endeared him to audiences for thirty years, he played on familiar conservative themes—less government, lower taxes, balanced budgets, family values, and peace through military strength. If these ideas had been associated mostly with ultraconservatives in 1964, by 1980 they were catch phrases that reached to the nerve center of America. Indeed, in the sixteen years since Goldwater had run, the country had grown more receptive to a conservative ideology. This was partly a consequence of the economic dislocation, or stagflation—recession combined with inflation—which had afflicted the nation through the seventies, and of setbacks in foreign affairs, defeat in Vietnam, mounting Soviet strength, and the Iranian defiance of American power by holding American citizens hostage in Teheran. Between 1973 and 1980, Reagan's chief pollster observed, "fewer than 20 percent of the country felt the nation was on the 'right track.' Seventy-five out of every 100 Americans thought the country was misdirected and in disarray." But it was not only events that favored a shift to the right in the country; blue-collar workers and ethnic Americans, many of whom had grown more prosperous and moved to the suburbs, now resented Great Society programs, government intrusion in their lives through high taxes and affirmative action for minorities. These people accepted Reagan's conservative assumptions.

Yet these middle-class Americans were not ready to abandon the New Deal gains of the previous fifty years or to see someone in the White House who would risk war out of antagonism to communism. To assuage these fears, Reagan spoke of "lasting world peace" and quoted Franklin Roosevelt. Most of all, he presented a moderate, reasonable face to the nation, calculated, in the words of journalist Elizabeth Drew, "to assure the national audience that this is a pragmatic, steady man who has ideas about government and who is reaching beyond the constituency that got him where he is tonight." [Reagan's speech embodied the two voices that had shaped his political career: on the one hand, he spoke to the conservative theme of freedom and independence for the individual, pledging "to restore to the federal government the capacity to do the people's work without dominating their lives"; on the other hand, he assured his listeners that he was no radical idealist courting defeat, but a sensible, thoroughly likeable American with a surefire formula for success that would please everyone. "Reagan is a vessel into which a lot of people are pouring their ambitions," Drew wrote. "He is the telegenic, easy-going ex-actor in whom people are finding, or hoping to find, what they want."[25]

Reagan's objective during the campaign was to preach the conservative wisdom without antagonizing moderate Democrats and independents. This was no simple task. As a campaigner Reagan was at his best when he spontaneously expressed his innermost beliefs. But by doing this he risked being identified with simplistic conservative views that appealed chiefly to right-of-center voters. The difficulty of holding the two sides in balance emerged at the start of his campaign. In August he went to Mississippi, where he avowed his faith in states' rights and pledged to restore the powers that properly belonged to state and local governments. He followed this in the middle of the month by calling the Vietnam war "a noble cause" and urging the nation to never again ask "young men to fight and possibly die in a war our government is afraid to win." At about the same time he told a press conference that fascism was the inspiration of the New Deal and that FDR's advisers, the members of the brain trust, admired the fascist system. Shortly afterward, while sending George Bush to Peking to assure the Chinese that no change would occur in relations between the United States and the People's Republic of China if he became president, he told the press that he intended to reestablish official relations with Taiwan. In the midst of this controversy he traveled to a Christian fundamentalist convention in Dallas, where he endorsed the teaching of creationism in schools. On Labor Day he compounded his difficulties by going to an opposite extreme when he attacked Carter for opening his campaign in Tuscumbia, Alabama, "the city that gave birth to and is the parent body of the Ku Klux Klan." The statement backfired because Tuscumbia was not the Klan's birthplace and because associating Carter with the Klan seemed a contrived device for making Reagan look more moderate than he was.[26]

These statements were the real Reagan, his inner feelings and beliefs for all to see. "There is no difference between Reagan's public and private statements," Theodore White believes. "His idea, voiced so often in public, is that the best way forward may be found by going back." Reagan is no intellectual, White added. "But he has ideas, and the ideas, simple and stubborn, are compulsive for him." Indeed they are, but not because he has carefully thought them through and finds them intellectually convincing. Rather, the ideology of individual freedom, conventional morality, patriotism, and passionate anticommunism perfectly reflects Reagan's deepest emotions. For Reagan, politics is a device for dealing with personal tensions that have plagued him since childhood. This may be fine for him, but it is hardly a reasonable way for a nation to wrestle with profound problems.[27]

In the last two months of the campaign Reagan and his closest advisers systematically acted to reestablish his credentials as a moderate and sensible man. They partly accomplished this by limiting his contact with the press and the spontaneous off-the-cuff remarks that had been getting him into trouble. In closing Reagan off from reporters, Elizabeth Drew observed, his aides were "trying to protect him from himself." "Reagan's campaign," she added, "is now designed to be as unrevealing as possible. That is in itself revealing." For Reagan himself this tactic was not an easy one. As Lou Cannon points out, "at nearly seventy years of age, he was forced to unlearn some of the habits of a lifetime." But he did it because he knew it could mean the difference between victory and defeat. And over and above the compulsive need to express his ideology was his need to be the successful hero, the winning candidate riding to the rescue of the nation.[28]

In the middle of September Carter unwittingly helped Reagan by attacking him as a racist and a warmonger. Carter pointed to the "stirrings of hate" in the campaign and predicted that the election would determine whether the country would be separated "black from white, Jew from Christian, North from South, rural from urban," and "whether we have peace or war." These exaggerated personal attacks allowed Reagan to appear as the more moderate of the two candidates, complaining to the press that he found it inconceivable that a president of the United States would say such things and that it was "beneath decency" for Carter to accuse anyone of deliberating wanting a war. Reagan effectively carried home these points in his October 28 debate with the president. Instead of seeing him as a racist and a warmonger, viewers received the impression of a pleasant, capable man who truly wanted peace. "I'm here to tell you that I believe with all my heart that our first priority must be world peace, and that the use of force is always and only a last resort when everything else has failed." If Reagan's demeanor and comments on peace were not enough to convince some voters that he was a reasonable man, his response to Carter's assertion that he had begun his political career by opposing Medicare added just the right touch. "There you go again," Reagan said in a measured tone, implying that Carter's whole campaign had been a series of overstatements about his ideas, record, and intentions.[29]

A week later Reagan won a decisive victory. Although he received only 50.7 percent of the popular vote, it was nearly 10 percent more than Carter's 41 percent. In the electoral college Reagan captured 489 votes from 44 states to Carter's 44 votes from 6 states and the District of Columbia. Gaining 12 Senate seats, the Republicans held a margin of 53 to 47, their largest majority in the upper house since 1928. In the lower house they gained 33 seats and reduced the Democratic advantage by almost 40 percent, from 276 to 243 Democrats and from 159 to 192 Republicans. With Reagan in the White House and the bulk of the new Republican representatives sharing his point of view, the election represented a pronounced shift to the right. But not nearly as great a shift as Reagan shortly pictured it. His election was as much, if not more, the product of voter disaffection from Carter as attraction to Reagan. It also depended on what the political scientist Walter Dean Burnham calls "the largest mass movement of our time," the failure of millions of Americans to vote. With only 55.1 percent of the electorate going to the polls in 1980, Reagan won the election with only 28 percent of the eligible vote. In short, Reagan's victory may have been less a turn to the right than a continuation of a trend toward voter alienation and nonparticipation dating from the 1960s.[30]

Yet whatever the explanation for his victory, for the first time in almost fifty years, since Herbert Hoover was president from 1929 to 1933, conservatives had a chance to direct national affairs and test the validity of their ideas. More to the point, Reagan now faced the same paradoxical problem he had confronted in California: could an advocate of less government, who was more concerned with curbing government's abuses than with using it to solve acknowledged economic and social problems, be a successful chief executive? In short, could someone rule who was constitutionally opposed to government power?

Part II

THE DOMESTIC
LEADER

CHAPTER THREE

Symbolic Victories

AS PRESIDENT, REAGAN faced a tangle of economic problems almost as difficult as those of the 1930s. In January 1981 inflation, interest rates, and the projected federal deficit stood at nearly record highs, and unemployment was 7.4 percent. A 13 percent increase in the cost of living during 1980, a 20 percent prime rate for borrowing money, a predicted $56 billion deficit, and an unacceptably high rate of joblessness presented the new administration with a formidable challenge. Reagan's answer was the same one he had been voicing since the 1950s: shrink the power and control of government and increase the freedom of individuals and private enterprise. Indeed, no president in American history entered the White House more determined to reduce the role and size of government than Ronald Reagan. Other presidents had come to power favoring the proposition that the government which governs least governs best, but none had built his political career so fully on this idea or had been so ready to make it the centerpiece of his administration.

Reagan's inaugural address was a forceful expression of this view, a declaration of faith that the way to overcome "economic afflictions of great proportions" was through less government. "In this present crisis," the new president said, "government is not the solution to our problem; government is the problem ... It's not my intention to do away with government. It is rather to make it work—work with us, not over us; to stand by our side,

not to ride on our back. Government can and must provide opportunity, not smother it; foster productivity, not stifle it." The
issue before the nation, Reagan asserted, was whether we will "do
whatever needs to be done to preserve this last and greatest bas-
tion of freedom." He saw this "freedom and the dignity of the individual" as now in jeopardy from an overgrown centralized
authority. "It is no coincidence," he said, "that our present troubles parallel and are proportionate to the intervention and intrusion in our lives that result from unnecessary and excessive
growth of government . . . It is time to reawaken this industrial
giant, to get government back within its means and to lighten
our punitive tax burden. And these will be our first priorities, and
on these principles there will be no compromise."[1]

When he first became governor of California, Reagan had
had no specific program for making his "principles" work. Now,
however, he had supply-side economics or, as this theory became
known under the new president, [Reaganomics, which was aimed
at reducing spending on social programs and lowering taxes.
Lower taxes were supposed to fuel a major economic expansion,
which, in turn, would cut unemployment and provide more tax
revenues to lower the federal deficit and pay for higher defense
spending. Described by George Bush during the 1980 Republican
primary as "voodoo economics," the program held out the unlikely hope of curing inflation and unemployment at the same
time. Bush had recognized and indirectly given voice to the fact
that this was not so much a realistic plan for overcoming economic ills as an expression of noneconomic values, an emotional
commitment to punishing the government and freeing prosperous Americans from controls] Although advertised as an economic program, Reaganomics was, in fact, a form of symbolic
politics, a means of liberating middle-class Americans from government tyranny and eliminating "immoral" deficits and the government's perceived preferential treatment of the needs of
minorities. It was a way to assure that government would now
defer to the wishes of the white middle class, which would once
again stand symbolically at the center of American life.[2]

[Because it is not clear to most people that Reaganomics is more a symbolic than a substantive economic program, because the Democrats' only alternative was the familiar one of more spending, and because Reagan is a superb salesman offering a plausible scheme for economic recovery, the country gave Reaganomics a respectful hearing] In a nationally televised speech on February 5, 1981, Reagan effectively described the problems facing the nation: "runaway deficits, of almost $80 billion" for the 1980–81 fiscal year, the first consecutive years of double-digit inflation since World War I, mortgage interest rates two and a half times higher than in 1960, a dollar worth only thirty-six cents of its 1960 value, an inflated housing market in which only one out of eleven families could afford to buy their first new home, an almost 100 percent increase in twenty years in the amount of federal taxes taken from earnings, 7 million unemployed Americans, and "the lowest rate of gain in productivity of virtually all the industrial nations with which we must compete in the world market."

If the problems were self-evident, so, according to Reagan, were their causes: unrestrained government spending and control. The federal payroll and budget were over 500 percent higher than twenty years before, government regulations added $100 billion a year to the cost of goods and services Americans buy, and the government was borrowing and expanding the money supply excessively. The answer to these difficulties, Reagan asserted, was to increase productivity by "making it possible for industry to modernize . . . And that means above all bringing Government spending back within Government revenues, which is the only way, together with increased productivity, that we can reduce and, yes, eliminate inflation." As specific first steps, he forbade government agencies to replace those who retired or left their jobs, and he set up a task force under Vice-President Bush that was to get rid of as many government regulations as possible. But recognizing that these were gestures, that it would "take more, much more" to overcome the nation's economic ills, he also announced his intention to propose cuts in tax rates and in government spending to stimulate productivity and to lower unemployment and inflation.

These cuts, he promised, would not reduce government spending below the levels of the previous year, nor would they be "at the expense of the truly needy." Rather, the rate of government spending would slow and budgets would continue to increase, but only at a pace comparable to increases in the population. Further, cuts in social programs would affect only those "not really qualified" or not deserving of help. By these means he hoped to "restore the freedom of all men and women to excel and to create," and to "leave our children . . . liberty in a land where every individual has the opportunity to be whatever God intended us to be."[3]

The plan took more specific form on February 18, when Reagan presented a State of the Union message to Congress on economic recovery. Reviewing the "grim" economic picture he had described in his earlier address, Reagan proposed a "comprehensive four-point program," consisting of reductions in the growth of government spending and in taxes, elimination of unnecessary, unproductive, or counterproductive regulations, and encouragement of "a consistent monetary policy aimed at maintaining the value of the currency." Specifically, he asked Congress to reduce direct federal spending by $41.4 billion in fiscal 1982. This would still allow, he said, an increase of $40.9 billion above 1981 spending, which would assure a "social safety net" for the poverty-stricken, the disabled, and the elderly. Social Security and Medicare payments would not be cut, and almost $216 billion worth of programs aiding tens of millions of Americans would be fully funded. At the same time he asked for a 30 percent across-the-board cut in tax rates over the next three years. He also proposed a comparable cut in taxes on unearned income and an increase in depreciation allowances for businesses. Pointing to the "virtual explosion in Government regulation during the past decade" and to the quadrupling of expenditures for these regulatory agencies, he promised to "come to grips with inefficient and burdensome regulations—eliminate those we can and reform the others." Finally, he urged the independent Federal Reserve System not to "allow money growth to increase consistently faster than the growth of goods and services."

The enactment of his full program, Reagan declared, would reduce inflation and interest rates, expand business, add three million jobs to the economy, sharply curtail bureaucratic red tape, and eliminate waste from social programs without in any way injuring the truly needy. Of those who had expressed opposition to his plan, Reagan said: "Have they an alternative which offers a greater chance of balancing the budget, reducing and eliminating inflation, stimulating the creation of jobs and reducing the tax burden?" Since they did not, he warned that the failure to enact his program would "put an end to everything we believe in and our dreams for the future."[4]

If Reagan's program appealed to millions of middle-class Americans who saw their values reflected in his plans, it also offered an irresistibly easy way out of the economic morass. Although most sophisticated economists considered the benefits promised by Reaganomics as too good to be true, Congress and the country as a whole could not resist a program that promised lower taxes, business expansion, more jobs, less inflation, lower interest rates, smaller deficits, and greater military strength. In February, after the president's two speeches, according to one poll, more than two-thirds of Americans approved of the Reagan economic program.

Congress, under skillful prodding by Reagan, was not far behind. Sympathizing with all the president's aims, having no comprehensive alternatives to offer, and fearing that opposition would be political suicide, Congress was predisposed to follow Reagan's lead. Of course, some strong liberal opposition emerged: "I do believe a lot of your assumptions are hallucinogenic," one New York congressman told Secretary of the Treasury Donald Regan. The Reagan program was "jellybean talk," another congressman said. House Democrats developed an alternative budget resolution costing $25.5 billion more than Reagan's plan. It contained more money for social programs, less for the military, and a smaller, one-year income-tax cut instead of a larger cut over three years. It also promised a significantly lower deficit for the 1982 fiscal year. But because it offered little besides greater spending and higher taxes, this budget became an easy target for conservatives, who asserted that the Democrats were reverting to the tired answers they had relied on and failed with in the past.[5]

Reagan prevailed. His courageous response to and recovery from the wounds he suffered in an assassination attempt in March pushed his popularity ratings in some surveys to the highest for a president in polling history. His appearance in behalf of his economic program before a joint session of Congress only a month after the attempt on his life gave added vigor to his influence. After wooing 47 conservative House Democrats from the South and the West, the president won a decisive victory for his budget bill on May 7, when the lower house gave him a favorable vote of 253–176. Sixty-three Democrats, more than a quarter of the party's House membership, defected to the president. The following week the Senate also put its stamp of approval on the president's budget by a lopsided vote of 78 to 20. In June a White House request for an additional cut of $5.2 billion to hold down the budget deficit provoked a sharper fight. Despite complaints from one Democratic leader that the White House wanted Congress to "lie down submissively" and let it "dictate" every last scintilla" of the 1982 budget, Reagan won again. Although he gained the key House vote this time by only 217 to 210, he emerged from the budget struggle with "just about everything he wanted." "Step 1 of the Reagan revolution in government economic and social policy," *Time* magazine concluded, "was just about accomplished."[6]

Step two was the president's three-year, 30 percent tax cut. Fears of higher budget deficits and increased inflation, however, made this part of the program harder to sell to Congress. Giving ground to this opposition, Reagan agreed to limit the first year's reduction to 5 percent and to delay its start until October 1. But the 10 percent cuts in the following two years were to remain intact. The president was unmoved by Democratic assertions that the across-the-board reductions favored the rich. "The President may be a real tightwad when it comes to programs that help working families," House Speaker Thomas P. (Tip) O'Neill complained. "But when it comes to giving tax breaks to the wealthy of this country, the president has a heart of gold." "Our proposal is not a 'rich man's windfall' . . ." Reagan replied. "It is fair, it is equitable, and it is compassionate."[7]

Despite these congressional reservations, Reagan again won the debate: at the end of July the House voted 238 to 195 and the Senate 89 to 11 to cut taxes by 25 percent over three years. The bill, in the words of Lou Cannon, was also "adorned with a clutch of special provisions which had little to do with any economic theory except greed." Indeed, the law gave generous tax breaks to the oil industry; savings and loan associations; recipients of unearned income on stocks, bonds, and real estate; married couples with two incomes; all corporations; and people who owed inheritance or estate gift taxes. It was an "overladen Christmas tree" providing gifts to numerous special interests that had lined up behind the bill. Although these were conventional ways of getting a tax law passed, no one could deny that at the end of his first six months in office, Reagan had achieved something of a political revolution. No president since FDR, according to *Time* magazine, had "done so much of such magnitude so quickly to change the economic direction of the nation." Yet, as the magazine also concluded, no one could say with assurance just what the consequences of Reaganomics would be. "Pray God it works," said one moderate Republican. "If this economic plan doesn't jell, where are we going to get the money for anything?"[8]

It took the country more than another year to recognize how little the nation as a whole would benefit from the supply-side program, but some people understood at once that the budget cuts and tax reductions would bring not greater economic opportunity and widespread prosperity, but staggering deficits, recession, and suffering for the neediest members of the society. "The administration has promised vigorous expansion through supply-side incentives in combination with monetary policy that works through high interest rates and a powerful contraction of the economy," observed liberal economist John Kenneth Galbraith. "This contradiction can only be resolved by divine intervention—a task for the Moral Majority."[9]

[The first Reagan budget reduced the number of people who were eligible to participate in federal social programs and the amount of the benefits they could receive. Food stamps, Medicaid, public service jobs, unemployment compensation, housing subsidies, urban mass transit, student loans, child nutrition programs, Aid to Families with Dependent Children, and Legal Services—all these programs suffered significant cutbacks. Nor did the Reagan tax cut make up for benefits lost by low-income families.] The 31.7 million taxpayers making $15,000 or less a year were to receive only 8.5 percent of the reduction while the 12.6 million people earning $50,000 or more a year were to get 35 percent of the money given up by the federal treasury. Moreover, as a consequence of Reagan's tax program, the contribution made by corporations to federal revenues was reduced from 13 cents to 8 cents of each tax dollar.[10]

Spokesmen for poor Americans complained bitterly about Reagan's "welfare for the rich" and insensitivity to those in need. Benjamin Hooks, the head of the National Association for the Advancement of Colored People, saw the president's policies bringing new "hardship, havoc, despair, pain, and suffering on blacks and other minorities." Coretta Scott King, widow of Martin Luther King, complained that Reagan's program would take ["food stamps and school lunches . . . from poor children to finance an arms race."] Another black leader compared Reagan's actions to those of a landlord who, instead of throwing you out of your house, cuts off the "lights, water and gas." When the economy gets better, he will turn the utilities back on. Mayor Coleman Young of Detroit described Reagan's program as the "trickle down" theory of economics that had failed under Herbert Hoover and would fail again.[11]

But Reagan does not see matters this way. He is convinced that placing capital in the hands of those Americans who are most likely to save and invest—the country's wealthiest citizens and its principal corporations—will result in a more productive economy. He believes that black Americans will ultimately be better served by his program than by continuing the old system of government supports. Speaking to the delegates at the annual convention of the NAACP in July 1981, the president declared: "Many in Washington over the years have been more dedicated to making needy people government dependent, rather than independent. They've created a new kind of bondage. Just as the Emancipation Proclamation freed black people 118 years ago, today we need to declare an economic emancipation." This would come about, he predicted, through his recovery program, which would lift the "entire country and not just parts of it."[12]

Reagan was sincere. He was not hiding some secret animus toward blacks which he needed to disguise for political reasons. He genuinely believes that minorities in general and black Americans in particular will ultimately make substantial gains from his reforms. His faith is so great or, more to the point, his emotional commitment to reducing dependence on government programs and restoring "freedom" and "individual initiative" is so strong that he finds it nearly impossible to accept criticism of his ideas, or "to abandon a goal when it involves a fundamental belief." Reagan is a "true believer," the *Los Angeles Times* said in a story on how one of his longtime aides viewed him. "He absolutely 'knows' things to be true . . . 'His is a philosophy of self-reliance. He believes the more you depend on government, the greater the narcotic effect it has on you.' " He is convinced "that good ultimately triumphs, that guys in white hats win, that people pull themselves up by their bootstraps if they are poor and help the deserving if they are rich . . . When Reagan believes something, he believes it 100 percent and preaches it like gospel. There is no shilly-shallying."

His aide asserted that the president's economic program was little more than a convenience for reaching his principal ends. Reagan "would be trying to cut federal spending and taxes even if the nation's economy were not in a mess," the *Times* also described this official as believing. "Inflation, high interest rates, a soggy economy—these factors have merely given Reagan the excuse, and a politically salable urgency, to do what he would be trying to do anyway: cutting back on the size of government and turning back to the citizens more responsibility for their own lives. The economy was 'a window' of opportunity . . . And all the budget and tax cuts and deregulations are a means to the end."[13]

The president's adviser revealed more than he probably cared to: Reagan, he was indirectly saying, has little knowledge of or serious interest in economic questions; his objective is less to repair the economy than to restore particular values to the center of American life. One may carry the point a step further: he has so thoroughly identified his quest for independence with his economic plan that he is nearly incapable of assessing that plan rationally. When people point out the failings of his economic program, he responds "on a totally different track." In March 1982, Senator Robert Packwood of Oregon, chairman of the Senate Republican Campaign Committee, revealed that some senators' expressions of concern to the president about a huge projected deficit evoked "anecdotal non sequiturs": "You know a person yesterday, a young man," Reagan replied to Packwood, "went into a grocery store and he had an orange in one hand and a bottle in the other and he paid for the orange with food stamps and he took the change and paid for the vodka. That's what's wrong." A group of shoe industry representatives complaining about foreign competition was treated to "a presidential lecture on the difficulty nowadays of buying a pair of cowboy boots as good as the ones available in days of yore."[14]

Reagan's attachment to a kind of symbolic politics in which he focuses on shadow victories and ignores economic realities is further illustrated by his handling of entitlements, those social programs for which people qualify automatically by meeting some basic standard of eligibility. Social Security, Medicare, the medical care program for people over sixty-five, civil-service pensions, and military retirement pay are all in this category. These programs now account for almost 50 percent of the federal budget and promise to claim an even larger share of federal spending in future years. More than anything else, entitlements account for the upward spiral in government deficits in the last twenty years. To truly cap the growth of government and meaningfully reduce federal outlays, the Reagan administration will have to address the problem of entitlements. But almost nothing was done about the issue during Reagan's first two years in office because, unlike welfare programs for the poor, entitlements affect the great body of middle-class voters that Reagan leans on for support. To be sure, in May 1981 Reagan proposed some cost-saving revisions for Social Security, including a 40 percent cut for those retiring at age sixty-two and a gradual 23 percent reduction in benefits for all future retirees, but Congress would have no part of it. The Republican-controlled Senate rejected his proposal, voting 96 to 0 against "precipitously and unfairly" reducing benefits for pensioners.[15]

Stung by this defeat, Reagan refused to address the entitlements issue in any comprehensive way in 1981. Consequently, the president was unable to carry out "genuine budget reduction" in his first year, though, as he had done in California, he slowed the growth of spending on social programs for the least affluent and politically weakest members of society. By saying, however, that he had meaningfully cut the budget, he opened himself to criticism. "The administration closed 1981," Cannon says, "as it began, representing minor and symbolic achievements as major, substantive ones." It produced not a "real budget revolution" but "a symbolic one."[16] Yet this was in character with the rest of Reagan's economic program and with most everything he has done in political life since 1967. Matters of substance are less important than rhetoric and appearances. This is not to say that Reagan's actions are without substantive consequences. They have done serious injury to domestic social programs and have caused significant suffering for the poor. But for Reagan, who denies these realities, actual political and economic changes are secondary to the fact that advocates of "correct" thinking or conservative ideas are in positions of power, where they can speak for old values and honor their constituents' views. Reducing the size of government, restoring the economy, strengthening the national defense—all are symbolic expressions of heartfelt beliefs more than statements of rationally drawn plans for meeting public needs.

This is clearly reflected in the attitudes and actions of the people Reagan appointed to high office. In the introduction to *Reagan's Ruling Class: Portraits of the President's Top 100 Officials,* Ralph Nader points out that many of these people "expressed an enthusiasm at finding themselves in positions where their adversaries were sitting a short time earlier. They believed that it was their day in the sun and they were going for broke." The Reaganites, Nader also observes, show "a remarkable sameness . . . of attitudes, ideologies, and even styles of thinking and explaining." Most of the people a president appoints reflect that president's views, of course, but Reagan has carried this to an extreme. Apart from a few people on the far right, it is "difficult to find a maverick" on the Reagan team. It is "a homogenized government" of true believers with a "uniformity of outlook" that makes them "appear as a product of a giant cloning process."

Collectively, these people favor immobilizing, repealing, or reducing government operations. "Problems that their agencies are supposed to address are minimized, denied, or considered the business of the states." Like Reagan, they display "a studied insensitivity to facts and a calculated indifference to alternate means to solve undeniable problems." There is a "robotized" quality to their view of the world. They see things not in terms of people and their real problems, but from an ideological perspective that allows little room for flexibility and humane response. Their central concern is to inhibit the government from taking an active part in economic and social affairs and to discourage agencies like the Bureau of Land Management, the Forest Service, the National Labor Relations Board, the Federal Trade Commission, the Environmental Protection Agency, the Legal Services Corporation, the National Highway Traffic Safety Administration, the Occupational Safety and Health Administration, the Energy Department, and a host of other protective and regulatory bodies from carrying out their assigned duties. The Reagan appointees are acting in the name of free enterprise, which ultimately is supposed to allow everyone to prosper, but their attacks on government power and control are not so much systematic steps to restore economic well-being as symbolic acts of vengeance on a government that they see as out of step with conservative values.[17]

The attitudes and actions of Reagan's principal advisers illustrate the point. Edwin Meese, III, counselor to the president and his chief policy adviser, is a law-and-order conservative whose family is "the prototype of Norman Rockwell America." Patriotism, respect for the flag, and respect for authority are central to Meese's world view. During the sixties, as a deputy district attorney for Alameda County, California, he advocated taking a hard line against Berkeley protesters and directed Reagan's response to campus disorders. His enduring antagonism to student rebels who defied his values is reflected in his belief that James Rector, a twenty-five-year-old Berkeley resident who was killed in the People's Park demonstrations of 1969, "deserved to die." While serving in the White House during 1981, Meese attacked the American Civil Liberties Union "as being part of a nationwide 'criminals' lobby' that thwarts law enforcement." He is also an unyielding foe of Legal Services, which he views as made up of "turmoil-makers" rather than deliverers of legal aid to the poor. During the 1980 presidential campaign Meese ran the issues office without initiating any major policies. He "is for people being locked up. He's against sin and in favor of motherhood," a former director of the California Department of Corrections has said.

Aside from his passionate belief in strong law enforcement, Meese has few pronounced ideas on economic or foreign policy. Nevertheless, he supervises the president's domestic policy staff and is a member of the National Security Council. He is as close to Reagan as anyone in the administration except Michael Deaver and is sometimes described as the "deputy president" who transmits Reagan's ideas to others and acts as "the policy funnel into the president." Although Meese plays a large part in what some have described as Reagan's "delegated presidency," he is a disorganized administrator. Some who have worked closely with him believe that this is because he has difficulty in making decisions. This is not surprising. Conservative homilies and antagonism to governmental activism are imperfect guidelines for charting a clear, effective national course at home or abroad.[18]

Michael K. Deaver is even closer to Reagan than Meese. Although his title is deputy chief of staff, he is the president's right-hand man with a say on all issues. His association with the president, like Meese's, dates back to 1967, when he joined the governor's staff as coordinator of state administrative activities. He soon became Reagan's man Friday, running the governor's personal residence, overseeing his staff, protecting him from excessive demands on his time and energy, and acting as his liaison with other branches of government. He plays much the same role in the White House, where he is recognized as "a conciliator, a facilitator and a bearer of vital messages to the president." A small-town Californian with a background in public relations, Deaver is the "perfect adjutant," "loyal aide," and reflector of Reagan's world view. In the words of one commentator, he has been "a shadow, a surrogate son, a confidante and comforter for the President." He is an uncritical admirer of Reagan, whom he describes as "the only person I've ever met who doesn't have to weigh things—his ideas seem to come from the depth of the man . . . He seems to know what is right." His identification with Reagan is so complete that some journalists have pictured Deaver as a man without "an existence of his own." He thinks more "in terms of the Reagans . . . than in terms of Mike Deaver."

Deaver's ideas mirror Reagan's. He is for budget and tax cuts and a tough foreign policy. Why can't the United States tell underdeveloped nations to go fly a kite, he asked Secretary of State Alexander Haig before a meeting with Third World countries in Mexico. "That's the most Neanderthal idea I ever heard," Haig replied. Deaver may be Reagan's indispensable aide, the man with whom Reagan can relax and speak frankly, and on whom he can rely to sense his mood and needs, but he has contributed little to substantive plans for meeting domestic and foreign problems. He is the quintessential conservative, ready to cut, trim, and cap government power in the name of traditional values but without any clear recognition of the complexities troubling the national and international scene or any idea of how to use government to ease the dilemmas of our time.[19]

Chief of Staff James A. Baker, III, Reagan's third principal adviser, shares control of White House operations with Meese and Deaver, principally supervising intergovernmental, legislative, and political affairs as well as the offices of personnel, communications, press, and public liaison. Unlike Meese and Deaver, however, Baker is a comparative newcomer to the Reagan camp. Scion of a wealthy Houston family that helped found the city, educated at a Pennsylvania prep school and Princeton University, and a prominent corporate attorney, Baker does not fit the self-made mold of the other Reaganites. His family controls one of the dozen largest law firms in the country and a major Texas bank. Baker has been less ideological and more flexible than most of the president's other closest advisers, and he has a reputation as a skilled political manager. At the 1976 Republican convention, for example, he successfully organized President Ford's floor fight to hold off Reagan's bid for the nomination, and during the election campaign he helped plot the strategy that brought Ford from a 10 percent to a 1 percent gap in the popular vote won by Jimmy Carter. As George Bush's manager during the 1980 primary campaign, Baker worked hard not to needlessly antagonize Reaganites, placing Bush in a position to become the vice-presidential nominee and himself to become a special assistant to Reagan by helping him prepare for the debates with Carter and John Anderson. Because Baker is known as a pragmatist and has refused to push for the goals of the Moral Majority, he has become a whipping boy for ultraconservatives, who characterize him as an "Ivy League–Wall Street–Big Business kind of Republican."

Yet for all this, Baker is a man with strong conservative views who fits comfortably into Reagan's White House. During his campaign for the office of attorney general of Texas in 1978, Baker emphasized the need for tough law enforcement, urging "a war on drugs, fixed-length sentencing, swifter and more certain punishment, tougher parole requirements, and stricter juvenile justice." He also stressed his opposition to federal "encroachment," complaining of environmental, energy, and voting rights regulations, and made clear his antagonism to labor unions by declaring "strong support" for the state "right to work" law. Like Reagan, he resents the growth of a government that seems principally concerned with the interests of liberals, minorities, and labor unions and that "indulges" criminals who defy traditional authority. As an upper-class old-family American who seems to feel elbowed aside by current trends, Baker shares Reagan's desire to weaken federal authority and get the country back on a traditional track. For Baker this apparently consists less of an economic program than of a weakened government partly presided over by conservatives like himself. As he told the *Washington Post* shortly before Reagan became president, "Most policy decisions are made in the Oval Office with two or three people sitting around, and I'm going to be one of those people."[20]

The symbolic politics practiced by Reagan and his immediate staff extends to the rest of his government as well. The Justice Department under Attorney General William French Smith is a good case in point. Like Baker, Smith is a wealthy old-family American whose ancestors came to the New World on the *Mayflower* and fought in the American Revolution. A Harvard Law School graduate and multimillionaire corporate attorney, he "looks like an objet d'art that might be advertised in *The New Yorker* magazine, a sleek figurine called 'The Attorney,' manufactured by one of those companies that produce porcelain owls and bullfinches." He has been a close personal friend and business associate of Reagan's since the early 1960s and a principal architect of the president's political career. Like Reagan, he is a staunch foe of judicial activism and of courts that make laws rather than interpret them. "We will attempt to reverse this unhealthy flow of power from state and federal legislatures to federal courts—and the concomitant flow of power from state and local governments to the federal level," he announced in October 1981. More specifically, he wishes to curb the role of the federal courts in rulings on abortion, school busing, affirmative action, and bans on state-sponsored prayer in schools. In Smith's view, the federal judiciary has become the advocate of permissive, liberal ideas serving minorities and women and is unresponsive to traditional beliefs. His policy of judicial restraint aims at restoring old-style, conventional values to the place of honor in American life.[21]

Smith's commitment to this altered role for the federal government expressed itself in an abortive effort to change an Internal Revenue Service policy that denies tax exemptions to private schools that discriminate on the basis of race. In response to an appeal to the president from Trent Lott, a Mississippi Republican congressman, the Justice Department announced in January 1982 that it was asking the U.S. Supreme Court to dismiss suits involving schools in North and South Carolina that faced the loss of their tax-exempt status. The announcement evoked charges of racism against the president, who had advocated such a reversal of policy in campaign speeches and had accepted its insertion in the Republican platform of 1980. The outcry, however, produced a White House attempt—"operation salvage"—to correct the president's image as someone who is insensitive to black Americans.

To this end, Reagan submitted legislation asking Congress to make the IRS ruling law. In this way, he argued, an important social policy would be made not by government bureaucrats but by the elected representatives of the people. He had intended all along, he explained, to submit legislation codifying the IRS rule. There was no racism involved, it was only a case of poor timing. "This president is the most fair-minded man I've ever known," Deaver told the press. ". . . It's a shame his reputation has to be tarnished by faulty staff work." By this means the White House hoped to convert an embarrassing expression of Reagan's real belief into a symbolic victory satisfying everybody. Black Americans were supposed to accept the picture of a compassionate president opposed to discrimination, while conservatives were supposed to see his action as a victory over arbitrary bureaucrats and for the rule of law.

As explained by Deputy Attorney General Edward Schmults, the president's action involved "a very important principle. As a citizen . . . I am more concerned—it goes to my philosophy of government—about what I would call faceless bureaucracies than I am about misdeeds by politically accountable people because we can throw politically accountable people out of office . . . The bureaucracy . . . is extremely tough to deal with . . . I remain persuaded that there's no authority in the law for an agency [like IRS], rather than Congress, to make those decisions." Describing the episode as "unfortunate," Schmults felt that the administration simply had "to do a better job of explaining what it is we are trying to do." Schmults need not bother; it is already reasonably clear. Acting on its true instincts, the administration has lined up with suburban whites in opposition to government insistence on equal rights for minorities, thus signaling to white middle-class Americans that their values and influence were once again predominant in national affairs. When this stand threatened to damage Reagan's political and moral hold on the country, however, he identified himself with minority rights at the same time he soothed conservatives by proposing symbolic inhibitions on government "bureaucrats." But the attack on the IRS policy of denying tax-exempt status to private schools discriminating on the basis of race did not survive a Supreme Court review. In May 1983, by a vote of eight to one, the Court rejected the administration's claim that only Congress, and not the IRS, had the power to deny tax exemptions to private schools. In "a stinging rebuke" to the administration the Court described the IRS action as serving "a fundamental overriding interest in eradicating racial discrimination in education."[22]

The administration also fused conservative and liberal symbols in handling the extension of the 1965 Voting Rights Act. A product of the civil rights movement of the sixties, the law provided for federal intervention to help enroll voters in districts where 50 percent or more of the voting age population was unregistered. The measure helped to advance black registration in the South particularly, where the percentage of blacks registered to vote jumped dramatically. In Mississippi, for example, the percentage of registered voting-age blacks increased from 6.7 to 59.8 percent in just three years. Though the Reagan administration would not dare oppose the extension of a law that has been so transparently successful in righting a historic wrong and democratizing American politics, it hung back from leading the measure through the Congress. When the administration did support a revised version of the statute, it gave the impression of "being dragged kicking and screaming into the twentieth century." It grudgingly accepted a new congressional provision that "prohibited state and local officials ... from employing any voting procedure that *resulted* in discrimination against blacks or other minorities." This was an easier standard to enforce than one requiring "those challenging a voting system to prove that the state or local officials consciously *intended* to discriminate." The administration also discouraged passage of a provision that would have required federal clearance for an indefinite length of time for any changes in voting procedures in districts with records of past discrimination; instead the requirement was to stand for only twenty-five years.

Apparently the president felt he had given more to his conservative constituents than to blacks in his actions on the Voting Rights Act. On the same day he announced his support of the compromise extension bill, he made a dramatic visit to a Maryland black family—the Butlers—that had had a Ku Klux Klan cross burned on its front lawn five years before. The issue was timely because a federal court had just awarded them several thousand dollars in damages. As with the IRS ruling against private schools that discriminated, Reagan was on both sides of the fence: his lack of enthusiasm for an extension of the Voting Rights Act expressed conservative antagonism to federal activism in behalf of blacks, while his acquiescence to that extension and his visit to the Butlers reflected his recognition of the political need to give both substantive and symbolic comfort to black Americans.

The president's actions did not fool many advocates of minority and women's rights. In June 1983 civil rights activists accused the administration of fostering a renewed atmosphere of racism in the country, pointing to its opposition to court-ordered busing and affirmative action in hiring. Likewise, the U.S. Civil Rights Commission criticized the administration's reduction in appointments of minorities and women to major government posts. Where 12 percent of President Carter's appointees were black, 12.1 percent women, and 4.1 percent Latino, Reagan has given only 4.1 percent of his administration's high-level jobs to blacks, 8 percent to women, and 3.8 percent to Latinos. To disarm some of this antagonism, particularly toward three Reagan appointees being considered for Senate confirmation to the Civil Rights Commission, the administration in July filed a desegregation suit against Alabama's public higher education system and proposed tougher antidiscrimination provisions in the fifteen-year-old Fair Housing Act. While civil rights activists generally praised these actions, they nevertheless saw them as cynical political efforts to reduce minority hostility to an unsympathetic administration.[23]

Reagan's greatest triumph in melding conservative and liberal symbols was his appointment of Sandra Day O'Connor to the United States Supreme Court. A conservative, fifty-one-year-old State Court of Appeals judge in Arizona and a former state senator, O'Connor shared Reagan's opposition to judicial activism and busing, favored the death penalty, and was personally opposed to abortion. Leaders of the New Right and the Moral Majority objected to her votes in the Arizona legislature supporting the dissemination of "all medically acceptable family-planning methods and information" to anyone wishing it and labeled her a supporter of abortion who was unfit to serve on the highest court, but conservatives like Barry Goldwater and Senator Paul Laxalt of Nevada warmly backed her appointment. Moreover, liberals found it difficult to object to someone with a reputation as a fair-minded legislator and jurist who would become the first woman to serve on the Supreme Court. Speaker Tip O'Neill called the choice "the best thing" Reagan had done since becoming president, while Senator Edward Kennedy said: "Every American can take pride in the president's commitment to select such a woman for this critical office." Her appointment received unanimous approval in the Senate.

(For Reagan it was the greatest symbolic triumph of his first year.] The seating of a wholesome, sensible, solid conservative on the highest court in the land was a source of enormous satisfaction to most of the president's supporters, especially when in June 1983 she led two other dissenting justices in opposing the Court's reaffirmation of its 1973 decision that made abortion a constitutional right. Yet at the same time O'Connor's appointment was a demonstration of how flexible and politically effective the president could be. (Reagan, the staunch opponent of the Equal Rights Amendment, had broken a 191-year tradition by appointing a woman justice to the Court.)"The appointment of O'Connor is a master stroke," declared liberal Democratic Congressman Morris Udall. "It shows a flexibility, a bigness that the Ronald Reagan stereotype doesn't recognize. It shows a political savvy on the part of the president that I had assumed was not there."[24]

For liberals, however, the O'Connor appointment and the voting rights extension bill were aberrations in an administration devoted to advancing conservative values by limiting the size and power of government. No one in Reagan's administration reflects this mentality better than Interior Secretary James Watt. Raised in the rural farm communities of Lusk and Wheatland, Wyoming, Watt was a model child, "an exceptionally good boy" who joined the Boy Scouts, became the high school valedictorian, "resisted unwholesome peer-group pressure," never drank beer, liquor, or coffee, graduated with honors from the University of Wyoming, and married his high school sweetheart. Taught rigid rules of conduct by his parents, who were ramrod Christians and devoted Republicans, Watt developed "high ideals," from which, his mother says, he still does not "deviate an inch." He "has lost none of that astringent seriousness of his Wyoming boyhood," one news account of him observes. "Even more, he still seems powered by youth's missionary energy, the sense of absolute righteousness that maturity usually softens." After college he earned a law degree and served in Washington as a legislative aide to Wyoming's conservative Senator Milward Simpson. There, during the sixties, the formative years of the Great Society, when western Republicans of the Goldwater stripe were held in low esteem, he remembers, according to a member of his current staff, being "treated like manure by those in power. Watt hasn't forgotten that." The staff member believes that residual feelings of resentment account for some of Watt's present antagonism to government regulators and environmentalists.

After eleven years in Washington, in 1977 Watt became the head of the Mountain States Legal Foundation, a conservative public-interest law firm in Denver. During almost four years in that job he fought against lower utility rates for the elderly and disabled in Colorado, federal strip-mining regulations, a proposal to make "part of a Wyoming oil field a protected wilderness area," and a federal prohibition on motorized rafts in the Grand Canyon. The purpose of the foundation, Watt said, was "to fight in the courts those bureaucrats and no-growth advocates who create a challenge to individual liberty and economic freedoms." Identifying himself with the "Sagebrush Rebellion," a conservative movement of westerners opposed to everything from the fifty-five-mile speed limit to the proposed deployment of MX missiles in Utah and Nevada, Watt told a congressional hearing in 1979 that "we of the West believe that in too many instances our states are being treated like colonies. 'Foreigners'—bureaucrats who seem to be out of control—are making the decisions affecting the land, water, and resources which are the foundation of wealth for the West and indeed in many respects, the Nation." Watt questions the patriotism of conservationists: "What is the real motive of the extreme environmentalists, who appear determined to accomplish their objectives at whatever cost to society?" "Is it to simply protect the environment? Is it to delay and deny energy development? Is it to weaken America?"[25]

Watt views his appointment to the Interior Department as a mission to which God has called him. He sees himself as part of

Reagan's "crusade for America," in which he must "emotionally, spiritually and intellectually . . . withstand the onslaught" of liberals who are not Americans. He says that his objective as Interior Secretary is to assure that the country "will mine more, drill more, cut more timber to use our resources rather than simply keep them locked up." To this end, Watt proposed making a billion acres of offshore potential oil lands available for drilling between 1981 and 1986—"more than ten times the amount of offshore acreage offered for oil-exploration leasing in the entire history of the United States." He also urged a moratorium on the acquisition of national park lands, encouraged private concessionaires to expand their activities in the parks, and proposed changing the existing permanent ban on future mining and drilling leases in the remaining 80 million acres of pristine U.S. wilderness so that within eighteen years all wilderness lands would be open for exploitation.

Watt's policies are sharply at odds with the opinions of the majority in Congress and the nation. Sixty-seven percent of those questioned in a nationwide poll expressed a desire to maintain existing conservation laws even at a cost in economic growth. In 1981 the House of Representatives voted overwhelmingly to support continued expansion of the national parks, and in 1982 it unequivocally rejected Watt's plan to modify the prohibition on wilderness leasing. Yet none of this deters Watt. He seems purposely to seek out unpopular issues on which he cannot win but by which he hopes to make a symbolic point. Indeed, he seems far more interested in provoking fights and trumpeting his principles than in gaining his ends. "Even by his own standards," one evaluation of his performance concludes, Watt is "not an especially effective Secretary of the Interior. The pendulum was already swinging toward development" when Watt took office. He "could have nudged the national consensus further in the development direction if he had convinced the public that esthetic, recreation and wildlife tradeoffs were being made judiciously. But he lacked a political temperament . . . He had such a proclivity for polarization that he refused—or was unable—to curb his tongue even when his comments undercut his own objectives. He picked needless quarrels with congressmen, ruined the morale in several Interior agencies, and triggered dozens of environmental law suits." In the opinion of one former Interior official, Watt and his assistants have "out-Reaganed Reagan . . . but their effort to impose their own theory about how government should be run is going to end up hurting their efforts to get things done, especially for those resource development constituents whom they want to assist."

But one has to wonder whether Watt really cares. Although he is ostensibly an advocate of the interests of big business, the mining and oil industries, and real estate developers, Watt himself is a man of limited means with net assets of only $65,000—"an austere zealot in a cabinet of genial millionaires." Indeed, judging from his actions, Watt is less interested in assuring economic gains for developers than he is in fighting a moral crusade against liberals and government power—against those whom he sees scoffing at his values and demeaning him and against governmental authority which, one suspects, is a substitute for an earlier parental force he found impossible to challenge. In sum, like Reagan, whom Watt describes as his "soul mate," he uses politics as vocational therapy: public advocacy is a way to relieve his inner tensions and heighten his self-esteem; it is a means of turning substantive issues into symbolic ones, of making social questions serve private, psychological ends.[26] If it were possible to probe in depth the psychology of most Reaganites, I suggest that one might find a shared problem with authority stemming from childhood. I speculate that the conservative world view is based on an inner need that is satisfied by fighting against excessive power and control in government.

Reagan's cut, trim, and squeeze approach to government has not been without impact. If Watt has not been totally successful in opening up federal lands and resources to private development, others in the Reagan administration have been more effective in weakening and eliminating government controls. Anne (Gorsuch) Burford, the former head of the Environmental Protection

Agency, for example, was an uncompromising foe of federal regulation. She favored putting "environmental decision-making" in the hands of local governments and said she took the EPA position "because I think this president has an enormous opportunity to change the way this government does business. And in no place is that opportunity more important or more relevant than in the environmental area." Under her aegis the agency's budget was cut to half of the amount people think is necessary for it to carry out its statutory responsibilities efficiently; the EPA backed revisions in the Clean Air Act "that would drastically weaken the law"; it urged "substantial revisions in the regulations governing hazardous wastes that will reduce protection on existing sites"; and it reduced enforcement actions to about one-eighth of what they were under the Carter administration. In short, when she resigned in March 1983 because of the controversy over her handling of the $1.6 billion superfund for cleaning up toxic waste dumps, she was "already well on the way toward pulling back the EPA from key programs overseeing hazardous wastes, toxic substances, clean air, and clean water." A former agency official believed that the Reagan-Burford policies were tearing "EPA up by the roots. It would take a new Administration that gave top priority to restoring this institution of public protection seven or eight years to get back to the 1980 level of competence." To counter this politically damaging view, Reagan, in a striking demonstration of pragmatism, replaced Burford with William D. Ruckelshaus, who was the first head of the EPA in 1970 and who is known for his skill in balancing environmental concerns fairly against the needs of business.[27]

Under Terrel Bell, a former U.S. Commissioner of Education and head of the Utah System of Higher Education, the Education Department is also shrinking in size and influence and was initially slated for elimination as a Cabinet-level agency. "This is a states-right administration," Bell has said, and he is doing all he can to turn responsibility for education back to the states. Departmental budget cuts have affected elementary and secondary school programs and reduced the amount of government aid available to college students. At the same time federal efforts to enforce civil rights regulations concerning schools and promote school desegregation are being reduced.\ In response to the New Right, Bell has appointed the Reverend Bob Billings, executive director of the Moral Majority, to the department's Office of Non-Public Education, has supported parent groups that oppose "immoral" books in school libraries, and has said that children should be guaranteed "the right not to read" such materials. Former Education Secretary Shirley Hufstedler describes the administration's policies as "an undeclared war on children" and predicts that if all Reagan's proposed changes are approved, it will take "multiple administrations" to repair the damage.

In the spring of 1983, however, when an administration-appointed national commission on education described a "rising tide of mediocrity" in the nation's schools, Reagan said nothing more about plans to eliminate the Education Department as a Cabinet-level agency and began talking instead about the need for improved quality in American education. He stated that his administration had not reduced funds for education but had only cut proposed budget increases; congressional leaders responded by describing his statement as "a fundamental, basic, gross untruth" which ignored the fact that the administration's three budgets had called for cuts in education totaling $9 billion, or nearly 20 percent of the federal education budget for those years.[28]

Between 1981 and 1983 the Department of Health and Human Services under Richard Schweiker, a former senator from Pennsylvania, also avidly pursued a program of reduced services. "This is our last opportunity and best opportunity" to reduce social programs, Schweiker declared after Reagan presented his economic plan in February 1981. "If we don't do it now, we never will." Schweiker pushed for major cuts in a broad array of health and welfare programs, particularly in Medicaid, health care services for the poor administered and partly funded by the states, and in Aid to Families with Dependent Children, a welfare program also shared by the states. A $1 billion reduction in Medicaid funding in fiscal 1982, combined with changes in the law governing the AFDC program, made one million welfare recipients ineligible for AFDC support and Medicaid benefits. Health and welfare cuts, a report of the American Hospital Association points out, "have triggered a much more rapid deterioration in health status than most officials responsible for the cuts are now willing to acknowledge ... Cuts in food stamps and school lunch programs are sending more persons with malnutrition to hospital outpatient departments. The tensions associated with an ailing economy have increased the reported incidence of attempted suicide, traumatic injury, and battered children, which has worsened in some areas because of fewer social workers assigned to deal with the problem." The report concludes, "Cuts already enacted for fiscal years 1982–1984 represent a serious threat to the health status of the most disadvantaged segments of our population."

The administration's determination to save money led the Social Security Administration to arbitrarily eliminate some 355,000 beneficiaries from its disability rolls. Appeals to administrative law judges resulted in the restoration of some 90,000 of these, and a U.S. District Court judge characterized the Social Security Administration's ending of payments to 72,800 physically disabled persons as arrogant. Margaret Heckler, who replaced Schweiker as head of Health and Human Services in March 1983, then announced a liberalization of rules for supporting handicapped Americans, although one Legal Services attorney called Heckler's action a "façade ... an attempt to create an image of compassion."

He was largely right. Reagan and others in the White House apparently were little concerned about the suffering the administration was causing. One may conclude that they view such cuts in social programs not in terms of the people affected but as symbolic victories over government control of the individual and in behalf of old-fashioned values identified with the white middle class. The consequences of the reductions do not register clearly on Reagan and the advocates of his ideas because their attention is focused almost exclusively on the psychologically satisfying assault on government power. They either ignore or deny the results of their actions by thoughtlessly repeating unrealistic clichés about the role of private, voluntary philanthropy. As the American Hospital Association report concluded, "The difficulty with the assumption that the voluntary sector can effectively assume responsibility for programs undergoing reductions in government support . . . is that the public and private sectors in the United States have formed a complex and unique partnership that is peculiarly American. The result is that the nonprofit, private sector is not an alternative to government—the two sectors are intertwined . . . Government cutbacks are inevitably private cutbacks." Moreover, if corporate and private philanthropies are to compensate for government reductions, their contributions will have to triple. There is no evidence that this is taking place. Reagan's failure to acknowledge this fact demonstrates his indifference to going beyond cuts in government spending and power to develop positive means of solving social problems.[29]

The same point can be made about the president's deregulation of the automobile industry. With the help of Transportation Secretary Andrew (Drew) Lewis, a millionaire businessman and prominent Pennsylvania Republican, the administration has moved to restore economic well-being to auto manufacturers by giving them tax breaks and reducing regulations. Because "automobiles have been one of the nation's largest sources of air pollution; a principal cause of accidental death, injury, and property damage; and major users of petroleum products," they have been increasingly subjected to "social" regulation. These facts, however, did not deter the administration, in the spring of 1981, from announcing that thirty-four automobile safety regulations and Environmental Protection Agency rules would be delayed, weakened, or eliminated. These included the required installation of passive restraint systems, airbags, or automatic seat belts; a requirement that bumpers be able to withstand the impact of a crash at speeds of at least five miles per hour; the testing of vehicles on assembly lines to assure that they meet federal emission standards; and fuel economy standards for cars and trucks manufactured after 1985. Reagan claims that these changes will save the automobile industry approximately $1.3 billion over five years and will reduce costs to consumers over the same period by $8 billion. Others are not so sure. Insurance companies and safety engineers contend that "the economic benefits of a crash protection standard (passive restraint) would be ten times greater than its cost."

The administration rejects this conclusion. *The Reagan Experiment,* a study by the Urban Institute, asserts, "It appears that the overriding reason the requirement was withdrawn was because passive restraints represent precisely the kind of government paternalism that the Reagan administration has expressly rejected. Thus, despite the fact that benefits arguably exceeded costs, cost-effectiveness proved an insufficient rationale for going forward with the regulation." As described by staff members in the Transportation Department, Lewis's attitudes reinforce the idea that the administration is much more interested in implementing preconceived views about government than in giving considered answers to complex questions. He "hates" government, one of them said, and he has little interest in transportation issues, many of them feel. "I don't have a sense that he cares at all about improving the transportation system," one official observed. "I don't think he really cares whether there's a DOT five years down the road."[30]

Nowhere did this passsion for symbolic victories over government find clearer expression than in Reagan's response to the air traffic controllers' strike in the summer of 1981. In August, after the 13,000-member Professional Air Traffic Controllers Organization failed to win from the federal government a shorter work week as a remedy for job stress and as a way to improve air traffic safety, it decided to strike. For Reagan their strike was a chance to make a point about government being the servant and not the master of the people. Whatever the merits of the case, he refused to consider any compromise. "I respect the right of workers in the private sector to strike," he announced. "Indeed, as president of my own union, I led the first strike ever called by that union." But these were government employees violating a no-strike pledge and threatening to interrupt "the protective services which are government's reason for being ... They are in violation of the law, and if they do not report for work within forty-eight hours, they have forfeited their jobs and will be terminated." When the controllers refused to give ground, three former Republican secretaries of labor offered to mediate the conflict. Reagan refused the offer. Although he acknowledged that it would cost the government $1.3 billion to train new controllers and that the consequent reductions in flight schedules would negate "many of the benefits of airline decontrol," the president fired all the strikers and decertified the union. Whatever the human and material costs, Reagan saw the strike as a chance to make a point: government and its employees would no longer exercise arbitrary control over individuals or over the course of American life.[31]

In the first year of the Reagan administration, wherever one looked, the pattern was much the same: cuts in federal programs spawned more by a reflexive antagonism to government than by considered analysis of the consequences. In the Energy Department, Secretary James Edwards, a dentist and former South Carolina governor, supported "a drastic reordering of priorities" and ultimate abolition of the department. Funds for nonnuclear energy research were cut by 85 percent from their 1980 level, to a total of $331 million for the 1983 fiscal year, while money for nuclear energy development was scheduled to increase to $1.68 billion in 1984, a rise of some 15 percent from the previous year. "Edwards's energy budget was shaped by blind bias," a former department official in charge of solar research complains. "Even as the country's most promising energy options are being gutted, a herd of technological losers will be getting fat at the public trough." This, of course, is the criticism of a solar energy advocate, but it is difficult to dismiss his observation that the administration is acting more out of a pronounced bias than from a balanced estimate of what kinds of research will serve the country's long-term energy needs.

In the Labor Department, presided over by Raymond Donovan, a millionaire builder from New Jersey, there was an $8 billion, or 23 percent, cut in the 1982 budget, with job-training programs particularly hard hit. The Department's Occupational Safety and Health Administration is, for all practical purposes, being dismantled through reduced enforcement of health and safety rules protecting workers. This is being done without any clear indication that it will make the American economy more productive. As the Urban Institute study concluded about Reagan's whole program of "regulatory relief" after one year, "The euphoria has died . . . The belief that [de]regulation could have an immediate and visible impact on the economy has faded."[32]

It was not just in government deregulation, however, that hopes had faded. During Reagan's second year the wide-ranging symbolic victories over government, which had given conservatives so much satisfaction, turned into substantive defeats for the whole country. Indeed, as the second year of the Reagan term revealed, symbolic politics may be a fine way to release psychic tensions and help people strengthen their self-esteem, but it is a poor way to overcome economic and social problems that afflict the nation and the world.

CHAPTER FOUR

Real Defeats

"REAGANOMICS IS DEAD," the journalist Robert J. Samuelson wrote in December 1982, "not because it failed, but because it never existed. Ronald Reagan never really had an economic program. Mostly, he had a social program to reduce domestic spending, to cut taxes and to increase defense spending.'Supply-side economics' was an expedient afterthought, meant to reconcile Reagan's desire for higher defense spending and lower taxes by making unbelievable claims for the beneficial effects of tax cuts." Above all, Samuelson concludes, Reaganomics symbolizes "a political and journalistic addiction to meaningless phrase-making and, more important, an addiction to the personalization of policies." In a word, Reaganomics is symbolic politics; it is an attempt to promote the president's personal values through a program that is ostensibly economic.[1]

Reaganomics does not work. It may help salve the amour-propre of Reaganites, but it does not answer the economic or social dilemmas of our time. To the contrary, it makes matters worse, injuring the poor and serving the interests of the rich. Reaganomics has plunged the country into an economic morass from which it will not easily escape, partly because Reagan insists that the country "stay the course." But he can hardly urge otherwise: Reaganomics is less a set of intellectual assumptions open to revision than an expression of felt values to which the president and his followers are emotionally tied. And when they do shift

94

ground, they deny that their approach to public affairs has changed in any way. Similarly, though proposed New Right legislation banning abortions, requiring balanced budgets, and legalizing prayer in public schools runs counter to majority sentiment and squanders political capital, Reagan has advocated congressional approval of these measures. Like his economic program, they are less the product of rational calculation serving the national interest than a means for Reaganites to ask the country to defer to their values.

A review of the Reagan economic program in the two years after it was begun is illustrative. From the outset the plan was a contradiction in terms, promising contraction and expansion at the same time. On the one hand, Reaganomics stood for monetarism, the policy of reducing inflation by curbing the growth of the money supply, maintaining high interest rates, and strengthening the dollar. On the other hand, Reagan's program consisted of supply-side economics—tax cuts that were supposed to produce savings, investment, and work incentives leading to a high rate of economic growth. This in turn was supposed to generate tax revenues that would ultimately pay for the tax cuts. When combined with reductions in government expenditures for social programs, supply-side policy was expected to curtail and eventually eliminate budget deficits. And this was promised despite a projected $1.8 trillion rise in the defense budget in five years.

During the first six months of his term Reagan hailed the coming economic boom. He predicted a falling rate of inflation, a revitalized dollar in the international money markets, and "businessmen and investors" committing themselves to "industrial development, modernization and expansion, all of this based on anticipation of our program being adopted and put into operation." He also pledged to "create 13 million new jobs, nearly 3 million more than we would have without these measures." The three-year tax package was to "have an immediate impact on the economic vitality of the nation, where even a slight improvement can produce dramatic results." Finally, though the federal government would run another large deficit in the fiscal year ending September 30, 1981, the Reagan program would make the deficit smaller than "it might have been and starting next year, the deficits will get smaller until in just a few years the budget can be balanced."[2]

Numerous economists and Wall Street financiers responded to the president's program with skepticism, if not outright disbelief. As one economist observed, "It looks as though one group was working on real growth, another on monetary policy, and a third on inflation. When you put the numbers together, they don't make sense." By the end of August, a month after the Reagan program was in place, the stock market had dropped more than a hundred points from its high point in the spring, and the economy had fallen into a recession. "Don't give me a lot of supply-side economic theory about what happens when you cut taxes," one Wall Street economist declared. "Don't tell me that in theory people should save more, and that in the end everything will be all right. Just give me the arithmetic and the reality." Businessmen and investors were frightened by swelling government deficits and rising interest rates, evidenced by six-month treasury bills discounted at a record 15.85 percent. These facts made themselves felt during the fourth quarter of 1981, when the Gross National Product fell 5.3 percent, factory use dropped 4.5 percent to 74.8 percent of capacity, expenditures for new plant and equipment contracted by 8.5 percent, and unemployment rose 0.9 percent to 8.3 percent of the working force. The only good news was that the annual rate of inflation had fallen to 7.7 percent. By the close of Reagan's first year in office, the average citizen either was no better off or was worse off than the year before.[3]

The contradictions and unrealism behind the president's economic program found dramatic expression in November 1981, when William Greider, a *Washington Post* editor, published a lengthy article in the *Atlantic* magazine on David Stockman, the director of the Office of Management and Budget. Based on eighteen tape-recorded interviews in which Stockman gave candid assessments of Reaganomics, the article revealed that one of the principal architects of Reagan's program doubted the wisdom of

much that was being done. As early as January 1981, Stockman
revealed, he had anticipated that the president's three-year tax cut
and increases in defense spending would produce a series of unprecedented peacetime federal deficits. To sell the president's program, Stockman and his assistants "changed the economic
assumptions fed into the computer model," and made the likely
results of the administration's actions far more attractive than
they initially seemed. "Instead of a double-digit inflation, they assumed a swift decline in prices and interest rates. Instead of the
continuing pattern of slow economic growth, the new model was
based on a dramatic surge in the nation's productivity. New investment, new jobs, and growing profits." Although critics of the
administration argued that "the supply-side premises were based
upon wishful thinking, not sound economic analysis," Stockman
and company publicly refused to give ground.

But behind the scenes it was a different story. Stockman recognized that smaller deficits and ultimately a balanced budget would
require not only a $40 billion reduction in social programs in fis-
cal 1982 but also $30 billion in savings on defense waste over the
next few years and the closing of tax loopholes benefiting oil and
other business interests, amounting to about $20 billion. Al-
though Stockman got nowhere on his defense cuts, and the president "just jumped all over my tax proposals," he persuaded
himself that the administration was on the right track. Buoyed by
the ease with which Reagan was able to work his will on Capitol
Hill, Stockman dismissed his own reservations as "inconsequen-
tial" and praised the president as having "a very clear philosophy"
and knowing "when something's wrong."

But Stockman's self-deception did not last out the year. By
the fall, with the economy faltering, he had to concede that the
economic situation was out of control. "None of us really understands what's going on with all these numbers," he told Greider.
". . . People are getting from A to B and it's not clear how they
are getting there. It was obvious to him, however, that balancing
the budget would require less defense spending, smaller tax cuts,
and reductions in safety-net programs like Social Security and

Medicare. Moreover, Stockman now had strong doubts about the whole supply-side theory. "I've never believed that just cutting taxes alone will cause output and employment to expand," he said. He "began to disparage the grand theory as a kind of convenient illusion—new rhetoric to cover old Republican doctrine." The supply-side argument, he conceded, was nothing more than a cover for the old idea of reducing taxes for the wealthiest individuals and largest enterprises in the belief that benefits would "trickle down" through the economy to less affluent Americans. "It's kind of hard to sell 'trickle down,'" he told Greider, "so the supply-side formula was the only way to get a tax policy that was really 'trickle down.' Supply-side is 'trickle-down' theory."[4]

Yet even though Stockman was voicing fears about the adequacy of Reagan's whole economic plan, he had been in the forefront of those who urged paying more attention to "the psychological climate" than to "the hard numbers of free-market transactions." In a memorandum of December 1980 entitled, "Avoiding a GOP Economic Dunkirk," Stockman had called for "an orchestrated policy offensive" in which the administration's initial economic program was "so bold, sweeping, and sustained that it totally dominates the Washington agenda during 1981; holds promise of propelling the economy into vigorous expansion and the financial markets into a bullish psychology; [and] preempts . . . debilitating distractions." The "fundamental point" to be considered is that "achieving fiscal control over outlays and Treasury borrowing *cannot be conducted as an accounting exercise or exclusively through legislated spending cuts in the orthodox sense.* Only a comprehensive economic package that spurs output and employment growth and lowers *inflation expectations* and interest rates has any hope of stopping the present hemorrhage."

As Greider describes it, "This was essentially a call to faith. It is a political vision of how symbolic political action might change hearts and minds, rather than an economic argument about how markets work." For all of Stockman's economic wisdom and his need to publicly voice his doubts about Reaganomics, economics for him is a matter more of the heart than of the mind. Indeed, despite his recognition that the administration's policies are a confusing hodgepodge producing little good result, he continues as Reagan's chief budget officer and as a leading proponent of Reaganomics. "I would not be here now, nor would I have worked sixteen hours a day for nearly a year if I did not believe in the president and his policies," Stockman said after the *Atlantic* article appeared.[5]

If Stockman keeps faith with the president, it is partly because the president himself has never lost faith in his economic plan. The publication of the Greider interviews brought Stockman a sharp rebuke from the White House. Although the difficulty of finding an adequate replacement saved Stockman from being fired, Reagan was sadly disappointed by his indiscretions and told him so in what Stockman described as a "visit to [the president's] woodshed." "For old-movie freaks," the economist Robert Lekachman writes, "that painful luncheon inevitably recalled those venerable Andy Hardy flicks in which a stern Judge Hardy (Lewis Stone) confronted his errant son, Andy (Mickey Rooney), and administered severe, character-building punishment. Few can be better qualified than the president to revive the Judge Hardy role. For his part, Stockman at his contrite press conference demonstrated considerable aptitude for the juvenile lead." However reminiscent of a grade B film, the "visit to the woodshed" made an important point: the president had no intention of abandoning his plan, which, as the dramatics with Stockman made clear, was more a moral commitment than a thoughtful design for restoring the nation's economic health.[6]

Reagan was more explicit about his determination to stick to his economic plan in an interview with the *Los Angeles Times* in January 1982. Asked why he placed a defense buildup and tax cuts ahead of a balanced budget in his scale of priorities, Reagan rejected the assumption that deficits must follow from tax reductions: "Reducing the tax rate can result in even the government getting more money," he said. "Tax cuts . . . are to restore a balance in government and private spending that will increase productivity, broaden the base of the economy, and help provide the jobs for those people who are unemployed, and when all that happens, as it did in the Kennedy years, the government itself ended up getting more money." "Do you see any circumstances where you might want to delay or cancel the tax-rate cuts to balance the budget?" asked one interviewer who pressed him to deal with current economic realities. "No," Reagan replied. "As a matter of fact . . . I firmly believe . . . that had we not been forced to compromise . . . the actual tax cut for 1981 is only about 1¼ percent . . . not exactly the stimulant to the economy we had in mind . . . Had we not had to compromise, very possibly we wouldn't have had this recession and, if we had had it, it would not be as severe as it is. So, rather than push it (the tax cut package) back or postpone, no, the thing that I would yield to if it could practically be done would be to move it forward."[7]

Despite Reagan's continuing optimism that his economic plan would work, the economy during the first three months of 1982 sank into a deeper recession, with unemployment climbing to 8.9 percent, the prime interest rate holding at 16.5 percent, capital spending contracting rather than expanding, business failures running at the highest rate since the Great Depression of the thirties, and federal deficits projected at nearly half a trillion dollars over the next three years. Reagan's answer to these difficulties was simply to persist in what he had begun in 1981. In his State of the Union speech on January 26, 1982, he asserted that "we have made a New Beginning, but we have only begun." He promised that his tax cuts would "put us on the road to prosperity and stable growth by the latter half of this year," and he reaffirmed his determination not "to balance the budget on the backs of the American taxpayers."

He also urged the case for a New Federalism, by which he hoped to transfer some three-quarters of the federal government's present domestic responsibilities to state and local governments. Under the president's program, the federal government was to assume full responsibility for a reduced Medicaid program, while the states were to take over food stamps and welfare and were to accept "a turnback" of forty-three federal programs, including health, education, local transportation, and social services.[8]

In an economic report to Congress in February and in his budget for fiscal 1983, Reagan echoed the same themes. The causes of the "fundamental deterioration" in the country's economic performance since the 1960s, he told Congress, could be found in the increased economic activities of the federal government—government regulations that raised production costs, high taxes which are disincentives to hard work and savings, and "transfer payments" for Social Security and welfare, which undermine a free market economy by also reducing incentives to work. "The long-term cost of paternalism," the report concludes, "may be to destroy an individual's ability to make decisions for himself." Consequently, the president's 1983 budget called for additional cuts of $26 billion in social programs and, despite a projected budget deficit of almost $100 billion, no tax increases that might discourage the savings, investment, and economic expansion that would be beneficial to the entire nation.[9]

By March, fourteen months into the Reagan term, with government cutbacks and the recession causing significant hardships for the disadvantaged, widespread objections to the president's actions began to be voiced across the nation. Lane Kirkland, president of the AFL–CIO, complained of an administration trying to achieve economic recovery by dismantling "the federal government until it is left with no function but to raise armies and coddle big business." In comparison with Reagan, Ford now looked like a liberal to Kirkland. Similar complaints began to be heard from the president's own party. Marc L. Marks, a Republican congressman from Pennsylvania, who had voted for every major economic program supported by Reagan, called for "thinking women and men everywhere to raise their voices against this murderous mandate that is being carried out." Marks urged the country not to support the destruction of a compassionate federal government "by a president and his cronies whose belief in Hooverism has blinded them to the wretchedness and to the suffering they are inflicting . . . on the sick, the poor, the handicapped, the blue-collar, the white-collar workers, the small business person, the black community, the community of minorities generally, women of all economic and social backgrounds, men and women who desperately need job training, families that deserve and desire the right to send their children to college or graduate school—in fact, anyone and everyone, other than those who have been fortunate enough to insulate themselves in a corporate suit of armor." J. Richard Munro, president of Time, Incorporated, also took up the cry against "this administration's retreat from federal aid for the less fortunate among us." He saw it as "doing grave damage to the quality of American life" and as "plain unfair" to the poor, who were bearing the burden of soaring deficits and economic dislocation caused by Reagan's policies.[10]

Reagan's response to this criticism was to describe it as unfair, slanted, and destructive to the national good. In March 1982, when television network news programs emphasized the country's economic problems in general, and unemployment and individual hardships in particular, Reagan attacked the TV coverage for slowing the nation's economic recovery. "In a time of recession like this," he said, "there's a great element of psychology in economics. And you can't turn on the evening news without seeing that they're going to interview someone else who has lost his job or they're outside the factory gate that has laid off workers—the constant down-beat that can contribute psychologically to slowing down a new recovery that is in the offing. Is it news," Reagan asked, "that some fellow out in South Succotash someplace has just been laid off . . . or someone's complaint that the budget cuts are going to hurt their present program?" The president wondered whether the networks "aren't more concerned with entertainment than they are with delivering the news . . . They're looking for what's eye-catching and spectacular." David Gergen, White House communications director, complained that the media were creating a false perception of the president's economic recovery program as unfair to lower-income and middle-income people. To counter this, on April 3 Reagan gave the first of a series of five-minute Saturday radio broadcasts. It was his way of getting the administration's message to the public unfiltered by the news media and of bringing the facts to the people without the confusion generated by anonymous sources and critics. As for the message itself, it was largely a repetition of his determination to cut taxes and government spending and a prediction that this program would begin to work in July when the 10 percent tax cut and reduced spending took hold.[11]

Reagan's determination to hold his ground came as no surprise to his critics. The president is an ideologue, they said, who "is firmly committed, not simply to solving the nation's economic problems, but to implementing his particular antigovernment, antitax principles." He "cares more about cutting taxes for the wealthy and eliminating social programs than he does about helping the nation's economy." Another critic pointed out that his "arguments concerning government explain virtually nothing about present economic problems. They amount to little more than a macroeconomic veil of modesty for the administration's political objectives: to redistribute income and well-being toward the rich and away from the poor; to redistribute health and education and security toward much the same people who would already have enjoyed them before the Second World War, or before the New Deal."

Some of this criticism seems overstated. Although the poor have fared badly under Reagan, middle-class Americans have seen little change in their government benefits. At the end of his second year, Reagan accepted a judicious set of reforms for rescuing the Social Security system from insolvency. Unlike his harsh proposals for cuts in benefits, which were rejected in 1981, the changes he approved in March 1983 won widespread approval. By endorsing the recommendations of the National Commission on Social Security Reform for higher Social Security taxes, a delay in cost of living raises, a change in the age for full retirement benefits from sixty-five to sixty-seven, and a requirement that new federal employees join the system, Reagan helped strengthen the national retirement program on which the great bulk of middle-class Americans depend for support in their advanced years.[12]

Still, one cannot ignore the fact that Reaganomics is a selfish program aimed at serving the interests of the wealthy—Reagan's class—at the expense of the less successful, less affluent members of society. For all his rhetoric to the contrary, there seems little question that Reagan's program is more the product of special-interest, or group-interest, politics than of concern with the national interest. To be sure, he sees little distinction between the two, but his refusal to depart from policies that in practice benefit mainly the well-to-do tells a great deal about his priorities.

Something else is at work here as well. Reagan's program not only serves the interests of his group, it also satisfies his own compelling psychological needs—to promote freedom and individual independence and punish government, or ruling authority. Indeed, for Reagan himself the emotional rewards of liberating people from federal controls seem to outweigh the material returns. [His insensitivity to the suffering of the poor has less to do with enriching himself or other wealthy Americans than it has to do with his antipathy to their dependence and their failure to achieve the self-reliance he gained for himself.] The needy remind him of his dependent father, from whom he has tried to separate himself all his life.] Stated another way, for Reagan to alter his program and accept higher taxes and more spending for the poor would be a blow to the assumptions and values that govern his life.

The extent to which these values governed his economic thinking became more evident during the spring and summer of 1982, when deteriorating economic conditions brought Reagan under mounting pressure to revise his economic plan. By July unemployment had reached 9.5 percent, the highest rate since 1941, bankruptcies were running at almost three times the rate of 1979, industrial production in June had slumped for the tenth time in eleven months, and the federal budget deficit for 1983 was expected to run well over $100 billion. The economic recovery,

which was supposed to have been under way by spring, was nowhere in sight, and public confidence in the administration's program to reverse the downslide was rapidly evaporating. In a
nationwide poll 58 percent of the respondents doubted that the
president's July 1 tax cut of 10 percent would produce the re-
bound he had promised. Republican hopes for major gains in the
1982 congressional and state elections were being extinguished,
replaced by fears of losing up to forty seats in the House of Representatives. The pollster Louis Harris saw "a huge counterforce of
public opinion building against many Reagan Administration
policies .. The chances of a Reagan conservative earthquake leg-
acy that will parallel that of [the New Deal]," Harris told leaders
of the American Public Health Association, "not only are remote,
but there is every indication that just the reverse is happening." A
Los Angeles Times poll in mid-July confirmed Harris's conclusion
that Reagan's policies were losing support, but it did not see "a
huge counterforce" building. It found that 52 percent of Americans saw the country as in either a recession or a depression, and
they lacked confidence that the Republicans or the Democrats
could repair the economic damage.[13]

Even in the face of these developments, Reagan refused to
accept the need for any fundamental change in his program. He
was unmoved by warnings that he would have to reduce defense
spending and delay or rescind the 1982–83 tax cuts to limit budget deficits that threatened to sustain high interest rates and forestall a recovery. In a meeting with congressional leaders on April
28, he dismissed Democratic contentions that his program was
hurting low- and middle-income people as newspaper propaganda.
"I read that crap about my program." But "we haven't thrown
anybody out in the snow to die," he said. To reassure the financial
markets that budget deficits would be brought under control, he
went on national television to predict that his policies would
bring the deficit down to $44 billion in 1985, "with an actual bal-
anced budget occurring sometime thereafter." To ensure that the
country would keep a balanced budget for many years after he had
left office, he asked Congress to pass, as soon as possible, a consti-

tutional amendment requiring balanced federal budgets. Only by this means can we "stop government's squandering, overtaxing ways and save our economy." In the short run, however, he saw no way to avoid a $100 billion deficit, and he urged Americans to help him win congressional approval for his current budget. The president's support of the balanced-budget amendment, as columnist Joseph Kraft observed, is "a classic example of the drunk preaching temperance."[14]

Others echoed these complaints, but they fell on deaf ears. In public appearances in the Midwest in May, Reagan argued that continuing high interest rates, which are understandable when prices are rising, "can no longer be justified on the basis of inflation . . . The only thing that's keeping the interest rates up and preventing a speedier recovery," he explained, "is the lack of confidence on the part of the private sector that government will stay the course" and restrain spending while moving toward a balanced budget. The "quickest way" to reduce unemployment, he added, was to pass the budget he was backing, because that will show financial institutions that the government is serious about holding down spending and the deficit. For Reagan, the immediate budget deficits were less a *real* economic problem than a perceptual one: if he could convince financiers that he would not break his vow to reduce the size and cost of government and that deficits would *eventually* disappear, all would be well. Economics, like so much else in Reagan's view of public affairs, has more to do with a personal outlook than with facts and figures on a balance sheet. Bankers, however, who had been some of his strongest supporters, refused to see things this way. They argued that high interest rates were the result of a variety of forces beyond their control, and they called Reagan's plea to lower rates "unrealistic in light of current economic conditions."[15]

Reagan could not accept their conclusion. Instead, he pictured the country as "on the verge of a tangible and lasting recovery," denounced "the proponents of negativism—the advocates of 'No,' " and reiterated the need for Congress to approve his budget plan. Moved chiefly by the need to break a five-month stalemate, in late June Congress gave the president most of what he asked—a budget that raised defense spending by 13 percent, reduced domestic programs by another $27.2 billion over three years, projected an additional $33 billion cut in domestic costs through modified enforcement procedures, and forecast budget deficits of $103.9, $84, and $60 billion for the fiscal years 1983–1985. Following Reagan's lead, Congress based their numbers on highly optimistic forecasts of national economic performance and savings, figures that one budget analyst described as having "no historical precedent." The budget deficits "can only drift up," one economist predicted. The financial markets will be "quite jaundiced" about the budget, another economist said. "There's a lot of air in it. The system is too fragile right now to deal with the truth." Reagan nevertheless congratulated Congress for passing a budget that "recommits this government to a clear course toward a lower growth of spending, steadily declining deficits and eventually the ability again to live within our means."[16]

Despite a widespread conviction among professional economists and the public generally that the economy would not improve during the rest of the year, Reagan continued to foresee an imminent upturn. "Interest rates and unemployment may remain stubbornly high for a time," he said on June 30. But "if we stick by our plan and keep the Congress from going back to runaway spending, the recovery will take hold, strengthen and endure." Referring to the 10 percent tax cut taking effect on the following day, Reagan declared: "Tomorrow, July 1 marks the beginning of brighter days for everyone who works, saves and helps our economy grow . . . The buying power of Americans is growing for the first time in years," he added. "Many Americans are still hurting economically but we are beginning to make progress." The president's confidence in his program, aides reported later in the month, was demonstrated by the fact that the administration had not prepared a fallback plan in case the recession continued or deepened. Although conceding that the economic improvement would be gradual and that it might even be another year before positive results were achieved, White House spokesmen maintained that in the long run the program will work. If further evidence were needed to show that the president intended to "stay the course," he gave it at a rally for the balanced-budget amendment on July 19. Calling the drive for the amendment "the people's crusade," he declared that "the people have had it [with] runaway government," and urged the need "to wean ourselves from the long misery of overtaxing, overspending, and the great myth that our national nanny always knows best."[17]

The White-House-sponsored rally, House Democratic Leader Jim Wright complained, was "unabashed show business . . . a Hollywood extravaganza." There was something unreal, a quality of play-acting, Wright implied, about "the all-time budget unbalancer . . . the Babe Ruth of deficit financing" leading the cry for such an amendment. "Politics is not only the art of the possible, but also the science of symbolism," the columnist Robert J. Samuelson pointed out. "When President Reagan plugs the balanced-budget amendment . . . he is engaging in this age-old ritual . . . But this is one case where the real world's complexities overwhelm the symbol's simplicities." Posing as an effort to control spending, which by itself it cannot do, the amendment "allows Congress to evade difficult political choices." These points were made all the more poignant by the fact that six days after the rally Treasury Secretary Donald Regan predicted a 1983 budget deficit of possibly $114 billion, well above the record $98.6 billion deficit the administration had forecast in February, and other economic forecasters saw even the larger figure as an underestimate. The nonpartisan Congressional Budget Office estimated the 1983 deficit at $140 billion, considering the administration's expectation of a 4.5 percent growth rate in the economy during the second half of 1982 as too high. "The Administration that is in power and its economists will always see happening what they need to have happen," John Kenneth Galbraith observed, in response to the administration's prediction.[18]

The president's push for the balanced-budget amendment was partly an attempt to offset other, less palatable actions he now felt compelled to take. With the federal treasury moving to borrow a record $140 billion to pay its 1982 debts, unemployment rising to 9.8 percent of the work force in July, and a third of those who voted for him in 1980 saying, according to a poll, that they would not support him again because his economic policies had been unsuccessful, Reagan acted to break the economic impasse. Implicitly conceding that lower interest rates, business expansion, and economic recovery could not occur without smaller federal deficits and less competition for loans, he now backed a tax increase of $98.9 billion over three years. The bill included provisions for doubling the excise taxes on cigarettes and telephone services, for withholding 10 percent of interest and dividend payments paid by banks and corporations to savers and investors, for allowing medical deductions only above 5 percent, rather than 3 percent, of income, for increasing the minimum tax for wealthy people, and for increasing business taxes by reducing tax credits for purchases of new equipment and by restricting opportunities to abuse the liberalized depreciation allowances that had been written into the 1981 tax act.[19]

Reagan coupled his support of the tax bill with denials that he was in fact raising taxes. This was his way of explaining his action to rebellious conservatives and to himself. "The Republican party is in danger of making a U-turn back to its familiar role of tax collector for Democratic spending programs," a group of conservative House Republicans told him. When a noncongressional group of conservatives publicly denounced the tax bill, Reagan called two of them to the White House to ask: "Are you trying to scuttle my presidency?" Publicly the president explained that he had "had to swallow very hard" before backing the bill, but "this was the price we had to pay to get a reduction in [spending] outlays." More important, he announced in a series of speeches that this was not so much a tax increase as it was a tax reform aimed at making those who are well off and pay little in taxes "pay their fair share." He predicted that the bill would have "very little effect on the majority of individual tax payers," and he asked: "Would you rather reduce deficits and interest rates by raising revenue from those who are not now paying their fair share, or would you rather accept larger budget deficits, higher interest rates and higher unemployment?" Without the tax bill he doubted that he would be able to preserve the 10 percent tax cut scheduled for 1983 and the later indexing of tax rates. As Reagan described it, this was a tax bill to save a tax cut.

He also emphasized that it was "plain hogwash" to call the measure the largest tax increase in American history. It was "80 percent tax reform, not tax increase." The law would essentially provide for better "collection of taxes owed under present law that are not being paid" and the closing of special-interest loopholes. The bill, Reagan insisted, "absolutely does not represent any reversal of policy or philosophy on the part of this administration—or this president." Conservatives also raised the reasonable objection that the Senate-initiated bill would violate the constitutional provision that all laws for raising revenue must originate in the House, and they were not persuaded by the president's rhetoric. Nor was the majority in the Congress, although on August 19 they passed the bill, seeing it as a necessary measure for improving the tax system and generating higher taxes to meet government costs. The bill appealed to liberals and troubled conservatives chiefly because it repealed some of the favors given to business in the 1981 tax law. "Rarely has the art of camouflage been stretched as far as it was by the Administration's effort to pretend that its $98.3 billion tax increase was just the latest logical chapter in the ongoing saga of Reaganomics," *Washington Post* columnist David S. Broder observed. "Liberal Democrats . . . knew that it was a reversal of the earlier Reagan dogma and embraced it. Conservative Republicans . . . knew the same thing, and rejected it."[20]

Reagan, however, refused to see it that way. Although he recognized that the bill represented something of a departure from his beliefs, he persuaded himself that at bottom he was not breaking faith with his principles. Reagan is so deeply tied to his ideology, so inclined to turn public questions into an extension of his own emotional needs that he cannot acknowledge that his programs ever seriously depart from his beliefs, even when they do.

His insistence that the tax bill represented no change in policy or philosophy was not just political posturing, it was sincere.

The administration's departure from monetarism in the summer of 1982 also went unacknowledged. Although the money supply and the interest rate on loans to member banks are technically controlled by the independent Federal Reserve Board, the White House does influence policy. At the start of his term Reagan warmly supported monetarist ideas about increasing the quantity of money and credit no faster than the growth of the GNP, approximately 3 percent a year. In July and August of 1982, however, with the economy showing few signs of recovery and seeming likely to slide further downward, the Federal Reserve, with the blessing of the administration, reverted to the liberal doctrine of expanding the money supply and lowering the discount rate to fuel economic recovery. Cutting interest rates four times in six weeks, thus bringing them down from 12 to 10 percent, their lowest level in almost two years, the Federal Reserve showed its determination to pump life into the economy. "The easing is an indication that the recession has gone on for a dangerously long time and a signal by the Fed that they don't see a recovery and are worried about the snowballing bankruptcies of financial institutions," one economist explained. The president had no complaint about the Fed's actions, and when the stock market staged a bullish rally that carried trading volume and the Dow Jones industrial average to new highs, Reagan attributed it to his economic policies. Of course, it was not Reaganomics that fueled the rally, but the move away from tight money which eased interest rates and held out hopes of a sustained recovery.[21]

Though he could also point to the slowing rate of inflation, which, as a consequence of the recession, was running at under 5 percent in the second half of 1982, the president had little else to cheer about. At the end of August he vetoed a $14.2 billion supplemental appropriations bill that increased spending for a variety of federal programs during the last month of the 1982 fiscal year. He particularly objected to $981 million for such programs as government-backed loans for college students, part-time work for unemployed people over age fifty-five, education for poor children and the handicapped, and unemployment benefits for those living in states that could not meet this obligation. In Reagan's estimate the bill was a "budget-buster") which would impede recovery. Despite vigorous lobbying on his part, both houses of Congress overrode his veto, handing him the biggest defeat of his first eighteen months in office. With the cooperation of eighty-one Republicans in the House and twenty-one in the Senate, Congress rejected Reagan's contention that the bill would break the budget and voted to support popular programs for the elderly, students, and the handicapped. The president's congressional opponents, having stripped $2.1 billion for the military from the bill, pointed out that he had backed an appropriation that was $1.9 billion larger than the one they had passed. The issue was not budget busting, congressmen explained, but priorities. "One would have to have a glib tongue, an effervescent personality and a stone heart to vote against this bill," Tip O'Neill said, referring to Reagan. Answering that he was "terribly, terribly hurt" by the override and that he intended to keep on vetoing "budget busters," the president used the defeat to regain some of the credibility he had lost with conservatives over his tax bill.[22]

The override signaled the growing determination of Congress to separate itself from the president's faltering program. Developments in September and October added to this determination. On Labor Day, in an article titled "A Holiday of Fading Hopes for Many," the *Los Angeles Times* featured the plight of Rockford, Illinois, where "1 in 5 Can't Find Work." In the middle of the month the paper reported another 0.5 percent drop in industrial production in August, the eleventh decline in output in thirteen months. Hopes for a consumer-led recovery based on the July tax cut were now being written off for the third quarter, with economists predicting little or no growth for the whole year and only a slow recovery in 1983. Needing a growth rate well above 4 or 5 percent to absorb new laborers coming into the work force and to reduce unemployment, the economy seemed likely to fall "far short of that required for sustained recovery." By

October unemployment had moved above 10 percent and was still rising. In the week ending October 9, for example, the number of people receiving unemployment benefits hit 4.66 million, the most since this aid program was started in 1935. Additional bad news was that the federal deficit for 1982 had reached a record $110.7 billion, more than $40 billion above the previous high of $66.4 billion in 1976.[23]

"The economy is simply going nowhere," one economist observed, "and I don't think we're going to see any major improvement until 1984." Reagan's supply-side economics, said Nobel Laureate George Stigler, is "a gimmick, a slogan that was used to package certain ideas." Although it had sharply reduced inflation, the president's overall program was a bust. "From the beginning everyone knew, or should have known," economist Lester Thurow wrote in October 1982, "that you could not put together huge tax cuts, gigantic increases in defense spending, a modest slowdown in the rate of growth of social welfare spending, and tight monetary policies without bringing on disaster. High interest rates had to throttle the economy and that is exactly what happened . . . Failure is upon us and . . . a new, completely different strategy is needed."[24]

But for political and psychological reasons, Reagan continued to deny this reality. In a news conference on September 28, he described the country as "better off today than we were" before his election. "We still have a long way to go, but together we pulled America back from the brink of disaster." He pictured the economy as "going around the corner or the curve" on the way to recovery. The further downturn in leading economic indicators for August was just a "glitch" on the chart, and unless there was "a palace coup" or he was "overtaken or overthrown," he saw no need for a tax increase in 1983. The following day he urged voters to make the November elections a referendum on his policies, and he attacked Democrats for an "economic binge" that had left the country with "a pounding national hangover." Out on the hustings, before partisan crowds and away from the constraints of executive decisions and responsibilities, he reverted to old campaign tactics, attacking the Democrats as "big spenders" and proponents of big government, and acting as if he, as president for almost two years, bore no substantial responsibility for current economic conditions. There was only one cause of unemployment, he said—inflation. "And that is why inflation must be the main target so that we can reduce unemployment." The choice on November 2, he declared, was between the Democratic party, which "puts its faith in pipe dreamers and margin scribblers in Washington," and the Republicans, who believe "in the collective wisdom of the people and their commitment to the American dream." Unemployment, he said in another campaign appearance, was so bad because congressional "big spenders" had inflated the economy. Americans were now "paying the penalty" of earlier Democratic policies of "spend and spend, tax and tax . . . borrow and borrow."[25]

But the president's attempt to blame the recession on the Democrats generally and the Carter administration in particular did not persuade many people. The president might be able to change a few votes with this rhetoric, the *Los Angeles Times* concluded, "but he cannot change the economy itself with speeches . . . He should be talking less about what happened and more about what next." But when Reagan spoke to this point in mid-October, his only advice was "stay the course." "Make no mistake," he told a national television audience, "America is recovery-bound and the world knows it . . . We have still got a long way to go before we restore our prosperity, but . . . at long last, your government has a program in place that faces our problems and has already started solving them."

Professional economists remained skeptical. "President Reagan points to the stock market to bolster his arguments that '. . . America is recovery bound,' " Lester Thurow pointed out. "Why do you suppose that President Herbert Hoover said recovery was just around the corner in the spring of 1931? Answer: The stock market rose almost 20 percent in the first eight weeks of 1931. The Reagan administration first said a recovery would occur in the fall of 1981, then in the fall of 1982, now in the spring of 1983. As in 1931, recovery is always just around the corner but forever fading out of sight." In attacking the opposing party, praising his administration's record, and predicting good things to come from his policies, Reagan was not behaving very differently from other presidents in other midterm elections. It was not his rhetoric or tactics which were objectionable, but the fact that he believed his own words. In his uncompromising view of the world, the Democrats had caused *all* the problems of the recession and Reaganomics was the *only* way out of the woods.[26]

A majority of those voting in the 1982 elections, however, were not convinced. The congressional and state races amounted to a modest victory for the Democrats. In the House of Representatives, where the shift away from the party controlling the White House after two years in office has usually been between 12 and 15 seats, the Democrats gained 26 seats, recouping most of the 33 positions lost in 1980 and widening their overall margin to 103—269 to 166. More important, those elected to the House seemed likely to be more liberal and far less susceptible to the president's control. In the Senate, however, where twice as many Democratic seats were at stake as Republican ones, the GOP maintained its fifty-four to forty-six edge. In gubernatorial contests, though, the Democrats also did well, capturing seven additional governorships, for a total of thirty-four to the Republicans sixteen. Similarly, the Democrats wrested control of one or more houses in nine state legislatures, giving them control of both chambers in thirty-four states, five more than before the elections. Still, the results did not amount to a repudiation of the president's policies. A survey of voters leaving the polls showed that while 36 percent saw Reaganomics as a failure and only 6 percent believed it a success, another 49 percent were ready to give the president's program more time before reaching a conclusion on its worth. Since the Democrats had made no fresh proposals to meet national economic problems, the public was in no hurry to abandon Reagan's solutions. If the elections, then, were not a pronounced expression of feeling one way or the other on Reagan's policies, they could be read "as a measured but sour response" to what the president had done.[27]

Those who were skeptical about Reaganomics found additional support for their views in developments during the closing months of the president's second year. Four days after the election it was reported that unemployment in October had reached 10.4 percent of the work force, 0.3 percent higher than in the previous month and the highest level since the end of the Great Depression in 1940. For blue-collar workers, the ones hardest hit by the recession, joblessness reached 15.9 percent. Unemployment among blacks was 20.2 percent. In November the recession deepened, with another 440,000 persons losing their jobs, and a total of 12 million Americans, or 10.8 percent of the labor force, out of work. Administration officials admitted that the figures were worse than expected and that they challenged their hopes for recovery. Unemployment for blue-collar workers in general climbed to 16.5 percent, and for construction workers in particular it was 21.9 percent. In December unemployment leveled off, with 12 million Americans still unable to find jobs. But this did not include a record 1.8 million laborers who had given up looking for work. These figures were given particular poignancy by the plight of some 2.5 million homeless Americans—nomads sleeping in public shelters, automobiles, bus stations, hospital emergency rooms, and beneath bridges, trying to keep warm under layers of cardboard. This group included hundreds of thousands of middle-class citizens driven into the streets by economic hardship. Half the men in New York City shelters, for example, were high school graduates, and 20 percent had attended college.[28]

Other economic news in the winter of 1982–83 was as bad. Estimates of the federal budget deficit for fiscal 1983 were now $170–175 billion, with the shortfall possibly reaching between $200 and $220 billion in fiscal 1984. Republican Senator Paul Laxalt, the president's closest adviser in Congress, described such deficits as "terrifying" and "probably intolerable." Worse yet, there seemed little likelihood that a rapid recovery of the economy would generate additional taxes to reduce the debts. Figures on industrial production in October, November, and December showed further drops of 1.1 percent, 0.7 percent, and 0.1 percent, evidence that the recession was continuing. According to the supply-side theory, capital spending was supposed to rise in response to the tax cut and lead the way toward recovery, but capital spending was down 4.8 percent for all of 1982 and was predicted to fall another 0.6 percent in the first half of 1983. With factories operating at under 70 percent of capacity there was little "incentive for companies to invest new capital in fixed improvements." Economic growth for all of 1983 was forecast at between 1.4 and 3 percent, the weakest recovery from a recession in the post–World War II period. Since a growth rate of 3 to 4 percent is needed just to absorb new workers coming into the labor force, unemployment was expected to stay at 10 percent or above during 1983 and to drop only to 9 percent by the end of 1984. Inflation, however, seemed likely to remain at a relatively low 5 percent for a second consecutive year. "Reagan has delivered a lower rate of inflation but . . . at a profound cost," one economist pointed out. "Those who did not receive their economic training at the University of Voodoo always knew inflation could be stopped by a deep enough recession. Few thought it a trade-off worth making."[29]

Reagan disagreed with this analysis of his policies. A deep recession for less inflation was not part of his program, although that seemed to be the current trend. In spite of that, he remained convinced that "we're on the right course," as he declared in November, and he predicted again that his policies would soon reduce unemployment. "I don't think that the president's faith in his program has diminished one iota," a White House spokesman announced in December. "He believes it's going to work." He would not increase taxes or substantially cut defense spending to bring down deficits. He "will not flinch in the face of stiffening congressional resistance and will press forward in 1983 with his familiar proposals of domestic program cuts, a massive arms buildup, and no substantial tax increases," a journalist paraphrased another White House official. In the lame-duck session of Congress, when Democrats tried to pass a $5.4 billion jobs

bill, the president warned that he would veto any such measure as
a "drag on the economy" that would slow down recovery. "We
will not solve the problems of the unemployed auto workers and
steelworkers with another giant, temporary public works program," he declared.[30]

The only concession he made in this direction was to support
passage of a five-cent-a-gallon gasoline tax to pay for repairing the
nation's highways and bridges. Saying this would be a "user fee"
rather than a tax increase, he also refused to call it a jobs bill, although most of the congressional majority backing it saw the
measure as a means of providing 320,000 construction jobs. The
only other economic solutions he seemed to find attractive were
to advance the 1983 10 percent tax cut from July 1 to January 1
and to fully tax unemployment insurance benefits. He apparently
believed that the first step would speed up a consumer-led recovery, while the second would provide money for federal job re-
training programs and make unemployment insurance less
attractive, supposedly giving recipients an added incentive to go
back to work. Congressional leaders and other officials, however,
rejected both ideas as likely to increase the deficit and punish
those who were already suffering. The president then backed away
from the programs, vowing to avoid emergency measures, "temporary Band-aids and placebos" which would do more harm than
good. It was time, he said, to "get on to the business of real [eco-
nomic] cure"—the program of Reaganomics which he thought
was beginning to work.[31]

By the close of his second year in office, it was clear that economic realities would not significantly alter the president's determination to reduce taxes and build up the armed strength of the
United States. He "simply does not believe the forecasts of his
own economists that his tax and defense policies are building
enormous deficits into the budget for fiscal 1984 and for many
years to come," *Time* magazine reported in December 1982. "Reagan thinks that his tax cuts and slashes in social spending will
shortly produce a boom that will fund lavish military spending
and shrink deficits too . . . Says one aide: 'He is absolutely con-

vinced that there will be a big recovery and that the economic picture in 1984 will be very conducive to his re-election.' "

Reagan is so insistent on sticking with his long-standing ideas that by the beginning of 1983 White House advisers had largely given up trying to change his mind on major policy issues. He has so often and so firmly turned aside their attempts to alter his thinking on taxes and defense spending that they no longer see any value in making the case. Reagan has not and will not budge on his beliefs—lower taxes and less social spending to shrink the size and power of government and greater military strength to face down the Russians—because they reflect his innermost feelings about self-reliance and freedom from authoritarian control. These are personal views to which he has adhered all his life and he finds it impossible to change now. Intrusive big government, which encourages dependence and denies freedom of choice, is a stand-in for the private situation in which he grew up. It symbolizes the dependency which blighted his father's life and from which he has struggled so consistently to separate himself.

Yet if Reagan demonstrates mostly rigidity in dealing with domestic problems that challenge his inner beliefs, he has also shown a capacity for compromise to assure his political success. His support of the $98.6 billion tax increase in the summer of 1982 and the gasoline tax in the winter of 1982–83 are two good examples. A third was his approval in March 1983 of a $4.6 billion emergency jobs bill—similar but slightly smaller than the bill he had rejected in December. It is entirely conceivable that Reagan will bend further in an effort to reduce deficits and promote recovery, but he will not admit that he is making any fundamental change. "Reagan can be induced to change his mind," *Time* points out, "but it is a complex and tricky process. The key, by unanimous agreement of all who work for him, is to argue that a new position is as compatible with his fundamental beliefs as the one he is urged to abandon. Then Reagan can justify a switch as a mere tactical adjustment rather than a reversal of his conservative philosophy."[32]

By the summer of 1983, however, Reagan saw less reason

than ever to back away from his original ideas. The economy began to show strong signs of recovery in the first seven months of the year, strengthening the president's conviction that his economic program was sound. Although unemployment fell only 1.3 percent to 9.5 percent, other economic indicators were more encouraging: inflation was running at less than 5 percent annually, interest rates were down to 10.5 percent, half of what they were at the start of Reagan's term, and the GNP was showing a steady upturn—a 2.5 percent annual growth rate in the first quarter and a 9.2 percent annual rate of increase in the second three months of the year. "All signs point to a strong recovery," the president said in June. "Our economic game plan is working."[33]

Yet if many economists were ready to forecast a solid immediate upturn, they were less certain about the long term, and they were reluctant to credit Reagan's policies with restoring the nation's economic health. With huge deficits of over $200 billion forecast for each of the next five years, many observers feared that the competition between business and government for loans would drive up interest rates again, rekindle inflation, and stall the recovery. Just as important, since the centerpiece of supply-side economics was a more productive, expanding economy, was that capital spending, or business investment in new plants and equipment, was, even with the projected recovery, expected to fall by anywhere from 3.8 to 8 percent in 1983. Economists remained unconvinced that Reaganomics was working or that a recovery was much more than the product of traditional Keynesian devices spurring a consumer-led recovery. Lower interest rates fueled by the Federal Reserve Board's easing of monetary controls, government tax cuts, and Pentagon spending, "an unpleasant variant of the public works advocated in a recession by good Keynesians," gave consumers the wherewithal to create a demand-side recovery. But even if thoughtful analysis concluded that the recovery had little to do with Reaganomics, it was good politics for him to claim this anyway. In economic affairs, it was clear after thirty months of his term that the president was particularly adept at making symbolic victories out of substantive defeats.[34]

Another case in point is the president's New Federalism, which has largely failed. In February 1982, a month after Reagan proposed to shift federal social programs like food stamps and welfare to the states, there was intense public resistance to such a plan. The Reagan program has a "nice appeal to local home rule and self-determination," one California legislator said, but "we are in the red, on the verge of bankruptcy, and there's nothing we could pick up." In nine states across the country, the *Washington Post* pointed out, "the New Federalism has produced only a few scattered cheers in state legislatures, and a lot of moans and sharp words . . . In the most economically crippled states, legislators can see only two unhappy outcomes from the president's plan to transfer programs . . . to the states: higher taxes or sharper cuts in state services." Indeed, under the weight of the recession and federal reductions in social spending, the states had to resort to both. In May 1982, the National Conference of State Legislatures reported that of the forty-five state legislatures that met that year, only nine "were able to avoid major budget cuts and increased taxes." In July an Associated Press survey of the fifty states found that eighteen had cut spending or raised taxes or had accepted state deficits exceeding $30 million, twenty had raised taxes or added new ones, while twenty states had placed freezes on hiring, laid off workers, or denied raises to state employees.[35]

In response to these hardships, Reagan cut his proposed transfer of federal programs to the states from $50 billion to $38.7 billion, agreeing to keep the $11 billion food stamp program under federal authority. Although the president insisted that the costs to the states would be balanced by state programs taken over by the federal government and by a federal transition fund, the majority of governors were not convinced. Richard A. Snelling, Vermont's Republican governor and chairman of the National Governors Association, announced in August that "the governors cannot support a plan that fails to provide for the medically needy, discourages adequate state welfare assistance, or ignores differences in state burdens." Because of this resistance, the administration felt compelled to pull back from introducing New

Federalism legislation in Congress before 1983. By the close of 1982, however, the administration had still been unable to convince many people that the New Federalism would work. A national coalition of social groups, for example, attacked the shift in 1982 of fifty-six federal programs to the states through nine block grants as a "cruel hoax" that would result in sharp reductions in social services. In December Richard S. Williamson, the president's assistant for intergovernmental affairs, acknowledged that the administration had been "unable to reach agreement on an overall package which all parties could endorse."[36]

But Reagan refused to concede that his New Federalism would not work. In an appearance before a convention of city officials in Los Angeles at the end of 1982, he urged the cities to rely less on Washington and more on local resources. "You must call on your imagination and creativity to find new local answers for today's urban problems," he declared. He also announced that "significant improvements" had been made in his original proposal and promised that the New Federalism would "not be a vehicle for budget savings" by federal, state, or local governments. By June 1983 he had still not made clear what these "significant improvements" in his program would be. By then, a majority of the country's mayors were even more skeptical of the New Federalism. At the annual mayors' conference many complained of increasing hunger among the unemployed in cities and of the "desperate need" for more federal funds to support "domestic programs that will strengthen the nation's economy, reduce unemployment, improve health care, and ensure a decent quality of life for all citizens." To find the money for domestic needs, Democrats urged a cap on the president's third-year tax cut, limiting the 1983 tax reduction to $700 for anyone earning over $47,000 a year. "It is time that the burden of Reaganomics is shared by those in the upper-income groups," Tip O'Neill said. "For two years, this group has benefited mightily from the Reagan tax program. This has been a program of the rich, by the rich, and for the rich." Reagan denied the accuracy of O'Neill's charge, and Congress failed to put any limits on the tax cut, but most economists agreed that the president's tax program favored citizens with the highest incomes.[37]

In contrast to the tax cut, his backing for the New Right social agenda was more symbol than substance. During his first year in office, while he was establishing his economic program, Reagan shied away from pressing for legislation barring abortions and forced busing, reinstituting prayer in public schools, and granting tuition tax credits to the parents of private and church school students. During 1982, however, he publicly advocated all four causes. In August, speaking before the annual Knights of Columbus convention, the president backed constitutional amendments to end "this national tragedy of abortion on demand" and to allow school children the same constitutional protection "that permits prayers in the houses of Congress, chaplains in our armed service and the motto on our coinage that says, 'In God we trust.' " Tax credits, he said, are necessary "so that our independent schools and our country, as a whole, will prosper from diversity and excellence." These measures, like his efforts "to clean up the federal fiscal mess and cut the size of government," were aimed at removing the restrictions on the "economic . . . political, and personal freedom of individual Americans. That's what we mean to restore." He intended to return "basic values" to "the highest levels of our government," where "intrusion into the life of the family and the local neighborhood—federally financed abortions, forced busing, [regulations] on many matters that government had no business dealing with—had reached unparalleled heights."[38]

For Reagan, action on these social issues amounted to "a crusade for national renewal." In an address at Kansas State University in September 1982, he preached that Americans should restore "to their place of honor the bedrock values handed down by families to serve as society's compass." He added, "The American people are hungry for a spiritual revival. More and more of us are beginning to sense that we cannot have it both ways. We cannot expect God to protect us in a crisis but turn away from Him too often in our day-to-day living." Praising the "frontier spirit," quoting from the Bible, urging his audience to "be proud of the red, white, and blue," Reagan declared that "here in the heartland of America lives the hope of the world." The speech was pure symbolic politics: a celebration of middle-class America and its values, an expression of regard for middle-class citizens whose conventional beliefs he wished to restore to the center of American life. "The crowd loved it," one observer reported, "interrupting the president's 37-minute speech 27 times with applause and cheers that roared through packed Ahearn Field House."[39]

Despite the president's support for the New Right's social measures and the vigorous efforts of conservative senators led by Jesse Helms of North Carolina, none of the proposals had won congressional approval by the end of 1982. The likelihood of getting such legislation through Congress in 1983 or 1984 diminished even further with the election of a more liberal House of Representatives in November 1982, but Helms and his supporters are not likely to give up on what they view as fundamental moral issues. The liberals who will oppose him on these social questions in 1983, Helms said, may "have to stand on their feet all night long," and they could "get a little tired."[40] Likewise, though Reagan did not press for these social issues as strongly as he did for cuts in domestic programs and taxes, he will not readily abandon the conservative agenda reflecting his innermost beliefs. If the economy improved sufficiently for him to shift his attention away from budget deficits, taxes, and unemployment, he would surely make a substantial push for the social reforms that mean so much to the New Right.

But even in the unlikely event that he and other conservatives got their way on these measures, they would ultimately find their success unsatisfying. Restrictions on abortions and busing, federal support of private and parochial education, and prayer in public schools will not permanently ease the concerns that trouble Reaganites. The enactment of this social agenda would not ensure long-term conservative influence on the national scene; it would be only a token triumph over national conditions that conservatives cannot fully reverse. As with the president's economic program, symbolic victories for New Right ideas will turn into real defeats.

Part III
THE WORLD LEADER

CHAPTER FIVE

Cold War Certainties

THE ORGANIZING PRINCIPLE of Ronald Reagan's defense and foreign policies is anti-Sovietism—the need to confront and overcome the Soviet Communist danger in every part of the globe. Reagan shares the legitimate concern, expressed by all American presidents since 1945, with the threat to America and its allies from a totalitarian Soviet Union hostile to their way of life. Unlike those predecessors, however, Reagan sees almost no room for reasonable compromise with the Soviets and looks forward to the day when the West "will transcend Communism. We will not bother to denounce it," he said in a 1981 speech, "we'll dismiss it as a sad, bizarre chapter in human history whose last pages are even now being written."

What explains this anti-Soviet evangelism? Reagan's rhetoric and actions suggest that in some fundamental way it is a symbolic protest against the state of his own nation. His anti-Soviet attitude arises as much from inner conservative tensions about government authority and social change as from any realistic understanding of Soviet aims and capabilities. For Ronald Reagan, the world outside the United States is little more than an extension of the world within: the struggle to defend freedom and morality abroad is a more intense version of the battle to preserve these virtues at home. In the eyes of Reagan and other conservatives, the communism of the Soviet Union represents the end point, the logical culmination of dangerous currents—big government, atheism, and relaxed moral standards—that they see running so powerfully in America. More broadly, as former *Harper's* editor Lewis H. Lapham has written, America sees in the Soviet Union "what it most fears in itself . . . Americans portray [it] as a monolithic prison, a dull and confined place where nobody is safe and nobody is free." It is a land of stereotyped commissars and peasants, of "cruel ideologues bent on world domination" and hapless victims of a repressive government. Through these caricatures, Lapham concluded, "Americans aim at the targets of their own despotism."[1]

Reagan's portrait of Soviet communism, unchanged since the 1950s, is of a ruthless, power-mad movement bent on the creation of a "one-world Communist state" in which individuals and the traditional Western concepts of freedom and morality count for nothing. Children growing up under Russian communism, Reagan said during his 1980 presidential campaign, are taught that a human being's "only importance is its contribution to the state—that they are wards of the state—that they exist only for that purpose, and that there is no God, they are just an accident of nature . . . This is why they have no respect for human life, for the dignity of an individual." At his first press conference in January 1981, the president made similar observations when asked if détente with the Kremlin were possible. Soviet Communist leaders had repeatedly affirmed their desire for "world revolution and a one-world Socialist or Communist state . . . Now, as long as they do that and as long as they, at the same time, have openly and publicly declared that the only morality they recognize is what will further their cause, meaning they reserve unto themselves the right to commit any crime, to lie, to cheat, in order to attain that, and that is moral, not immoral, and we operate on a different set of standards, I think when you do business with them, even at a détente, you keep that in mind."[2]

In speeches during 1981 and 1982 he struck similar themes when discussing world affairs. Quoting Pope John Paul II, in a commencement address at Notre Dame in May 1981, Reagan denounced "economic theories that use the rhetoric of class struggle to justify injustice, that in the name of an alleged justice the neighbor is sometimes destroyed, killed, deprived of liberty or stripped of fundamental human rights." Ten days later at West Point he told the cadets that after World War II the United States had "prevented what could have been a retreat into the Dark Ages. Unfortunately, another great power in the world was marching to a different drum beat, creating a society in which everything that isn't compulsory is prohibited. The citizens of that society have little more to say about their government than a prison inmate has to say about the prison administration."[3]

The danger to free peoples everywhere, he also emphasized, was that the Soviets aimed to export their totalitarian system to all points on the globe. He told the United Nations Special Session on Disarmament in June 1982 that the history of Soviet foreign policy since World War II was a "record of tyranny" that "included violation of the Yalta Agreements, leading to domination of Eastern Europe, symbolized by the Berlin wall, a grim gray monument to repression . . . It includes the takeovers of Czechoslovakia, Hungary, and Afghanistan and the ruthless repression of the proud people of Poland. Soviet-sponsored guerrillas and terrorists," he added, "are at work in Central and South America, in Africa, the Middle East, in the Caribbean and in Europe, violating human rights and unnerving the world with violence. Communist atrocities in Southeast Asia, Afghanistan, and elsewhere continue to shock the free world as refugees escape to tell their horror."[4]

Reagan's description of Soviet communism is plausible. It has been a repressive, totalitarian regime at home and has exhibited an evangelistic fervor for influence abroad, especially when its national security is involved, as in Eastern Europe, where it has established a kind of imperial empire. Other American presidents and foreign policy makers have used language similar to Reagan's to describe the Soviets, but unlike him they have recognized that Moscow is also a self-interested nation-state that is open to a certain amount of give-and-take in world affairs. Reagan has been much less willing to accept this as a fact of international politics because his depiction of the Soviet Union is less a balanced realistic view of its internal conditions and external aims than an amalgam of conservative complaints about conditions in the United States. When Reagan speaks of Soviet statism, of Communist indifference to personal freedom and the dignity of the individual, he is referring as much to conservative perceptions of recent trends in America as to the state of Russian affairs. After World War II, Reagan told an interviewer in 1980, "when the Soviet Union—when it looked as if the world might go into a thousand years of darkness—Pope Pius XII said, 'The American people have a great genius and capacity for performing great and generous deeds. Into the hands of America, God has placed an afflicted mankind.' I want to see," Reagan said, "I want to help get us back to those fiercely independent Americans, those people that can do those great deeds, and I've seen them robbed of their independence, I've seen them become more and more dependent on government because of these great social reforms." To Reagan and a certain group of middle-class, educated, suburban conservatives, there are striking similarities between a Communist Russia and a welfare-state America that they see as abandoning its traditional spirit of rugged individualism. The mission for a conservative president, Reagan believes, is to oppose both forces at the same time—to limit the size and power of government at home while repelling and, if possible, destroying, Communist power abroad.

Although the United States had faltered for a while in its response to these dangers, he described this as only "a temporary aberration. There is a spiritual revival going on in this country, a hunger on the part of the people to once again be proud of America, all that it is and all that it can be . . . The era of self-doubt is over," he announced at West Point. "We've stopped looking at our warts and rediscovered how much there is to love in this blessed land . . . Let friend and foe alike be made aware of the spirit that is sweeping across our land, because it means we will meet our responsibilities to the free world. Very much a part of this new spirit is patriotism, and with that goes a heartfelt ap-

preciation for the sacrifices of those in uniform . . . Today, you are
. . . [a] chain," he told the cadets, "holding back an evil force that
would extinguish the light we've been tending for 6,000 years."[6]

For Reagan and some lower-middle-class Christian fundamen-
talists, anticommunism is also a crusade to restore traditional assumptions about God, family, and country to a central place in
American life. These people, Richard Hofstadter has written, "are
less concerned with the battle against communism in the world
theater than they are with the alleged damage it does to politics
and morals at home. The cold war serves as a constant source of
recriminations about our moral and material failure, but as an objective struggle in the arena of world politics it is less challenging
to them than it is as a kind of spiritual wrestling match with the
minions of absolute evil." The visceral, evangelistic anticommunism of these Americans is another way of demanding recognition
for their values and their importance as a social group. It is a way
of reasserting the conventional American verities they identify
with so strongly and of boosting their self-esteem.

Those upwardly mobile, middle-class Americans who make
anticommunism an extension of their fight for greater personal
freedom at home also derive a sense of status from their militancy
against the Soviets abroad. Indeed, both groups use the crusade
against communism as a demonstration of their Americanism and
their importance in preserving the nation. Superpatriotism, pride
in country, pride in the flag, pride in America's men and women
in uniform are central elements of this "cold war fundamentalism." An emotional patriotism has been a stock ingredient of
Reagan's speeches for years. His inaugural address celebrated
America's heroes and gave recognition to a fallen American soldier in World War I who cheerfully made the supreme sacrifice
for his country. This nationalism is also meant to compel a revival
of respect for America overseas, a renewed deference to the United
States by friends and foes. For its staunchest advocates, the aim of
this resurgent nationalism is to assure that other nations will no
longer defy or ignore America or, perhaps more to the point, ignore them. The deference these superpatriots demand from other

countries differs little from what they ask of their fellow citizens at home.[7]

Reagan's national security and foreign policy advisers all share these attitudes toward Soviet communism in one degree or another. Secretary of Defense Caspar Weinberger, a conservative corporate attorney with a Harvard law degree and strong credentials as a budget cutter of domestic spending, and an advocate of less government, came to the Defense Department after serving as Reagan's finance director in Sacramento and as President Nixon's director of the Office of Management and Budget and as secretary of health, education, and welfare. His efforts in these two positions to limit federal spending on social programs, even using the legally questionable method of impounding of federal funds, won him the nickname "Cap the Knife." Yet as secretary of defense, Weinberger has turned one hundred eighty degrees on spending and has been an unbending supporter of a huge arms buildup to combat Soviet power. Ronald Brownstein and Nina Easton, the authors of *Reagan's Ruling Class,* point out that despite massive budget deficits, Weinberger has "defended nearly every tank, missile, and machine gun, every . . . weapon system that has come across his desk. On arms control, on Poland, on trade with the Soviets, Weinberger has taken a harder line than even the most . . . [extreme] hawks in the Administration." In the view of one former admiral, he is "one of the few genuine anticommunist cold warriors in Washington." His anti-Soviet rhetoric, *Time* magazine has pointed out, is at least as bellicose as that of other leading hawks in the administration. "He strongly believes détente has worked to the strategic advantage of the USSR. As he told the NATO ministers: 'If the movement from the cold war to détente is progress, . . . we cannot afford much more progress.' " He comes across like "a Roman proconsul," a West German newspaper complained.[8]

Others in the Reagan defense establishment echo Weinberger's anti-Soviet views. Deputy Secretary of Defense Frank Carlucci, an ex-foreign service officer and former deputy director of the Central Intelligence Agency, is said to have been involved in coups d'état and assassination plots in Third World countries. Though none of these charges has ever been "irrefutably proven," Carlucci prides himself on his anticommunism and freely tells of being accused of plotting "the assassination of Patrice Lumumba in the Congo, the overthrow of Allende in Chile and Abeid Karume in Zanzibar and of Goulart in Brazil." He shares Weinberger's belief, which is disputed by many, that the United States has fallen behind the Soviet Union in "nuclear-war-fighting capability" and must now develop the same capacity to fight and win a nuclear war. Similarly, Fred Ikle, under secretary of defense for policy, depicts the United States as militarily inferior to the Soviet Union, which is as determined as ever "to expand the Communist empire." Ikle is an outspoken exponent of an arms buildup which will close America's military "window of vulnerability" and prevent the ultimate subjugation of the West by Soviet power. However, he opposes the proliferation of nuclear weapons and the deterrence theory known as Mutual Assured Destruction (MAD); according to this theory the U.S. nuclear arsenal should be able to absorb a first strike and answer with a massive assault on the enemy's population. Other leading figures in the Defense Department, like Secretary of the Navy John Lehman and Assistant Secretary for International Security Policy Richard Perle, share an apocalyptic vision of the Soviet danger, which they consider little different from the threat posed by Nazi Germany. Like the Nazis, the Soviets have built up their military power and are ready to use it. They are prepared to fight, survive, and win an all-out nuclear war.[9]

Reagan's State Department does not trail far behind his defense officials in taking a hard anticommunist line. Although considered moderates in the Reagan administration, former Secretary of State Alexander Haig and his successor George Shultz are vigorous advocates of standing up to the Soviets. As a prominent member of Henry Kissinger's National Security Council and as Nixon's White House chief of staff, Haig was identified with détente and was attacked by the radical Right as a compromiser who was willing to reach agreements with the USSR. But any rational estimate of Haig's record suggests that he was an appropriate head of the State Department in the conservative Reagan administration. A former general and commander of NATO, a veteran of the Pentagon bureaucracy and Washington's political wars, a hawk on Vietnam—Kissinger described him as a deciding voice in the Christmas bombings of 1972—an alleged architect of United States efforts to overturn the Allende regime in Chile, Haig had impeccable credentials as an anti-Soviet cold warrior.

On foreign policy in general and the Soviet Union in particular, *Time* magazine said in March 1981, Haig's "ideas dovetail so neatly with Reagan's that the President hardly considered anyone else as his No. 1 foreign policymaker . . . The essence of their combined view: the prime threat to peace and stability in the world is Soviet expansionism, and the U.S. must restore the confidence of its allies and the entire free world that it can and will contain such aggression." While Haig considered the United States as being opposed to "anything military" since the Vietnam war, he described the Soviets as transforming "a continental and largely defensive land army into a global offensive army, navy, and air force fully capable of supporting an imperial foreign policy." Although the Soviet military buildup is unquestionable, Haig was too quick to view it as principally serving an aggressive and expansionist foreign policy. Yet, like Reagan, "for all his somber view of Soviet power, he believes that the historical tide is running against Marxism, and that with a prompt buildup of American military might and a consistent policy of checking Soviet adventurism, including strong support for all anticommunist governments around the world, the United States will come out on top." Stated another way, Reagan and Haig see the United States as holding the fate of the world in its own hands; the struggle to eclipse the USSR depends less on what happens overseas than on what we commit ourselves to in the United States.[10]

When Haig resigned in June 1982, Reagan replaced him with another conservative Republican, George Shultz, a professional economist who had served as Nixon's director of the Office of Management and Budget, secretary of labor, and secretary of the treasury. Shultz, a fiscal conservative and an advocate of free trade, helped shape Reagan's initial economic program. He is widely viewed as a pragmatist with a flair for reconciling conflicting positions. His appointment aroused the ire of archconservatives, who see him as part of the Nixon-Ford-Kissinger establishment backing détente, and as even more of a "détentist" than Haig. "We had only two seconds to enjoy Haig's firing," one radical Right leader complained. Shultz's selection as secretary of state moved another New Right critic to observe: "Now we've got what we helped to prevent." As an Ivy League graduate and former dean of the University of Chicago Business School, Shultz is much too understated for the evangelistic conservatives who are moved by rhetorical bombast about Communist evils. Unlike Reagan, who speaks that sort of language to the Moral Majority, Shultz is a reserved, quiet man who prefers compromise to confrontation.

He is less moderate than he has been given credit for, however, and his credentials as a stern anticommunist are unassailable. Disturbed by the strategic arms limitation (SALT) agreements with the Soviet Union, Shultz was a founding member in 1976 of the Committee on the Present Danger, a group of prominent American foreign policy experts who considered Reagan's predecessors' approach to the Russians as much too soft. At the time of Shultz's appointment, Washington insiders predicted that he would "focus more sharply on exerting economic and political pressure against the Soviet Union." He "would probably take a harder line [than Haig] toward dealing with the Soviets," one senior White House official believed. Emphasizing that Shultz had been Reagan's original choice for secretary of state, the White House encouraged the belief that the new secretary would be more attuned ideologically to other Reagan advisers on the issues that had separated Haig from the president. Although these assertions may be seen as part of the administration's effort to disarm New Right hostility to someone it considered too moderate,

Shultz does genuinely share Reagan's concern with advancing the cause of freedom against Communist totalitarianism, as his tenure in the State Department has demonstrated.[11]

Other national security and diplomatic assignments have given the New Right less reason to complain. Reagan's selection of Richard Allen as national security adviser softened conservative complaints about having first Haig and then Shultz as secretary of state. Initially "the Right's principal spokesman in internal Reagan administration debates on national security matters," Allen is an evangelistic anticommunist who was a member of conservative think tanks at Georgetown and Stanford universities. In the 1970s he served on Nixon's National Security Council, from which he resigned after personal and political clashes with Henry Kissinger. During his year in the Reagan administration he fought repeatedly with Haig over policy and power. In March 1981, two months after becoming national security adviser, Allen told the Conservative Political Action Conference, in a speech not cleared by the State Department, that America's West European allies should be upbraided for their "pacifist sentiments" toward the Soviet Union. Richard Pipes, a professor of Russian history at Harvard and a member of Allen's National Security staff, reinforced the picture of a new cold war militancy in Washington when he declared that détente was at an end and that the Soviets would have to choose between evolving along Western lines or going to war. A hallmark of Allen's career, a news magazine pointed out, has been controversy over his "unyielding hostility to the Soviet Union."[12]

In January 1982 Allen's fights with Haig and the impropriety of his acceptance of gifts from Japanese journalists embarrassed the administration and forced him to resign. He was succeeded by William Clark, a former California attorney, Reagan's chief of staff in Sacramento, and a state supreme court justice. Clark came to the National Security Office with only limited experience in foreign affairs, having been appointed deputy secretary of state under Haig in 1981. As his Senate confirmation hearings demonstrated, Clark's only credentials for the job were his long-standing relationship with the president, a flair for administration and for resolving conflicts between strong-minded officials, and a devotion to conservative principles and patriotic sentiments. His inability to identify the leaders of South Africa or Zimbabwe or the names of the NATO countries opposed to long-range nuclear missiles on their soil and his open acknowledgment that he could speak only in the most general terms about major foreign policy questions exposed the administration to ridicule in the world press. Yet he has been effective as national security adviser to the president by being a "conciliatory presence" rather than an abrasive self-promoter, and he has staunchly supported Reagan's tough approach to the Russians and his military buildup to meet the Soviet challenge, attitudes that have endeared him to the Right.[13]

No one in the field of foreign affairs in the administration has done more to satisfy the Right than Ambassador to the United Nations Jeane Kirkpatrick. A former political science professor and member of the Center for Strategic and International Studies at Georgetown University, as well as a resident scholar at the conservative American Enterprise Institute, Kirkpatrick caught the president's attention in 1979 with a *Commentary* article entitled "Dictatorships and Double Standards." An attack on Jimmy Carter's human rights policy, the essay distinguished between right-wing authoritarian governments that were friendly to the United States and left-wing totalitarian regimes that were linked to the Soviet Union and threatened American security. Kirkpatrick criticized Carter's "posture of continuous self-abasement and apology" toward leftist "autocrats" and his antagonism to rightist rulers like Nicaragua's Somoza and the shah of Iran as destructive to the United States. Where the left-wing governments were clients of the Soviets, the right-wing ones were "not only anticommunist, they were positively friendly to the U.S." As ambassador to the UN, she has been an outspoken advocate of American support for South Africa's government and the anticommunist military regimes in Chile and Argentina. She has explained Third World revolutions as the product of Soviet expansionism and has urged American intervention in Third World countries like El Salvador to defend ourselves against the Soviet threat.[14]

Kirkpatrick's view of the world, like Reagan's and that of his other principal foreign policy advisers, rests upon an exaggerated fear of Soviet power and control. This is not to imply that the Soviet Union is a benign, reasonable state with which the United States can easily achieve an accommodation. The Soviets' suspicions, illusions, and aggressive determination to serve their own interests make the USSR a difficult and dangerous adversary which will take advantage of any sign of idealized hopes and timidity in international exchange. But the Reagan picture of a power-hungry, evangelistic nation inspired by an unyielding determination to fasten totalitarian communism on all parts of the globe reveals more about Reagan's conservative inner tensions over issues of authority, dependence, and control than about Soviet capabilities and aims. Most conservatives, having had a rigid, stern, authoritarian upbringing, are both submissive to and rebellious against authority. Advocates of traditional values and the moral life, to which they insist all Americans must conform, conservatives oppose an oppressive government seeking to stymie initiative and personal freedom. And yet the paradox is that they themselves are authoritarian. They are ready to exclude many freedoms nonconservatives consider important—the right to have an abortion, to breathe clean air, and not to have a religion are but a few examples. It is not surprising that they are tolerant of right-wing regimes abroad that they see sharing their values of family, church, and country. Jeane Kirkpatrick, for example, describes rightists in Latin America as "traditional rulers in semi-traditional societies." In contrast, they see leftist regimes as defying the conventional wisdoms American conservatives live by and as extensions of liberal impulses in the United States which subject the individual to excessive government restraints on economic choices and social actions. Going well beyond the genuine fears of the Soviet Union's imperialistic and totalitarian drives, the Reagan administration's foreign policy is less a realistic response to actual conditions abroad than a kind of symbolic objection to conditions in the United States.

Reagan's defense buildup is a good case in point. Throughout his campaign for the presidency and from his first day in office, Reagan stressed the need to expand America's military might to meet the Soviet threat. "Let us not delude ourselves," he said in 1980. "The Soviet Union underlies all the unrest that is going on. If they weren't engaged in this game of dominoes, there wouldn't be any hot spots in the world." More important, according to this view, Soviet adventurism is supported by a massive growth of military power. The administration argues that although the United States still holds a nine-to-seven advantage over the Soviets in the number of nuclear warheads, Moscow has nearly a two-to-one edge in the megatonnage, or destructive power, of its nuclear weapons. Moreover, the Soviets have achieved a clear superiority in land-based ballistic missiles, and administration defense specialists describe this as part of a plan to achieve "military superiority in all fields."

Where Moscow depicts its reach for nuclear parity as essential to its security, the administration interprets it as a drive for an offensive advantage. "It is neither reasonable nor prudent to view the Soviet military buildup as defensive," Secretary Weinberger told the Senate Armed Services Committee in March 1981. The administration's answer to this danger was to propose the largest and most expensive peacetime expansion of military might in American history. In the five years between 1981 and 1986 the annual defense budget was to more than double, from $171 billion to $367.5 billion, with the total expenditure amounting to $1.8 trillion. The program in part called for expanding the navy from 456 to 600 ships to counter the recent expansion of Soviet naval power. "Control of the seas is as essential to our security as control of their land borders is to the Soviet Union," Weinberger said.[15]

Development of nuclear weapons was considered an equally pressing priority. Warning that the United States faced "the prospect of Soviet strategic superiority" unless it built up its land-based missiles and bomber forces, Weinberger advocated yet again, even though it had been declared unneeded by earlier Congresses, a new manned bomber capable of penetrating Soviet air defenses. He also pushed harder for the MX intercontinental ballistic missile system, to be based in Nevada and Utah. As for the SALT agreement that the Carter administration had negotiated with the Soviets, Weinberger, despite the contrary view of many reputable arms control experts, dismissed the treaty as permitting "an enormous further increase in Soviet offensive capability while presenting the danger of lulling us into a false sense of security." Though Weinberger also avowed that the administration was "not abandoning hopes for arms control," it still had not identified an arms control strategy after six months in office. At his confirmation hearings in June 1981, Eugene V. Rostow, Reagan's proposed director of the Arms Control and Disarmament Agency, admitted that the administration had not yet settled on a policy. "It may be that a brilliant light will strike our officials," Rostow said. "But I don't know anyone who knows what it is yet that we want to negotiate about." Moreover, Rostow estimated that it would be at least another nine months before the administration was ready for any serious new SALT talks.[16]

The administration's plans immediately produced a barrage of criticism. Former government officials and defense experts contended that the Reagan-Weinberger rearmament plan rested on an exaggerated view of the nation's present and future strategic vulnerability. They argued that the manned bombers and land-based missiles the administration wished to construct would be useful in fighting the kind of war the United States was least likely to confront: a nuclear conflict with the Soviets. Critics also pointed out that such weapons would do little to deter limited Soviet aggression in such places as Poland or Central America. To meet this challenge the United States would have to strengthen its conventional forces, and while the administration had indicated its intention to do so, it had offered no persuasive blueprint for how this would be done. Indeed, critics complained that Reagan and Weinberger wanted to spend billions of dollars on defense without a close assessment of what the money would buy. The experts wanted to know: "What kind of global strategic doctrine will govern the deployment of U.S. forces? What kind of weapons are needed to carry out that doctrine? What is the proper mix of spending between strategic nuclear forces and conventional forces? . . . Can U.S. industry, for which military production is essentially a sideline, turn out weapons in the quantity required by the buildup Ronald Reagan contemplates?" As *Time* magazine observed, critics worried that the administration was "preparing to spend indiscriminately for everything the Pentagon can think of—missiles, ships, planes, tanks, guns, ammunition, spare parts, training, military pay—in the hope that money alone will solve all problems, which it emphatically will not." Had the Democrats been the sponsors of this defense plan, Reaganites would surely have described them as simply "throwing money at a problem."[17]

Liberal economists like Lester Thurow also expressed fears that the Reagan defense program could "wreck the economy" by gobbling up scarce resources and causing runaway inflation. "The military build-up that is currently being contemplated," Thurow wrote in May 1981, "is three times as large as the one that took place during the Vietnam War." Johnson's failure to raise taxes to pay for that war and the Great Society, which he refused to spend less on, "wrecked the economy." Thurow saw Reagan's determination to cut taxes and have an even larger military buildup as a recipe for long-term economic catastrophe. He foresaw "tremendous strains . . . on the domestic economy, unless measures are taken to restrain private consumption. Without tax increases the military can only get the necessary capital capacity, skilled manpower, and raw materials by paying more than the civilian economy is willing to pay. This drives up prices and creates civilian shortages."

Cuts in domestic programs would come nowhere near making up the difference. "President Reagan talks as if his cuts in civilian government consumption are going to pay for the extra military spending. But he also talks as if those civilian budget cuts are going to pay for the loss in revenue from business tax cuts and from the 30 percent cut in personal income taxes ... But the sums that will be spent and saved do not match. A $138 billion cut ... in civilian expenditures ... simply does not counterbalance a $196 billion tax cut and $181 billion increase in military spending." Nevertheless, the administration saw the burden of total government spending shrinking "not because of a decrease in that spending, but because there will be an explosion of economic output" of some 23 percent in the next five years. But Thurow considered this supply-side wisdom as unconvincing and damaging. With the growth in American economic productivity slowing down since 1965 and running at a negative rate for the three years before 1981, Thurow challenged the assumption that productivity would "return to a 3 percent rate of growth almost instantly ... Such an increase in productivity has never happened before in our history," he said, "and there are good technical reasons for believing that it will not happen now." What made the whole thing particularly dangerous, Thurow concluded, was that Reagan's mistakes would not become obvious until long after they had been made, and by then it would be too late to correct them.[18]

Why is the administration so much on the wrong track in its arms buildup? If the threat from Moscow is less than what the administration sees, why does the White House exaggerate the Soviet danger? Again, it is because the Soviets are a convenient whipping boy for conservative concerns. Moscow does represent a genuine danger to the United States, so conservatives have not had to invent the peril, only to make more of it than actually exists. It is not simply the actual Soviet threat with which conservatives are engaged but also the Soviet Union as the symbol of those unpleasant developments at home they are striving to combat.

Principally for this reason, none of the criticisms of the Reagan defense plans had any perceptible impact on the administration's military buildup. In the summer of 1981 Weinberger gave Reagan a proposal for regaining nuclear superiority over the Soviet Union within this decade. According to the *New York Times,* the plan went "well beyond previous plans to strengthen those forces" and would "encompass intercontinental ballistic missiles, long-range bombers, Trident submarines armed with more accurate missiles and, especially, a vast rebuilding of the extensive communications apparatus through which the strategic forces are controlled." It aimed to create "a capacity to fight nuclear wars that range from a limited strike through a protracted conflict to an all-out exchange."[19]

At the same time the administration announced that it would build the neutron bomb, a weapon "designed to kill as many people as a regular hydrogen bomb ten times its size, and yet cause less damage to nearby buildings." American military chiefs described the weapon as the best way to deter or counter a massive Soviet tank assault across Central Europe. Opponents of the bomb warned that its restricted effects might encourage NATO generals to use it hastily against a Soviet attack, making it "the catalyst for escalating a conventional war into a nuclear confrontation." When the Soviets attacked the action as a "further spiraling of the arms race," the president replied: "They are squealing like they're sitting on a sharp nail simply because we are now showing the will that we are not going to let them get to the point of dominance where they can someday issue to the free world an ultimatum of 'Surrender or die.'" Reagan added that some of those opposing the decision "are really carrying the propaganda ball for the Soviet Union."[20]

In the view of Reagan and his defense advisers, the principal point is that the Soviets had undertaken a huge buildup of ICBMs and were ready to use them, should a crisis require it. "The Soviets have sufficient forces to attack and destroy our ICBMs," Lieutenant General Edward Rowny, Reagan's chief arms control negotiator said in August 1981. "I have no doubt that we could still launch a second strike with our other missiles and wreak untold damage on the Soviet Union, causing more than 100 million casualties. But the fundamental problem is that the Soviets don't believe that. They believe nuclear weapons are there to be used . . . So we must think about nuclear exchanges not because they will ever occur necessarily but because as long as the Soviets believe they're possible, they will have the power of blackmail over us." It is difficult to follow Rowny's logic. Does he see the Soviets as doubting our second-strike capability or the will to use it? Is he saying that only the Soviets think of using nuclear weapons and that this opens us to blackmail? If this is his argument, then he himself refutes it by planning for a possible nuclear exchange. His assertion is also countered by the fact that the president also thinks in terms of a possible nuclear war. In October 1981 Reagan made clear that he was determined to prevent the United States from being blackmailed by announcing that this country would begin producing MX missiles and B-1 bombers and by indicating, in a conversation with newspaper editors, that he could imagine a limited nuclear war in Europe. The Soviets were now to understand that the United States was as ready as Moscow to use its nuclear arsenal.[21]

Revelations by Thomas K. Jones, deputy under-secretary of defense for strategic and nuclear forces, about the administration's civil defense plans gave further indications of the president's determination to face down the Soviets by preparing to fight and survive a nuclear war. In an interview with Robert Scheer, a national reporter for the *Los Angeles Times,* Jones predicted that the United States would be able to fully recover in two to four years from an all-out nuclear exchange with the Soviet Union. Jones's optimism rested on the assumption that people could be evacuated from cities to the countryside, where they would dig holes and cover them with a couple of doors and three feet of dirt. Jones believed that in this way the American people could survive a nuclear war. "It's the dirt that does it," he told Scheer. "What is truly astounding about my conversation with T.K.," Scheer wrote, "is not simply that one highly placed official in the Reagan administration is so horribly innocent of the effects of nuclear war. More frightening is that T. K. Jones' views are all too typical of the thinking of those at the core of the Reagan administration, as I have discovered through hundred of hours of interviews with the men who are now running our government. The only difference is that T.K. was more outspoken than the others."[22]

Jones's ideas were dismissed by informed people as preposterous. The *New York Times* ridiculed his views in an editorial entitled "The Dirt on T.K. Jones": "Is the Thomas K. Jones who is saying those funny things about civil defense . . . only a character in 'Doonesbury'? . . . Or is T.K. . . . the peace movement's mole inside the Reagan Administration?" Yet, as Scheer points out, "Jones's notions of civil defense, odd as they may have seemed, are crucial to the entire Reagan strategic policy." Central to the administration's thinking about nuclear war is the conviction that the Soviets have developed an effective civil defense plan, including fallout shelters and city evacuation plans, and that this program has allowed the Russians to assume that they could reasonably survive and win a nuclear conflict. As long as the United States fails to imitate the Soviet civil defense program, the administration's defense planners believe, we are vulnerable to a Soviet first strike. The prime objective, Jones told Scheer, is to convince the American people that they can survive a nuclear war if they learn how to build and supply a proper shelter. "In the business of nuclear war," Jones declared, "what you don't know can kill you."[23] But surely it is Jones's fantasy of millions of evacuees from cities sheltering themselves in shallow holes covered with "a couple of doors and three feet of dirt" that is more likely to kill us. The belief that any such civil defense program could allow the country to survive a nuclear conflict encourages the administration to contemplate fighting such a war. Jones' presence in the Defense Department is enough to make any sensible person lose all trust in the administration's ability to lay rational plans for the security and survival of the United States.

The administration's optimistic plans for delivering the mail after a nuclear attack also testified to its determination to prepare the country for such a conflict. "Those that are left will get their mail," the Postal Service Civil Defense Coordinator told a House subcommittee. First-class mail "would be delivered even if the survivors ran out of stamps." One subcommittee member could not believe his ears: "There will be no addresses, no streets, no blocks, no houses," he exclaimed. Denouncing the postal plan as "idiotic" and "deceitful," subcommittee members said "there would also be no trucks, trains or airplanes for delivering the mail." One defense policy expert reinforced the committee's skepticism: "I can assure you that while neither snow nor rain nor heat nor gloom of night will stay the postal couriers from the swift completion of their appointed rounds, nuclear war will."[24]

The administration now came under a barrage of criticism for its so-called defense plans. The diplomat and historian George Kennan pointed to "the futility of any war fought with these weapons." He reminded the country that every president from Eisenhower to Carter had emphasized that "there could be no such thing as victory in a war fought with such weapons." He warned against the continued multiplication of these devices, saying that we and the Russians together had achieved "levels of redundancy" in destructiveness "of such grotesque dimensions as to defy rational understanding." To those who would invoke the need for deterrence, Kennan replied: "If the same relative proportions were to be preserved, something well less than 20 percent of these stocks would surely suffice for the most sanguine concepts of deterrence . . . Whatever their suspicions of each other, there can be no excuse on the part of these two governments for holding, poised in a sense against each other and poised in a sense against the whole Northern Hemisphere, quantities of these weapons so vastly in excess of any demonstrable requirements."

While asserting that Moscow had contributed its share to getting us into "this dangerous mess," Kennan urged against "blaming it all on our Soviet adversaries . . . It has been we Americans," he said, "who, at almost every step of the road, have taken the lead in the development of this sort of weaponry. It was we who first produced and tested such a device; we who were the first to raise its destructiveness to a new level with the hydrogen bomb; we who introduced the multiple warhead; we who have declined every proposal for the renunciation of the principle of 'first use.' " Whatever then might be blamed on the Russians, and "they too have made their mistakes," Kennan allowed, ". . . let us not, in the face of this record, so lose ourselves in self-righteousness and hyprocrisy as to forget the measure of our own complicity in creating the situation we face today."[25]

Men more knowledgeable about nuclear weapons than Kennan echoed and expanded upon his point of view. Hans Bethe, a Nobel Prize-winning physicist, a prominent figure in the development of the atomic bomb, and a leading adviser to the U.S. government on issues relating to strategic nuclear weapons, spoke for numerous other American scientists when he publicly took issue with the administration's assertions about the need for a nuclear buildup to eliminate Soviet superiority to the United States in ICBMs. In testimony before the Senate Foreign Relations Committee in May 1982, Bethe disputed the idea of American inferiority: "We have more nuclear warheads than the Russians, and I consider this to be the most important measure of relative strength." Our so-called vulnerability, Bethe said, rests on the belief that the Russians will soon be able to use their ICBMs to destroy our land-based ICBMs. Even if this were technically feasible, which it may not be, Bethe claimed "that such a first strike would give no significant military advantage to the Russians." Since ICBMs make up only one-fourth of the U.S. strategic nuclear forces, "invulnerable nuclear-powered submarines" and bombers carrying cruise missiles could effectively retaliate. Dismissing the argument that our submarine-based missiles do not have "sufficient accuracy," he described numerous targets for which these "missiles would have plenty of accuracy." Moreover, he outlined the United States' significant progress in the development of sophisticated submarine warheads, which "permits our submarines to operate over most of the North Atlantic, and to still hit Russia."

But the most important addition he saw to America's arsenal was the cruise missile. It "can penetrate into the Soviet Union. No defense system against it exists. The elaborate and costly Russian air defense system has been made obsolete by the cruise mis-

sile, 3,000 of which are to be installed on our B-52 bombers . . .
Because the cruise missile can penetrate the Soviet Union as no
bomber can, and because it has extreme accuracy, we do not need
a new bomber, the B-1, and even less its follow-up, the
STEALTH." The need for these new bombers would be made su-
perfluous by the cruise missile, which would be able to do the job
"much more effectively and cheaply." Given the substantial invul-
nerability of our submarine and bomber forces, Bethe thought it
"a futile expenditure of money" to deploy additional land-based
ICBMs, which had become increasingly vulnerable to attack. Indeed, because the Soviets rely mostly on land-based strategic weapons, and the United States has more nuclear warheads overall, it is
in fact this country that has superiority. "If anyone has a window
of vulnerability, it is the Soviet Union." The greatest threat to our
national security, then, is not from our inferiority to the Russians
in strategic armaments, but from "the grotesque size and continuing growth of both nuclear arsenals."[26]

Other strategy experts and scientists supported Bethe's conclusions. Herbert Scoville, Jr., a former deputy director of the
CIA, denied President Reagan's claim that the "Soviets now have
a definite margin of superiority over the United States . . . The
president doesn't seem to realize," Scoville said, "that even if all
our . . . [ICBMs] are destroyed, we would still have 3,000 warheads at sea placed on invulnerable submarines and another 2,000
on bombers on alert status. Each of these warheads has an explosive force many times that of the bomb that destroyed Hiroshima.
These can destroy military as well as industrial targets. They could
contaminate hundreds of thousands of square miles with deadly
radioactivity." George Kistiakowsky, a Harvard professor of
chemistry, who had been science adviser to President Eisenhower,
and George Rathjens, a political scientist at Massachusetts Institute of Technology and a former official in the State and Defense
departments, joined Scoville in complaining, that "on arms control, Reagan hasn't earned our trust." "The president has asserted
that our strategic forces are inferior to those of the Soviet Union,
that we could not deter a Soviet attack on this country, and that

we must postpone arms control and procure new weapons to deal with what he calls a 'window of vulnerability.' But he ignores three-quarters of our strategic forces, our invulnerable submarine missiles and alert bombers, which provide us with a much more survivable overall deterrent than that of the Soviet Union. This poor-mouthing of U.S. strength does great disservice to our security and undercuts our influence on friend and foe."[27]

In response to what many people now perceived as the administration's "negative and hopeless ... cold war policies," promising "increasing political tension and nuclear danger," an antinuclear war movement spontaneously began to spread across the United States and Western Europe. At the heart of this movement, George Kennan said, are "some very fundamental and reasonable and powerful motivations: among them a growing appreciation by many people of the true horrors of a nuclear war; a determination not to see their children deprived of life, or their civilization destroyed, by a holocaust of this nature; and finally ... a very real exasperation with their governments for the rigidity and traditionalism that ... prevents them from finding, or even seriously seeking, ways of escape from the fearful trap into which the cultivation of nuclear weapons is leading us." Echoing Kennan's ideas, Admiral Hyman G. Rickover, the developer of nuclear-powered ships, called for an international conference to outlaw nuclear weapons and nuclear reactors. Pointing to the Washington Arms Conference of 1921–22, Rickover said that "it would be the finest thing in the world for the President of the United States to initiate immediately another disarmament conference" to halt and reverse the arms race.[28]

A solid majority of Americans agreed. Fourteen months into the Reagan term, 57 percent of those asked in a nationwide poll favored "an immediate freeze on the testing, production and deployment of nuclear weapons by the United States and the Soviet Union." In spite of the president's insistence on the need for a nuclear buildup to assure national security, a majority of Americans, regardless of age, sex, or political allegiance, said that increased production of these bombs would not make them feel more secure. At the same time 140 congressmen publicly offered backing for nuclear freeze petitions, and local and state governments across the nation did likewise. Calling the president's military buildup "voodoo arms control, which says you must have more in order to have less," Senator Edward Kennedy joined Republican Senator Mark Hatfield of Oregon in supporting a bipartisan resolution urging a bilateral freeze by the United States and the Soviet Union in the production and deployment of all nuclear weapons, as a prelude to arms reduction talks. The resolution was simply a recommendation; it did not compel the United States to halt its nuclear buildup, and any freeze would occur only in conjunction with the Soviets. In June 1982 more than half a million people jammed Central Park in New York in support of an end to the arms race. Described as possibly the largest protest meeting in American history, it included many people who had never been to a demonstration in their lives, seeming to confirm George Kennan's belief that the movement was achieving dimensions which would make it impossible "for the respective governments to ignore it. It will continue to grow until something is done to meet it," Kennan said.[29]

Yet at the same time, another poll showed that majority opinion in the United States favored a defense buildup and a tougher stance toward the Soviet Union. Although 60 percent of the respondents in this poll believed that a war with the Soviets would turn into an all-out nuclear conflict, they favored the United States getting "tougher with Russia, even if that means risking war." In increasing the defense budget and taking a harder line with the Soviets, one political commentator noted, "Reagan has given the public exactly what it asked for, and the public understands and appreciates that fact. Americans are increasingly aware, however, that the *cost* of a defense buildup and a tough anti-Soviet line is a greater risk of war. They do not want Reagan to abandon those policies. Rather, they want some assurance that he will not push those policies any further without making an equally strong commitment to pursue an effective arms-control policy that will alleviate the threat of nuclear war."[30] As in domestic affairs, where they want reduced government costs with no cutback in major social programs, Americans want both a strong defense capacity and a smaller likelihood of nuclear war, however contradictory these two goals seem.

Outwardly, the president gave the public what it asked for, a defense buildup and peace overtures. At the same time that he was winning the increases in defense spending he had proposed to Congress, he also mounted a well-publicized peace campaign. In a speech before the National Press Club in Washington in November 1981, Reagan outlined a plan for reducing the number of intermediate-range land-based nuclear missiles in Europe. In December 1979, after the Germans and the British had asked Washington to counter a growing Soviet buildup of missiles pointed at Western Europe, the United States had agreed to deploy Pershing II and ground-launched cruise missiles in West European NATO countries. Reagan now declared that this country would not deploy the intermediate missiles if the Soviets would dismantle all their SS-20, SS-4, and SS-5 missiles aimed at America's European allies. The president also indicated his intention to "open negotiations on strategic arms as soon as possible next year." In April 1982, in response to the mounting public pressure for a nuclear freeze, Reagan used his first televised prime-time press conference to emphasize his commitment to arms control: "I want an agreement on strategic nuclear weapons that reduces the risk of war, lowers the level of armament, and enhances global security," he announced. "We can accept no less." He also proposed that the United States and the USSR agree to a freeze on nuclear weapons, but only after the elimination of Moscow's "definite margin of superiority." Rejecting assertions that the two sides already had rough parity in nuclear arms, the president warned that an immediate freeze would give the Soviets no incentive to reduce their nuclear arsenal. Shortly afterward he spoke to the public about the "unimaginable horror of nuclear war," saying that "a nuclear war cannot be won and must never be fought. So, to those who protest against nuclear war, I can only say, I'm with you."[31]

In May, in a commencement address at his alma mater, Eureka College, Reagan proposed Strategic Arms Reduction Talks—START—that would lead to "verifiable, equitable, and militarily significant" agreements for smaller nuclear arsenals. As the immediate objective of these talks, he suggested that the United States and the Soviet Union reduce their stocks of long-range ballistic missile warheads to equal levels, at least a third below their current holdings. "To enhance stability," he asked that "no more than half of those warheads be land based." In practice, this would require the Soviets to give up more than the Americans. Since 72 percent of these Soviet warheads and only 25 percent of America's were land based, the Russians would have to dismantle more than half of theirs, while the United States would not have to abandon any. Instead, it would be able to meet the quota by eliminating smaller and less accurate submarine warheads. This first phase of talks was also to include "significant reductions in missiles themselves." In a second phase the two sides were to "seek to achieve an equal ceiling on other elements of our strategic nuclear forces, including limits on ballistic missile throw-weight at less than current American levels." This meant reductions in the lifting power of missiles, which in turn would limit the quantity and size of warheads. Not surprisingly, Soviet President Leonid Brezhnev rejected Reagan's proposal as an attempt to gain an advantage over the Soviet Union.[32]

In response the president used a trip to Western Europe in June 1982 partly to intensify his peace campaign. In a speech to the British Parliament he described the existence of nuclear weapons as threatening "if not the extinction of mankind, then surely the end of civilization as we know it." He pictured negotiations on intermediate-range nuclear forces in Europe and the START talks, which were to begin later that month, as "critical to mankind. Our commitment to early success in these negotiations is firm and unshakeable and our purpose is clear: reducing the risk of war by reducing the means of waging war on both sides." On the following day he told the West German Parliament that U.S. foreign policy is based on the principle: "Seek peace and pursue it."

To those who were marching for peace, he said: "My heart is with you." To a demonstrator carrying a sign that said "I am afraid," Reagan expressed sympathy for "that earnest plea." He called the nuclear threat "a terrible beast," restated his commitment to a "zero option" on intermediate-range nuclear missiles in Europe and to the strategic arms reductions outlined in his Eureka speech, and he introduced a proposal for mutual reductions in NATO and Warsaw Pact forces to 900,000 men on each side. "Let us build a cathedral of peace," he concluded, "where nations are safe from war, where people need not fear for their liberties." Also telling the West Germans that he was "determined to ensure that civilization avoids a nuclear war," he announced his intention to propose new measures for reducing the possibilities of a nuclear accident and of an accidental war.[33]

At the same time, led by Secretary Weinberger, the administration tried to dispel the idea that it was "planning to wage protracted nuclear war, or seeking to acquire nuclear 'war-fighting' capability." In a speech at the Army War College in June, Weinberger declared that there was "no place in our strategy" for the idea that a nuclear war can be won. He pictured the administration's military buildup as aimed solely at deterring a Soviet attack. In a letter sent to thirty U.S. newspapers and forty foreign publications in August, Weinberger attacked critics' assertions that this was not the aim of Reagan's policy as "completely inaccurate . . . The improvements in our strategic forces that the President has proposed . . . do *not* mean that we endorse the concept of protracted nuclear war." Instead, the policy was no more than the same one of deterrence that the United States had been pursuing since the start of the nuclear age. "Our entire strategic program," he concluded, "including the development of a response capability that has been so maligned in the press recently, has been developed with the express intention of assuring that nuclear war will never be fought."[34]

But the administration's critics were justifiably skeptical of these claims and of the president's whole peace campaign. They tellingly pointed to the Pentagon's five-year Defense Guidance

Plan, prepared in the spring of 1982, which "accepted the premise that nuclear conflict with the Soviet Union could be protracted" and asserted that U.S. nuclear forces "must prevail and be able to force the Soviet Union to seek earliest termination of hostilities on terms favorable to the United States." Despite Weinberger's denials, Hans Bethe said that the plan "contradicts and may destroy President Reagan's initiatives toward nuclear arms control." A former arms control official felt that the document provided "renewed evidence (is it still needed at this late date?) that our military planners, and the civilian leaders who direct them and listen to them, are ill-equipped, by training and experience, to address the realities of the nuclear age ... Our leaders' current course is a little short of suicidal." When Air Force General David C. Jones retired as chairman of the Joint Chiefs of Staff in June 1982, he warned that "it would be throwing money in a 'bottom-less pit' to try to prepare the United States for a long nuclear war with the Soviet Union." The following month fifty members of Congress told the president that they were "extremely alarmed with those sections of the [defense] guidance calling for planning to wage a protracted nuclear war. In our minds, such a strategy will result in a futile renewal of the nuclear arms race in which neither side will relent ... This policy completely contradicts your declared intentions to lessen the risk of nuclear war and under-mines the credibility of your offer to negotiate 'meaningful reductions' in nuclear arsenals with the Soviet Union."[35]

In an "open reply" to Weinberger's letter to American and foreign newspapers, the journalist Theodore Draper accused the administration of willful deceit in its defense and arms control policies. "We are now in the midst of a real arms race and an un-real arms negotiation," Draper wrote. "That is not what the world in general and the American people in particular have been given to understand ... The disparity between what you are doing and what you say you are doing cannot be concealed forever."[36]

The best evidence of the truth of Draper's assertion was in the administration's unrelenting military buildup in 1982–83. In

August 1982 the *Los Angeles Times* reported that the administration planned to speed up the development and testing of nuclear weapons and to modernize and expand the nation's facilities for producing arms. The White House asked Congress to provide $5.8 billion for nuclear weapons in fiscal 1983, an increase of 40 percent over 1981. At the same time the overall defense budget increased by 14 percent from 1982 to 1983, with full funding for the MX missile system and the B-1 bomber. In March 1983, when the Pentagon issued its next annual "Defense Guidance" document, it was, a journalist described a Pentagon official as saying, "carefully cleansed of inflammatory rhetoric about fighting a nuclear war in order to help polish the Reagan administration's 'softer' image on nuclear issues." Defense officials emphasized to the reporter, however, that despite changes in language, "none of the nation's military doctrine has changed." The document itself illustrated this by, on the one hand, conceding that "neither side could win . . . a [nuclear] war," and, on the other, speaking of being able to halt a Soviet attack if deterrence failed and "restore the peace." The "objective" of U.S. armed forces "would be to deny enemy war aims" and *"restore peace on favorable terms."* "As is written on the walls of the Ministry of Truth in the fictional fiscal year 1984," Emma Rothschild observed, " 'War is Peace.' "[37]

Despite assertions from the authoritative British Institute of Strategic Studies that the United States and the Soviet Union had parity in land- and sea-based missile warheads and that the United States was ahead if aircraft weapons were counted, the Reagan administration pressed ahead with its buildup. Soviet statements that they would match the U.S. advances only hardened the president's intention to expand America's military might. In October 1982, after Brezhnev called any Soviet lag in this competition "inadmissible," Weinberger publicly reiterated the need for America to upgrade its defense arsenal and attacked the idea of a nuclear freeze as likely to "increase the dangers of war" by weakening America's power to deter an attack and make it more difficult to negotiate reductions in nuclear arms. Weinberger and the president now also charged that foreign agents were manipulating the freeze movement. They pictured the Soviet Union as favoring a freeze because it was ahead in nuclear weapons. "There is no question about foreign agents that were sent to help instigate and help create and keep such a movement going," Reagan said. But, Joseph Kraft observed, "The fact is that Ronald Reagan and his advisers are mainly responsible for the antinuclear movement in this country." Early in 1983 the FBI implicitly confirmed this when it issued a report denying that foreign agents were responsible for or in control of the freeze movement.[38]

In the winter of 1982–83, when the president pressed Congress for $26 billion to deploy the MX missile in a controversial "dense-pack" configuration and for an additional 14 percent in defense spending, Congress rebelled. "MX stood up like a lightning rod. It took all the heat," one commentator said of the growing congressional resentment of the White House defense plans. The rejection of the president's plan to deploy the MX, Theodore White believes, broke "the American politics of consensus on defense. What has been provoked is this generation's reexamination of the defense posture of the United States." This view is borne out by Congress's response to the 1984 defense budget. Disturbed by projected deficits of $200–$300 billion and by continuing unemployment of 10.4 percent of the labor force in January 1983, the House Appropriations Committee voiced bipartisan opposition to additional large increases for defense. Having given the president 98 percent and 96 percent of what he asked for defense in 1981 and 1982, representatives and senators now responded to his request with "mockery," "ridicule," and "anger." Democrats and Republicans alike protested against the misappropriation of money for "exotic and farfetched weapons" and mocked alleged Pentagon savings as "ludicrous." In February, when Weinberger refused to discuss defense cuts in an appearance before the normally sympathetic House subcommittee on defense appropriations, its members criticized him for his inflexibility and warned that he was losing "grass-roots support for defense spending." Despite the president's willingness to reduce the increase in defense appropriations from 14 to 10 percent, and despite constant pressure from the administration to support that figure, the congressional budget resolution in June 1983 reduced the defense increase to 5 percent.[39]

Nothing seemed to confirm the administration's commitment to its all-out arms buildup more than Reagan's dismissal in January 1983 of Eugene V. Rostow as director of the Arms Control and Disarmament Agency. Although personal differences between Rostow and National Security Adviser William Clark contributed to the decision to get rid of Rostow, the more important reason was that the White House and some conservative senators, led by Jesse Helms, saw Rostow as "too soft" toward the Russians and too eager to respond flexibly to a Soviet peace offensive that included new arms-control proposals. Particularly disturbing to critics of the president's defense and disarmament policies was his appointment of Kenneth L. Adelman as Rostow's replacement. "Rostow favors a military buildup—he is an unreconstructed Nixon anticommunist," said a staff member of the Senate Foreign Relations Committee. "But he also felt you could do business with the Russians. Ken [Adelman] sees the Russians as the personification of evil itself, and it's very hard, if you have that view, to negotiate with them." Rostow's firing involved "more than bureaucratic battles," *The New Republic* observed. It resulted from his willingness to deviate from Reagan's "zero option" for eliminating six hundred Soviet intermediate-range missiles pointed at Western Europe and for dropping plans to install similar American missiles in December 1983. To get a Soviet-American agreement, Rostow was ready to accept a compromise which, in the view of *The New Republic,* "conforms to all the canons of parity, of stability, of deterrence." The fact that the administration wanted no part of it suggests that the zero option was never anything more than a strategy for silencing criticism. "The political intentions of our government's official position on intermediate-range nuclear weapons have been exposed," *The New Republic* concluded. "Arms control is not exactly among them."[40]

But in response to pressure from NATO allies to modify the zero option, at the end of March 1983 Reagan proposed an interim agreement with Moscow by which the United States would deploy fewer intermediate-range missiles in Europe than the 572 planned and the Soviets would reduce their 600 missiles already in place to an equal level. "If there must be some," the president declared, "it is better to have few than to have many." The Soviets promptly rejected this suggestion, however, as unfair: a proposal that failed to include the hundreds of NATO aircraft capable of delivering nuclear weapons, as well as 162 British and French missiles, announced Foreign Minister Andrei Gromyko, was "not a serious proposal."[41]

Gromyko also implied that the president was trying to give the appearance of flexibility when he had no interest in an agreement. Other critics found evidence that this was the case in the fact that the week before Reagan offered to modify the zero option, he had publicly combined a plea for his defense program with a theatrical suggestion for a long-term shift from the present defense system based on massive retaliation to an antiballistic missile system that would rely on lasers and microwave devices. The plan was belittled by many as a futuristic "Star Wars" fantasy, and critics objected that the idea was more a way for the president to polish his image as a peacemaker than a serious plan for advancing arms control negotiations.[42]

The same complaint was voiced in May and June of 1983 when the administration, by promising to be more flexible in its approach to arms negotiations with the Soviets, persuaded Congress to appropriate $625 million for development of the MX. "President Reagan is embarked on a public-relations campaign designed to persuade skeptics at home and abroad that he is committed to achieving equitable nuclear-arms reduction with the Soviet Union," Senator Alan Cranston declared. Reagan was following the recommendation of a presidential Commission on Strategic Forces, to emphasize warheads rather than the missiles that carry them and to "build down," that is, shelve two nuclear warheads for every new one deployed. But Cranston and other critics saw the decision as a device for bending Congress to the president's will rather than as a way to advance arms limitation talks with Moscow. "Although Reagan's revised proposal clearly is more flexible than the one he presented almost a year ago," two journalists pointed out, "it would still require the Soviet Union to cut back far more of its nuclear arsenal than the United States, and therefore may not be attractive to the Soviets." Perhaps most telling in this regard was the fact that the president failed to mention the most striking feature of the commission's report, the denial of the existence of the so-called "window of vulnerability." While concluding that the Soviets had an edge in land-based missiles and a capacity to threaten America's ICBMs with a first strike, the commission recommended that "the different components of our strategic forces should be assessed collectively and not in isolation," meaning, as *The New Republic* put it, that "a concern about our ICBMs" should not be promoted into "a concern about the state of our defenses in general."[43]

But it seems unlikely that the Reagan administration will desist from this approach and try to reach meaningful arms control agreements with Moscow. Reagan, Weinberger, and other leading defense officials will not let go of the conviction that the United States must increase its military power to hold the Soviets at bay. They cannot admit that there is now rough parity in strength between the United States and the USSR. Such an admission would open the way to serious negotiations and a possible return to détente, which would require a reversal of the attitude toward the Soviets that has informed conservative thinking for more than thirty-five years. It is not the comparative strength of the Soviet and American military arsenals that so disturbs Reaganites; it is Soviet Russia's totalitarianism and its symbolic embodiment of all those trends toward statism, atheism, and "immorality," against which conservatives see themselves holding the line. Reaganites do not acknowledge this; they sincerely believe that Moscow has gained an advantage over the United States in military power and that only a buildup of American strength can right the balance and preserve the peace. They will not be convinced otherwise because they are partly blind to their own hidden agenda: to reestablish American military superiority over the Soviet Union, as a step toward a symbolic triumph over the forces in this country promoting government power and undermining the conventions with which conservatives so thoroughly identify.

CHAPTER SIX

Cold War Confusions

THE SYMBOLIC CONCERNS behind Reagan's defense policy have also shaped his handling of foreign affairs. His approach to world problems, whether in Europe, Latin America, East Asia, or the Middle East, has been a kind of "cold war fundamentalism" or "ritualistic anti-Sovietism" in which global ills are seen as springing mainly from Moscow's actions. "This fundamentalist response," points out international relations specialist Stanley Hoffmann, "tries to find remedies in old verities: not in the spirit that led to past successes, but in the mythified recipes that worked before, in the rituals of national celebration, in the rationalizations that attribute troubles or temporary decline to internal dissolvent forces or evil men and ascribe recovery to a rediscovery of traditional ways." The Reagan foreign policy, another commentator observes, is the product of "a political leadership . . . provincial in background and isolationist in spirit," giving "top priority to domestic issues." It is the design of a president with markedly little interest in foreign affairs who "is content to receive a series of one-page 'minimemos' summarizing foreign and defense problems and . . . a foreign policy paper of ten pages or more only about once a month."[1]

Reagan's foreign policy is less a response to the outside world than another expression of his struggle to defeat values and trends that challenge conservative truths. The enemy or problem everywhere abroad is Soviet Russia or left-wing totalitarianism opposing conventional American ideals. In this scheme there is no room for close attention to regional and local differences; the political difficulties in Central America are very little different from the dangers troubling the Middle East. The Soviet threat to Western Europe is largely the same as the threat to Asia. Indigenous problems make little impression on Reagan and his foreign affairs advisers: conflicts between Arabs and Israelis, Indians and Pakistanis, Latin American peasants and land owners—these are distinctly secondary to the overriding issue of countering Soviet influence and power. The objective in international affairs is not to see the world for what it is and defend the national interest as prudently as possible but to assure the triumph of simplistic and conventional ideas that only the most rigid conservatives can support.

Early in Reagan's term it was clear to acute observers that the consequences of such a world view would be confusion and disarray in foreign policy. The Reagan administration's fundamentalism, Hoffmann writes, "is a disturbing evolution, because it shows not only a kind of collective inability to cope with complexity, but also an unwillingness to examine our present predicament seriously." As journalist Ronald Steel points out, "Anti-Sovietism as a foreign policy doctrine is vague, emotional, and reactive." Reagan's diplomacy "is not a policy, it is a stance. It promises a cold war victory, but can deliver only military frustration, economic distress, and political disaffection." Steel is largely on the mark, because Reagan's anti-Sovietism does not speak to foreign realities. Unlike a defense policy, international relations cannot be insulated from outside influences. The Reagan administration has been able to pursue an arms buildup despite differences with its allies and its adversaries, particularly over ICBMs and arms reduction proposals, but in trying to set a political or economic course abroad, it has had to take closer account of other governments and peoples. Consequently, where Reagan's cold war certainties have served as a catalyst for single-minded defense planning, they have become almost unmanageable in the face of external political and economic realities and have been a source of considerable confusion in the conduct of foreign affairs.[2]

The first year of Reagan's presidency was replete with examples of this difficulty, El Salvador being a major case in point. At the start of its term the Reagan administration described the situation in that country as a "textbook case of indirect aggression by Communist powers through Cuba." In a white paper titled "Communist Interference in El Salvador," the administration described the revolutionary struggle there as principally a Communist-inspired movement controlled by external forces and supplied by the Soviet bloc. "The Salvadoran guerrillas," one critic of this argument pointed out, "are not just a leftist opposition movement, but are agents of what we used to [unrealistically] call the international communist conspiracy." The administration believes "that the Salvadoran insurrection is being fed from abroad, that it is a communist plot orchestrated in Russia, coordinated by Cuba, and implemented by the Marxist government in Nicaragua." According to this view the struggle "has no true domestic causes"; it stems not from indigenous poverty and political repression, but from "a virus imported from Eastern Europe." As Tom J. Farer, a professor of law and president of the Inter-American Commission on Human Rights, stated the point, the administration practices "a heroic indifference to detail. The revolutionary who haunts their hysterical prose never acquires a face." Conservatives "ask no questions about the particulars of time and place and program, about why a man or woman has assumed the awful peril of rebellion; they never ask because, for their crabbed purposes, they have all the necessary answers. Having taken up arms—some of them Cuban or Russian or otherwise tainted—against an anti-communist government, the revolutionary is either a totalitarian communist or a foolish tool, not to mention a 'terrorist.' "[3]

To combat the Communist threat in El Salvador, the administration sent Secretary of State Haig to Capitol Hill, and sent State and Defense Department officials to Europe and Latin America to drum up support for military and economic aid to the

Salvadoran junta headed by President José Napoleón Duarte. Although his conservative regime had been accused of numerous human rights violations, including the murder of four American church workers by government security forces, it described itself as a centrist administration committed to some land reform and opposed to extremists of the left and the right. Turning a blind eye to the junta's faults, the Reagan administration increased material aid to Duarte's government, including the use of U.S. military advisers to help combat the guerrillas. El Salvador was to be a model of what the Reagan White House intended in foreign affairs: a "test case of U.S. determination and ability to draw the line against Red subversion." Instead of linking aid to El Salvador to the elimination of human rights abuses and progress on land reform, the Reagan government provided military and economic aid on the assumption that the rebellion in El Salvador was Soviet supported, making the conflict there "not a local affair but part of a larger East-West struggle."[4]

The inadequacy of such an approach to El Salvador was quickly shown. While almost no one disputed the assertion that there was Communist involvement in El Salvador or that arms were being shipped via Cuba and Nicaragua, a critical scrutiny of the administration's claims revealed that far fewer arms were reaching the rebels than the reports claimed and that the Soviets and the Nicaraguans, "who were bent on protecting their own revolution," were giving the guerrillas only grudging support. The *Wall Street Journal* "found only one instance of outright Soviet aid to the rebels—an airplane ticket from Moscow to Vietnam for one guerrilla." "There are a lot of people who are starting to wonder if this Administration is telling the bottom line—or only trying to sell one," one American official in Latin America declared.[5]

The administration's actions, arousing fears of another Vietnam, provoked substantial debate and opposition in the United States. *Time* and *Newsweek* ran cover stories on the Salvadoran conflict and American involvement, while major newspapers gave extended coverage to the bloodletting, including the widespread killing of innocent civilians by guerrillas and government security forces. Organized opponents of increased U.S. aid, particularly church groups, deluged Congress with pleas to defy the administration's policy. In response, congressional committees made additional aid to Duarte's government contingent upon "a concerted and significant" effort to limit human rights violations, hold free elections, introduce agrarian reforms, and negotiate for a settlement with "groups which renounce and refrain from further military or paramilitary opposition activity."[6]

Duarte agreed to hold elections for a constitutional assembly in 1982 and a presidential election in 1983, but the Reagan policy neither improved conditions in El Salvador nor made the United States or its allies more secure from threats to their economic and political well-being. In spite of American aid, the civil strife did not ease in El Salvador during 1981, and by the end of the year that Central American country was no closer to ending its civil strife than when Reagan came to office. In the eyes of many people "the problem seemed intractable." As stated by one Central American leader, "those who hold real power on both sides are beyond the reach of the democratic forces on both sides." Moreover, as one American commentator wisely foresaw, a tough policy in El Salvador was "not going to make the Russians fall in line in Africa and the Middle East, let alone in Poland. Nor is it going to protect U.S. interests in Central America." Indeed, the hard-line policy toward El Salvador was nothing more than "a dangerous distraction" from the work of rebuilding a dynamic economy at home and attending to true strategic interests in Latin America and other parts of the globe.[7]

Even the Reagan administration could not entirely resist these compelling truths. As one specialist on Latin America pointed out, by the close of 1981 Reagan's "resolve to 'draw the line' and contain the spread of communism had simmered down to grudging and conditional support for continued economic and military aid by a reluctant Congress, occasional aggressive remarks by the secretary of state about Cuban and Nicaraguan support for the guerrillas, and a general lack of enthusiasm for a civil war that seemed to have no solution. In September, when President Duarte came to argue his case on American television and in Congress, he received surprisingly little attention." Although the White House would not abandon its policy, it was widely agreed that the administration had made a serious mistake in turning "the ugly little war in El Salvador" into a showdown between Soviet expansionism and American resolve. By first "casting the Central American conflict in apocalyptic East-West terms" and then failing to achieve the quick military victory it sought, the Reagan government undermined its international credibility and fostered the view that it was ill prepared to deal with the realities of world affairs.[8]

The administration's actions toward the Soviet Union during 1981 produced a similar perception. In response to the president's familiar anti-Soviet rhetoric during the 1980 campaign and his first press conference in January 1981, Soviet President Brezhnev and Foreign Minister Gromyko threw Reagan on the defensive by making proposals to meet and discuss "outstanding differences." Declaring that it should not "rush to summitry for summitry's sake" and that issues like subversion in El Salvador and Soviet interference in Afghanistan should either be "straightened out" or on the table before talks were decided on, the administration resisted the suggestion. Yet at the same time the president felt compelled to send Brezhnev a hand-written, conciliatory letter in which he asked, "Is it possible that we have permitted ideology, political and economic philosophies and governmental policies to keep us from considering the very real, everyday problems of our peoples?" Shortly after, on April 24, in response to pressure from American farmers, the administration lifted the grain embargo President Carter had invoked against the Soviets after their invasion of Afghanistan.[9]

If these were supposed to be signs of a pragmatic response by Reagan, they were soon contradicted by fresh expressions of a tough anti-Soviet line. Four months after Brezhnev replied to the president's letter with a renewed suggestion for a "well-prepared" meeting at a "moment acceptable to both of us," Reagan had given no answer. During this time, from late May to the end of September 1981, the administration continued its steady drumbeat about building up military strength to eliminate the Soviet advantage and expressed its intention to use "our trade relations and our broader economic relations . . . [to] reinforce our efforts to counter the Soviet military buildup and its irresponsible conduct." When Reagan did answer Brezhnev on September 22, "the tone was sterner, the accusations crisper, the rhetoric more reminiscent of the campaign" than in his first message. But in the same letter he expressed interest in a "stable and constructive relationship" with Moscow and a desire for expanded trade and increased contacts "at all levels of our societies." In the fall the administration sent yet another double message: it opposed Western European financing and use of a natural gas pipeline from the USSR, on the one hand, and it proposed arms limitation talks, on the other.[10]

By the end of the year there was confusion on both sides of the Atlantic about what the Reagan administration intended in its dealings with the USSR. In the view of *New York Times* columnist Flora Lewis, by December 1981 the NATO "alliance had never been so gravely troubled and so uncertainly led . . . There were no clear sign posts on what kind of East-West relations Washington was seeking, what it expected from the USSR, beyond not taking advantage of weak spots on the earth's political crust. There was no visible plan for developing new relations with Moscow, only denunciation of the way things had been going." When reporters asked administration officials where they were heading, the answers produced more confusion. Secretary Haig vaguely described the American goal as winning "restraint and reciprocity" from Moscow, but other members of the government indicated that there was a deliberate policy vacuum, an attempt to put Soviet-American relations on hold until the United States rebuilt its military power. Meetings between the president and European leaders added to this impression: "Mr. Reagan listened, smiled a lot, repeated his message on the advantages of private enterprise and his determination not to be pushed around by Russians, and went his own way, apparently unmoved," Flora Lewis observed. "Gradually, Europeans wondered what role he actually played in his administration."[11]

The problem perhaps was not so much in Reagan's failure to use his authority as in his unwillingness to improve relations with Moscow. If there were overtures in this direction, they were more the product of political pressures generated at home and abroad than of any genuine determination to get on a better footing with the USSR. The central objective of the Reagan conservatives, which made a clearly articulated policy unnecessary, was not to engage the Soviets in any constructive way but to regain America's military edge as a way of establishing a kind of symbolic superiority. The goal, then, is less to construct a rational framework for resolving tensions with Moscow than to eclipse it actually in military strength and symbolically in competing ways of life.

In the Middle East the same preoccupation with the Soviet Union distracted the Reagan administration from making any progress toward a more permanent peace during 1981. This is not to imply that answers to the intricate and fierce conflicts besetting that area are within easy reach of even the most rational and imaginative American policy makers. As Middle East expert John C. Campbell wrote at the end of 1981, "As with its predecessors, the range of choice and the chances of success [open to the Reagan administration] were constricted by the policies and decisions of other states, the availability of resources, the interaction with policies in other parts of the world, the demands of domestic politics, and the unpredictability of events in the Middle East; indeed, the only certainty was that unexpected and upsetting events would occur there."

Yet the administration might have performed better than it did. Focusing on what Haig called a "strategic consensus," an anti-Soviet combination of Israel and moderate Arab states, the administration stressed military steps to deter a Soviet attack on the Middle East at the expense of diplomatic formulations for resolving local political conflicts. "In considering the year's events,"

Campbell says, "the most valid criticism to be made of U.S. policy may be that in concentrating on a stronger military posture it neglected political foundations." Stated another way, the administration viewed the Middle East less in terms of its special tensions and needs than in the context of America's global competition with the USSR.[12]

A review of that year's events underscores the point. In April 1981 Secretary Haig traveled to Egypt, Israel, Jordan, and Saudi Arabia to promote the idea that "Soviet expansionism represents as great a threat to the stability of the Middle East as the unresolved issue of Palestinian autonomy." Although Haig granted that continuing strife in the region "offers the Soviet Union troubled waters in which to fish," he had no fresh initiatives to offer for resolving those troubles. This did not sit well with the Middle East leaders he saw, particularly the Jordanians and Saudis. "We see two dangers," an adviser to Jordan's King Hussein said, "Soviet as well as Israeli expansionism. If the Americans want the Arabs to help them confront the first danger, why don't the Americans help us solve the second?" Denying that talks with Haig had produced a "convergence of views," Saudi Foreign Minister Prince Saud declared: "The Kingdom of Saudi Arabia regards Israel as the principal cause of instability and insecurity in the region." Israel's Prime Minister Menachem Begin was ready to give rhetorical support to Haig's "anti-Soviet clarion call," but when the United States announced its plan to give Saudi Arabia five radar early-warning aircraft, or AWACs, to "ensure overall security in the Persian Gulf," Begin rebelled. Fearing that the planes would be used to spy on Israel's air force, the Israelis predicted that "the AWACS would lay Israel naked to Arab eyes in the sky."[13]

The limitations of the policy the French call *mal soviétique*—the impulse to see the Soviets behind most of the problems in the Middle East—was further demonstrated in June 1981 when the Israelis destroyed an Iraqi nuclear reactor they feared would be used to build a bomb. The episode, *Newsweek* observed, threatened "the campaign of Secretary of State Alexander Haig to persuade the

Arabs that they have far more to fear from Moscow than they do from Jerusalem." Although the Reagan administration indicated its concern for easing Arab-Israeli tensions by sending Philip Habib, an experienced diplomat, to mediate Israeli-Syrian differences over Lebanon, it had nothing to offer on the explosive Palestinian question and Israel's continuing presence on the West Bank of the Jordan River. "With the Administration unable to offer the Palestinians anything but the prospect of the dead end autonomy talks up the road," *Newsweek* concluded, "Haig's dream of sidestepping the Palestinian issue and closing ranks with the Arabs against the Soviet Union seems hopelessly compromised or naive." It now seemed "more important than ever for the President and the Secretary of State to shape a more coherent Middle East policy than has emerged so far."[14]

But the White House showed little inclination to change course. Despite complaints by the State Department in the summer that the administration "has done nothing to develop a Middle East policy, and that the President has displayed a degree of innocence about the issues involved," the White House continued to press the case for an anti-Soviet coalition without first addressing more fundamental questions about local conflicts. In August the focus of Reagan's policy became the sale of AWACs to Saudi Arabia, which he insisted Congress should approve to strengthen U.S. ties to moderate Arab states. But instead of advancing the "strategic consensus" the administration was advocating for the Middle East, the proposed sale principally exacerbated Arab-Israeli tensions. Pointing out that the United States already had four AWACs planes in Saudi Arabia that could do the necessary surveillance, that five additional planes largely under Saudi control would menace Israel's security, and that the instability of the Saudi government might cause this sophisticated weaponry to end up in anti-American hands, opponents of the deal complained that the president's policy "consisted of little more than an obsession with Soviet expansionism."[15]

To push the agreement through Congress in the fall of 1981, Reagan had to mount a major political campaign, calling on the support of former national security officials like Henry Kissinger, Robert McNamara, and Melvin Laird, and telling senators that unless they gave him their votes they would be destroying his effectiveness in conducting foreign policy. He also argued that the assassination of Egyptian President Anwar Sadat in October 1981 made it all the more imperative that the United States support its few Arab friends in the area. Using these persuasive tactics, the White House won a narrow four-vote margin for its policy in the Senate. But it was something of a Pyrrhic victory: the Saudis ended up feeling "humiliated and insulted by the long process in which their stability, competence, and trustworthiness were questioned day after day," and the sale produced a "palpable" deterioration in American-Israeli relations. Amid "muffled talk of 'Reagan or Begin,'" the president declared that no foreign country was going to dictate the foreign policy of the United States.[16]

In these circumstances the situation in the Middle East went from bad to worse. With the United States offering no new proposals on the Palestinian and West Bank issues, the Saudis moved into the political vacuum and stated that Israel should withdraw from all occupied territories, that a Palestinian state should be established on the West Bank and in the Gaza Strip, and that all states in the area, implicitly including Israel, should live in peace. Although President Reagan called the proposal an encouraging development, Prime Minister Begin labeled it a plan for the gradual liquidation of Israel. When the Palestine Liberation Organization, Syria, and other "rejectionist" Arab states dismissed the Saudi plan at a conference in late November, it deepened Israeli militancy, with the Begin government pointing out that some Arabs had "rejected even a one-sided peace plan of Arab origin." Begin then persuaded the Israeli Knesset to approve a de facto annexation of the Golan Heights, which Israel had taken from Syria in the 1967 war. When the Reagan administration joined the U.N. Security Council in calling the action illegal and suspended strategic agreements with Israel, the "strategic consensus" Reagan and Haig had been preaching for almost a year was in a shambles.[17]

By the start of 1982 Arab-Israeli tensions had confounded Reagan's hopes for an anti-Soviet grouping in the Middle East. "More than in any other region," Hedrick Smith of the *New York Times* pointed out, "the Administration has met frustration. Sharp tensions between Israel and Saudi Arabia have dashed hopes of forging an anti-Soviet consensus, and Mr. Reagan has yet to establish a workable relationship with Prime Minister Menachem Begin of Israel. Each time the two governments paper over their squabbles, differences erupt again. While the Reagan Administration pursues the belief that American and Israeli interests are both served by accommodation with moderate Arabs, the Begin Government has reacted angrily to Washington's arms sales to Saudi Arabia and its favorable reaction to Saudi negotiating terms." Stanley Hoffmann summed it up best perhaps when he observed that Reagan had an ideology but not a policy for dealing with the world. "This ideology turned out to be utterly deficient as a strategy because it fails to address many real problems, it aggravates others, it provides no priority other than anti-Soviet imperatives and precious little guidance even in connection with the Cold War."[18]

The distorted diplomacy of using ideology as strategy extended to Asia as well, and to relations with the People's Republic of China and with Taiwan in particular. "What had been a relationship with some positive momentum and strategic weight," Sinologist Richard H. Solomon wrote at the end of 1981 about United States relations with Beijing, "stagnated over the year in distrust and uncertainty." During the 1980 campaign Reagan had denounced Carter's normalization of relations with the People's Republic and avowed his intention to fulfill the Taiwan Relations Act of 1979 by selling defensive weapons to the island's anticommunist Nationalist government. Shortly before his inauguration the president-elect expressed skepticism about cooperating with Beijing, describing China as "a country whose government subscribes to an ideology based on a belief in destroying governments like ours."[19]

Once in office, however, Reagan adopted a more moderate

position, accepting the need for normal relations with China, which the Nixon, Ford, and Carter administrations had encouraged. Under the prodding of Secretary Haig, a strong advocate of using China as a counterweight to the USSR or of adding it to a coalition of anti-Soviet nations, the president incorporated China into his global anti-Sovietism. Indeed, in June 1981 he sent Haig on a goodwill trip to Beijing and invited the Chinese to buy arms from the United States. At the same time the administration openly expressed its determination to sell arms to Taiwan and refused to accept that such sales would undercut relations with the P.R.C. Instead the White House focused strictly on the need to strengthen Soviet opponents, regardless of how these actions might affect other international questions.

Such a dual policy—almost a two-China policy—was deemed destructive by critics on two counts: it deepened Soviet antagonism to the United States and it alienated the Chinese. Former Secretary of State Cyrus Vance criticized the decision to sell weapons to the P.R.C. as "needlessly provocative" to the Soviet Union. "It smacks of bearbaiting rather than dealing seriously with the problems." He also asserted that it "virtually removed any influence we have left over the Soviet Union. We played the China card in no-trump." Likewise, it did nothing to conciliate the Chinese. Reluctant to be a cat's-paw in Reagan's anti-Soviet campaign or to accept arms sales to Taiwan passively, Beijing refused to send a military mission to Washington in the second half of 1981 and publicly expressed its interest in reopening discussions with Moscow on long-standing differences. By the end of the year, with Washington giving no indication that it would back off from its Taiwan policy, the official China News Agency warned that American arms sales to the island would violate Chinese sovereignty and would "gravely endanger the development of U.S. relations with China and lead to their retrogression." In less than a year's time the Reagan administration had brought relations with the P.R.C. to "the brink of a major disruption."[20]

The administration's general lack of success in its anti-Soviet approach to world affairs did not deter it from largely holding to

the same course in 1982–83. To be sure, a number of initiatives
and shifts made it seem that the White House was responding
more realistically to international conditions, but behind these
apparent changes the impulse to see the world simply as an unrelenting contest between American freedom and Soviet totalitarianism remained as keen as ever. At the end of May 1982, sixteen
months after Reagan had come to office, some in Washington believed that the responsibility of governing had "tempered the
President's hard-line thinking and moved him toward a more
moderate, tolerant, practical view of the world's other super-
power." His closest aides, however, denied the change; the president may have softened his language, they said, but not his
attitude. "He hasn't changed one bit in how he thinks about the
Russians," one of them explained. Since Reagan was about to
leave for Europe, where he would stress the peace initiatives he
had announced in the previous seven months, the emphasis on his
continuing antagonism toward Moscow may have been a political
sop to conservative supporters troubled by his apparently less militant approach to the Russians. This White House denial of a shift
in the president's view of Moscow undoubtedly had such a political aim, but it was also a statement of fact, as a review of Reagan's
foreign policies during 1982 and the first half of 1983 demonstrates.[21]

Latin America is a good case in point. In February 1982 the
president announced before the Organization of American States
that the United States would launch a Caribbean Basin Initiative,
an economic program which would make most Caribbean exports
to the United States duty free and give tax incentives to American
investors in the area. The proposal aimed to help "our neighbors
help themselves" and to blunt criticism that the administration
saw Central and South America only in terms of the strategic Soviet threat. But as Alan Riding, chief of the *New York Times*
Mexican Bureau, pointed out, the program was little more than a
gesture. It was "built largely on the dubious premise that private
enterprise could lift the region out of its slump." Moreover,
where the Central American republics estimated that it would

take $5 billion in emergency aid and $20 billion in long-term development support to produce economic recovery and political stability, the Reagan administration proposed to do the job with $350 million. "The Administration has not found the right answers" for the area, Riding wrote at the beginning of 1983, because "it has not asked the right questions." Instead of seeing political instability as indigenous, it blamed it on "external forces . . . Moscow, Havana and Managua." Instead of viewing depressed world commodity prices as the principal cause of the region's economic crisis, it attributed the problems to government profligacy and implied that Caribbean economic difficulties "can be resolved largely through internal austerity measures—as if communism can be combatted with poverty."[22]

Throughout 1982 and the first six months of 1983 the White House remained preoccupied with the security problem posed by Communist expansion. "A new kind of colonialism stalks the world today and threatens our independence," Reagan declared in his speech before the OAS. "It is brutal and totalitarian. It is not of our hemisphere but it threatens our hemisphere and has established footholds on American soil for the expansion of its colonialist ambitions." Pointing to "the expansion of Soviet-backed, Cuban-managed support for violent revolution in Central America," the president warned that a failure to "act promptly and decisively in defense of freedom" would result in "new Cubas . . . totalitarian regimes tied militarily to the Soviet Union . . . exporting subversion" and driving their citizens to flee to the United States. Since an "outside power" was supporting "terrorism and insurgency," he intended "to help friendly countries hold off those who would destroy their chances for economic and social progress and political democracy."[23]

The president's words were given particular meaning in El Salvador, where the administration continued its military efforts to combat a leftist revolution against a repressive conservative government. As a number of critics in this country and abroad pointed out, the president's concern with Communist expansion in Central America was not wholly artificial or the product of blind anticommunism; Soviet-Cuban efforts in El Salvador, Central America, and the Caribbean Basin do pose some threat to the security of the United States. "Half of U.S. trade, including two-thirds of all oil imports, passes through the Panama Canal or the Gulf of Mexico," one commentator has observed. Yet the impulse to see the danger to the United States as emanating principally from Moscow and Havana and to see the answer in military repression of leftist insurgents is a simplistic and ineffective way to meet a complex problem. But this is what the White House continued to do in 1982 and 1983. Turning aside suggestions from Mexico, Venezuela, Panama, France, and the Socialist International for a negotiated settlement in El Salvador and with Nicaragua, the Reagan administration pressed the case for more military aid and a more determined effort to defeat the "communist threat." At the end of February 1983, with the war going poorly for the Salvadoran government and no prospect of an end to the fighting, Secretary Shultz "reiterated emphatically [before a Senate subcommittee] his determination that there be no negotiations with the guerrillas in El Salvador." He also expressed the conviction "that the assumption of power in El Salvador by the same group that is in power in Cuba and Nicaragua, with the same source of support, is bad news for the people of El Salvador, for the people of the United States and . . . for the churches of El Salvador. There's nothing great about the way religion is treated in the Soviet Union," he declared.[24]

This obsession with the Soviet threat was counterproductive because it persuaded the administration that "the most effective way out of the crisis in El Salvador is military rather than diplomatic." That "is a shortsighted strategy that will further entrap the United States in a political quagmire," the *Los Angeles Times* asserted. By late April 1983 the administration still showed no inclination to change its mind. When the House Foreign Affairs and the Senate Foreign Relations committees rejected the president's plea for additional military aid to El Salvador, and congressmen charged that the administration was supporting the guerrillas who were trying to overthrow Nicaragua's leftist Sandinista government, Reagan decided to address a joint session of Congress, only the fifth time he had done this during his twenty-seven months in office. His speech was a defense of his overall Central American policy. Declaring that "the national security of all the Americas is at stake in Central America," Reagan said: "If we cannot defend ourselves there, we cannot expect to prevail elsewhere. Our credibility would collapse, our alliances would crumble and the safety of our homeland would be put in jeopardy." He asked prompt congressional approval for economic and security programs which would allow the people of Central America to "hold the line against externally supported aggression."

Experts on the area did not agree with the president's analysis and prescription. The administration, Alan Riding argued, needs to be "guided by pragmatism rather than short term ... objectives." It needs to "embark on an open-minded endeavor to develop political stability and economic viability ... It would, of course, require a much greater economic investment than anticipated by the CBI [Caribbean Basin Initiative], as well as recognition that leftists exist." Indeed, such a policy would require accepting the fact that solving problems in Central America will take something more imaginative than counterinsurgency warfare against a "Soviet-controlled threat," that Central America must be viewed in regional terms rather than simply as an extension of the United States' struggle with the USSR.[25]

But the administration could not free itself from this thinking. In June Reagan appointed Richard B. Stone, a former Democratic senator from Florida, as a special envoy to the region to promote political solutions to its conflicts, and in July he appointed former secretary of state Henry Kissinger to head a study commission on Central America. But he also continued to press for military aid to combat Soviet-sponsored opponents seeking to spread Marxism throughout the area. In May and June he replaced Thomas O. Enders, the assistant secretary of state for inter-American affairs, and Deane R. Hinton, the U.S. ambassador to El Salvador, with men who would be more likely to support a hard-line or military approach to Central America. As many commen-

tators observed, it was not that Enders and Hinton were antago-
nistic to military aid or were prepared to accept the triumph of
Marxism in El Salvador and Central America; they were not. But
they were experienced diplomats who recognized that a successful
policy depended upon flexibility and political negotiation as well
as upon military power. Their replacements, Langhorne Motley,
an Alaska land developer and former ambassador to Brazil, and
Thomas R. Pickering, a career foreign service officer who had
served in Africa and the Middle East, seemed to be less knowledgeable about Central America but more in harmony with Reagan's emphasis on military progress. In July, in line with this,
Reagan announced U.S. military maneuvers in the region on an
unprecedented scale. The president's actions, one U.S. foreign policy expert observed, demonstrated the administration's "abysmal
ignorance of the nature of Marxist 'wars of national liberation.' . . . The Administration strategy . . . touches none of the
root causes of left-wing insurgencies, and will only spread the
conflict and provoke an anti-American backlash." A former
American ambassador to Panama echoed the point: the United
States needed to encourage economic and political reform in El
Salvador, discourage government repression by "death squads,"
and get other countries in the region involved in finding a solution to El Salvador's problems.[26]

The administration's limited perspective on Central America
also undermined its ability to deal effectively with South America.
"Reagan regarded South America as important more for its potential contribution to the U.S. effort in Central America than for
itself," Latin American specialist Susan Kaufman Purcell wrote at
the end of 1982. "South America's military governments were
seen as possible providers of training and weapons to their belea-
guered Central American counterparts." This attitude played a
significant part in Argentina's decision to invade the Falkland Is-
lands in the spring of 1982. Having "an exaggerated sense of their
importance to the United States" in building an anticommunist
alliance, Argentina's ruling military leaders mistakenly assumed
that the Reagan administration would not oppose their invasion

of the Falklands. Secretary Haig added to this misperception: in his shuttle diplomacy between London and Buenos Aires to mediate the conflict, he never made clear to Argentina that if negotiations failed and war resulted, the United States would side with Britain. Bound by its preoccupation with the Soviet threat and its need to see Argentina's conservative military regime as an unshakable ally in the anticommunist struggle, the Reagan government could not bring itself to state this reality until it was forced to do so. Although there could be little doubt, outside of Argentina, that the United States would side with its strategically more important ally, Britain, and with the principle of self-determination, which Britain was clearly defending in the conflict, the administration gave open backing to London only after the fighting began.[27]

This provoked considerable bitterness toward Washington in much of Latin America, which Reagan decided to soften by traveling to Brazil, Colombia, Honduras, and Costa Rica for a five-day visit at the end of 1982. Although he made a concerted effort to focus on the region's economic problems, especially in Brazil, where a $72 billion foreign debt was straining the country's financial limits, the president could not resist pressing his anticommunist theme. At the same time that he announced a $1.2 billion loan to help ease Brazil's financial crisis and expressed confidence in the country's long-term economic prospects, he warned of the danger of "counterfeit revolutionaries . . . who are . . . armed by the surrogate of a faraway power . . . whose goal is the destabilization of our governments and economies. This is aggression, pure and simple," he declared.[28]

In Colombia Reagan received a stern lecture from President Belisario Betancur on the short-sightedness of excluding Cuba from inter-American forums, of holding Cuba responsible for armed revolution throughout Central America, and of encouraging expenditures on arms instead of on economic and social improvement. Despite this admonishment, Reagan stressed the anticommunist idea as strongly as ever on his stops in Central America. In Honduras he met with Guatemala's military ruler,

President Efrain Rios Montt, the leader of a regime "universally condemned as one of the most brutal and corrupt governments in the world." Reagan praised Rios Montt as "totally dedicated to democracy," saying that he viewed Guatemala's government as "getting a bum rap" and that he wished to restore its military aid, which moved one columnist to observe that the insensitivity of Reagan's administration to "human cruelty will ... stain the name of the United States." Although his trip to Latin America achieved some gains for the United States, a number of commentators agreed that he was still a long way from settling on a policy that would effectively advance U.S. national security throughout the hemisphere.[29]

The administration's dealings with the Soviet Union and Europe during 1982 were even more destructive to the national interest. Seweryn Bialer pointed out that after two years in office Reagan's "conduct toward the Soviet Union is guided less by a comprehensive and consistent long-range policy than by a general ideological orientation ... The result of this approach ... has been a sharp worsening of U.S.-Soviet relations to a level of serious new confrontation and mutual suspicion." The focus of Reagan's anti-Sovietism at the end of 1981 was the repression of Poland's Solidarity movement when Warsaw introduced martial law in December. Hard-liners in the administration, led by Defense Secretary Weinberger, urged Reagan to adopt economic sanctions against Warsaw and Moscow and to threaten to foreclose on the Polish debt unless America's allies joined in punishing the Poles and Russians. But the White House, following State Department advice, limited itself to unilateral sactions, chiefly an embargo on American-made parts for the natural gas pipeline between Siberia and Western Europe.[30]

The president's decision provoked considerable controversy. Conservatives in the United States complained that he was being too timid, that the sanctions were no more than a gesture which amounted to a tacit acceptance of Poland's failure to regain its freedom from Soviet Communist control. By contrast, Americans and Europeans who were opposed to the sanctions objected that they would simply worsen relations with the Soviets and Western Europe without advancing the cause of Polish independence in any way. They also questioned the rational judgment of an administration that was selling the Soviets millions of tons of grain and at the same time berating its allies for subsidizing the Russian pipeline. Supporters of Reagan's policy answered that while grain sales would make the Soviets dependent on the United States for food supplies, the pipeline would give Moscow control over Western Europe's natural gas supply. But the Europeans denied both assertions, arguing that during the Carter grain embargo the Soviets bought grain elsewhere, while the pipeline would not be the principal provider of natural gas in Europe and would not make them vulnerable to Soviet blackmail. A German journalist asked: "How could trade be cynical business-as-usual when countenanced by France, Germany or Italy, while its American counterpart was touted as a strategic advance for the West? Why was deference to the ailing steel industry in Europe more sinful than President Reagan's appeasement of Midwestern farmers beset by overproduction and falling prices—and in an election year to boot?" The Europeans were particularly cynical about the administration's argument that their "gas purchases would contribute vital resources to the tottering Soviet economy while American grain sales would sap it even more by extracting billions in scarce cash." In fact, the reverse was true: the grain imports would allow the Soviets to free resources—labor and capital—to produce more valuable oil and natural gas.[31]

Partly to iron out these differences, Reagan met with America's principal allies—Britain, Canada, France, Italy, Japan, and West Germany—at Versailles, France, in early June 1982. The meeting produced some heated exchanges between Reagan and his European allies, especially West German Chancellor Helmut Schmidt, in which the president insisted that they agree to reduce credits to the Soviets because these allowed the USSR to channel scarce resources into a massive military buildup. Although the allies committed themselves to "commercial prudence in limiting export credits to the Communist countries," the conference agreement, in the words of one commentator, was a "convoluted communiqué" that "solved precisely nothing." Ten days later French President François Mitterand made clear that there was no agreement on limiting credit subsidies to Moscow. Reagan then acted, in the view of some Europeans, to injure his adversary by punishing his friends. On June 18 he ordered an extension of his December embargo on American pipeline suppliers' sending parts to their subsidiaries and license holders in France, Germany, England, and Italy. When three of the European countries encouraged subsidiary suppliers under their jurisdiction to defy the president's ban, the White House imposed a general export embargo on the defiant companies.[32]

The conflict stirred what many people in Europe and America thought were the worst strains in the alliance in twenty years. "We are not speaking the same language anymore," French Foreign Minister Claude Cheysson complained publicly. "The United States appears to be totally indifferent to our problems." "If the Kremlin had plotted this policy," Republican Senator Charles Percy observed, "they couldn't have done a better job." "Why launch a policy that could not change anything important even if it succeeded, and that from the start is known to be unacceptable to the allies, and therefore must do more harm than good?" one American journalist wondered. The only answer he could find was that the administration could not distinguish between a principle and a practical, workable policy. Many Europeans reached the same conclusion. In their view the administration's opposition to liberal credits and pipeline exports rested less on a desire to punish Moscow for martial law in Poland than "to destabilize the entire Soviet system." The aim of Reagan's actions, in short, was not stricly to save Poland or to keep the Europeans from becoming dependent on Soviet gas supplies but to fight an "economic war" that would sap Soviet power.[33]

Finally realizing that pipeline sanctions were doing more to undermine relations between America and its European allies than to hurt Moscow, Reagan was persuaded to reverse his course in November. Announcing on November 13 that the United States had reached a "historic" accord with its allies on principles for conducting future East-West trade, the White House declared an end to all pipeline curbs. But the British and French at once disputed the assertion that they had made an agreement with the administration. No deal had been made on East-West trade, they said, which would lead the president to abandon his sanctions. It was "a unilateral decision," British Foreign Secretary Francis Pym announced. One former State Department official called the Reagan-proclaimed trade agreement with America's allies a "fig leaf" to cover up the fact that the administration was changing a policy that had "disrupted the alliance and damaged several major American industrial concerns." One European newspaper called the embargo "the flop of the year," while a West German journalist described "the President's plunge into unilateralism" as "a blunder of almost historic proportions." It also raised a "painful question": after two years in office, was the Reagan administration "equipped to conduct a foreign policy commensurate with America's power and purpose in the world?" The decision to ease differences with America's allies on East-West trade issues, however, did open the way to better relations. At a summit meeting of industrialized nations in Williamsburg, Virginia, at the end of May 1983 the Reagan administration was able to reach agreements with its European allies and Japan on economic steps to overcome the worldwide recession and on deployment of intermediate-range nuclear weapons in Europe.[34]

Still, this did not convince administration critics that the president was on a new track toward a successful foreign policy. The contrast between Reagan and Yuri Andropov, the man who became Soviet president after Brezhnev's death in November 1982, raised further doubts. In only two months Andropov was able to design a coherent arms control policy toward the United States and Western Europe which encouraged the impression that Moscow was more eager than Washington to negotiate a treaty. Although Soviet proposals for reductions in long-range and intermediate-range nuclear missiles were more a propaganda ploy than an acceptable offer, Washington's quick rejection of the proposals

enhanced the view in Europe as well as at home that the Reaganites were so rigidly anti-Soviet that they would not enter into serious negotiations. As one columnist summed up the situation at
the end of Reagan's second year in office, "It is in precisely the
area of how to deal with the Soviet Union that Reagan would
collide with himself in any serious effort to alter course. Here we
are not talking about tactics or dogma . . . We are talking about
something evangelical: a profound philosophical conviction that
communism is evil." With good reason, administration critics
doubted that the Reagan White House would find solutions to
"the big problems of arms control and defense affecting relations
with the Soviet Union."[35]

That Reagan's administration might lack the intellectual
range and the will to deal with the increasingly serious problems
of the Middle East was also apparent through the summer of
1982. During the first four months of the year, actually, the picture in the area brightened just a bit. Although Egyptian-Israeli
talks about autonomy for the West Bank Palestinians seemed
hopelessly deadlocked by Jordan's refusal to join the negotiations
and by Israel's expanding settlements, Washington's support of
the 1978 Camp David accords helped assure the final withdrawal
of Israeli forces from the Sinai Peninsula in late April. Yet at the
same time the administration's failure to shift its focus decidedly
"from primary concern over the Soviet strategic threat to the un-
derlying indigenous problems of the region" contributed to the
deterioration of conditions for peace and did nothing to deter the
Begin government from invading Lebanon in June to destroy the
military power of the PLO. "American activism in the peace process has a deterrent effect on violence in the area," former Under
Secretary of State Joseph J. Sisco believes. "American realism and
optimism as an operational principle is a necessary psychological
antidote to pessimism, despair, frustration and fear, and America's
determined and persistent involvement and leadership is indispensable. The parties cannot do it by themselves." To this Sisco
added that "the near-exclusive emphasis on strategic consensus
early in the Reagan Administration gave Israel the impression

that the United States was not too concerned over the stalemated autonomy talks. There has been a tendency to undulate between harsh criticism and undue accommodation toward Begin's policies. This confused both the Likud and Labor in Israel and tended to confound the Arab world as well." Even the most determined White House effort might not have been able to head off the events of the summer of 1982, especially when one considers how determined the Begin government was to destroy the PLO in Lebanon and to expand Israeli settlements on the West Bank. But the administration's failure to make more of an effort to resolve the problems of the Middle East did make those events more likely.[36]

The Begin government, with little evidence that Washington wanted to undertake a new Mideast peace initiative, and convinced that Egypt would not intervene and that the United States would grudgingly accept Israeli action against the PLO in Lebanon, sent its forces across the border on June 6. As it became clearer that Israel planned to drive Palestinian forces not just out of southern Lebanon, but also out of Beirut and the whole country, the urgency of a fresh American effort to address fundamental issues in the Middle East became all the more obvious. As Charles William Maynes, the editor of *Foreign Policy* magazine wrote in mid-June 1982, "What must now happen is that Israel must withdraw and the United States must join with all parties in the Middle East to induce both the Israelis and the Palestinians to make the kind of mutual concessions that will make progress in the peace process possible. For this to happen, President Reagan himself will have to play a major role in Middle East policy . . . Unless the President decides to play a more vigorous and fundamental role, the prospect in the Middle East is one of continuing crisis and repeated wars, until one day the world finds that not only the Arabs and the Israelis, but also everyone else will have stepped over the edge."[37]

The appointment of George Shultz as secretary of state at the end of June gave additional momentum to the idea that the administration should shift its focus from creating an anti-Soviet consensus in the Middle East to seeing the region principally in terms of its own special problems. At his confirmation hearings in July Shultz declared, "The crisis in Lebanon makes painfully and totally clear a central reality of the Middle East: the legitimate needs and problems of the Palestinian people must be addressed and resolved—urgently and in all their dimensions." Henry Kissinger emphasized much the same point in the *Washington Post,* arguing that "the Lebanese crisis creates an opening for American diplomacy to overcome the deadlock in the autonomy talks between Egypt and Israel. The United States must demonstrate that its proposed course in Lebanon is motivated by its concerns to bring about a just peace in the area and not only to remove a threat to Israel's northern border. This makes it urgent that concrete meaning be given to the long-stalled autonomy talks regarding the West Bank and Gaza." Kissinger believed that "the peace process in the Middle East can thus be given a new impetus" if the United States "leads with decisiveness and imagination."

With the help of Shultz and Kissinger, Reagan put forward a new peace plan for the Middle East in a nationally televised address on September 1, 1982. A departure from Reagan's earlier vague expressions of hope for peace in the area, the plan offered a detailed formula for resolving Arab-Israeli differences over the fate of the Palestinians. Acting without the prior knowledge of either the Israelis or moderate Arab leaders in Egypt, Jordan, or Saudi Arabia, Reagan rejected the Israelis' insistence on incorporating the West Bank and the Gaza Strip into Israel and also rejected Arab demands for an independent Palestinian state in those areas. Instead, he called for a freeze on Israeli settlements on the West Bank, recognition by the Arabs of Israel's existence, a five-year transition period in which "the peaceful and orderly transfer of domestic authority from Israel to the Palestinian inhabitants of the West Bank and Gaza" would occur, and the ultimate creation of a self-governing Palestinian state associated with Jordan. He pictured these proposals as "fully consistent with Israel's security requirements and the aspirations of the Palestinians" and as offering "the best chance for a durable, just and lasting peace." In what many commentators saw as the wisest and most realistic action in foreign affairs of his presidency, Reagan seized upon the difficulties in Lebanon to propose a broader peace settlement and urged all the concerned parties not to let this opportunity "slip from our grasp."[38]

The Reagan plan did not bring about an immediate improvement in the Middle East. The Begin government rejected the proposals as dangerous to Israel's survival and resolved not to enter into any negotiations based on the president's ideas. Although Arab leaders reacted more positively, they also refused to embrace the central propositions in the president's plan, and by April 1983 King Hussein of Jordan had declared that his country was unable to play the role Reagan had described for it in his peace initiative. Unwilling, however, to concede that the administration's peace effort was dead, Secretary of State Shultz traveled to the Middle East in April and May to negotiate the withdrawal of foreign troops from Lebanon. Part of the secretary's aim was to convince Arab leaders that the United States could win an Israeli commitment to leave Lebanon as a prelude to the more difficult task of arranging Israel's withdrawal from the West Bank. Although Shultz could not budge the Syrians on taking their forces out of Lebanon, he did put the finishing touches on an agreement between Lebanon and Israel, ending their forty-five-year state of war and initiating the eventual withdrawal of Israeli troops.

Although this was only a small step forward, it, along with the earlier peace initiative, had a highly salutary impact on the situation in the Middle East. The Reagan actions, one expert suggested, "quelled much of the public outcry among the Arabs for the time being and gave new hope, or at least helped ease the despair, in the Arab world. They moved the focus from crisis control to the peace process and . . . brought the Palestinian issue to center stage . . . In the most basic sense, the importance of the Reagan high-risk but necessary strategy to reassert diplomacy over force lies in the major political debate, dialogue, and ferment it has stimulated in Israel and the Arab world." More specifically, the president's proposals and actions gave peace advocates on both sides of the Middle East dispute a fresh sense of opportunity. Although eleven months after the Reagan initiative no one could point to dramatic progress, there remained a feeling that the Reagan administration was now focused on the *real* problems of the area rather than on the less well defined Soviet threat.[39]

The administration's effort to adopt a more flexible strategy toward China did not work out as well. At the end of 1981 Secretary Haig tried to make the president understand that his aggressive talk about resuming arms sales to Taiwan had brought U.S.-China relations to a "critical juncture" and might bring about "a setback that could gravely damage our global strategic position." Also arguing that Taiwan did not need sophisticated fighter planes to counter Beijing's limited offensive military capability, Haig persuaded Reagan to launch an intensive effort to ease tensions with the P.R.C. This Reagan did by sending the assistant secretary of state for East Asian affairs to Beijing in January 1982, by communicating directly with China's leaders by letters in April, and by having Vice-President Bush visit the country in June. In this effort the president emphasized to the Chinese that he wanted a fresh understanding on the arms sales to Taiwan.

In what one commentator called "a victory of pragmatism and patient diplomacy over rhetorical bluster," the administration managed to work out an accord with Beijing in August. In a joint communiqué the two sides agreed to five major points: China was fundamentally committed to "a peaceful reunification of Taiwan"; America agreed not to infringe on Chinese sovereignty or to promote a "two Chinas" policy; it understood Beijing's desire for peaceful resolution of the Taiwan issue; it pledged not to make any long-term agreements to sell arms to Taiwan and to gradually reduce current short-term agreements, with sales not to be qualitatively or quantitatively higher than those made since 1978; and the two countries pledged to do everything possible to settle the issue of arms sales.[40]

Although the agreement forestalled the sharp downturn in relations that Haig had warned against, it by no means solved the problem. In September Chinese officials complained that weapons deliveries to Taiwan still hung like a "black cloud" over Beijing's relations with the United States and that until the matter was fully resolved there would be no improvement in ties between the two countries. A visit by Secretary of State Shultz to Beijing in early February changed nothing. Although the August agreement eased the Taiwan problem, Chinese officials said, "it did not restore confidence between the two countries or revitalize the relationship." Asking for "actual deeds rather than empty words and promises," the Chinese pressed the Reagan administration to provide a timetable for the reduction of arms sales to Taiwan and details of how they would be limited. When Reagan not only resisted this but also told the conservative journal *Human Events* in February 1983 that the United States "did not give an inch" in the August communiqué and that reduced arms sales depended on peaceful agreements being made between the People's Republic and Taiwan, Beijing accused Reagan of reneging on his agreement and taking "a grave step backward."[41]

The principal consequence of Reagan's continuing support of Taiwan was that Beijing shifted toward a more central position between Moscow and Washington. The Chinese responded positively to Soviet overtures for talks to reduce long-standing tensions and began to harshly condemn American policies in Latin America, Africa, and the Middle East. Sinologist Michel Oksenberg pointed out that during 1982 "Beijing chose to highlight its own independence from both superpowers. Its rhetoric began to lump the Soviet Union and the United States together. The label 'hegemonists' was no longer reserved for Moscow but was extended to include Washington as well . . . In short, while distancing itself somewhat from the United States, the P.R.C. sought to strengthen its identity as a developing country, becoming more active in its espousal of various Third World causes."

By late spring 1983 the Chinese leaders, apparently having lost hope that there would be any substantial improvement in relations with the United States as long as Reagan was president, seemed intent on taking a tougher approach to Washington. Agitated not only by the administration's continuing arms sales to Taiwan but also by quotas on U.S. imports of Chinese textiles, by America's failure to provide the advanced technology it had promised, and by the grant of political asylum to the Chinese tennis player Hu Na, the Beijing government canceled all official cultural and athletic exchanges with the United States and committed itself to pursuing better relations with Moscow and Eastern Europe and to separating itself further from the United States on international questions.[42]

In the first half of 1983 it was clear that the Reagan administration would not let go of the conviction that indigenous regional and national issues were secondary to the danger posed by the worldwide Communist threat. The relentless growth of Soviet military power is aimed at dominating the world, Caspar Weinberger declared on March 9. If the American arms buildup is allowed to stagnate, a journalist reported him as saying, "the United States will have to settle for permanent nuclear inferiority and thus be subject to nuclear blackmail by the Soviet Union." His remarks were meant to underscore the release of a Pentagon study, "Soviet Military Power," which asserted that the Soviets intended "to undergird the step-by-step extension of Soviet influence and control" not simply by military force but "by instilling fear and promoting paralysis, by sapping the vitality of collective security arrangements, by subversion, [and] by coercive political actions of every genre."

At the same time, in March 1983 the president told a meeting of Christian evangelists in Florida that America's conflict with the Soviet Union was a "struggle between right and wrong, good and evil." He called Soviet Russia an "evil empire" and totalitarian states "the focus of evil in the modern world." Reagan coupled his attack on the Soviets with renewed pledges to seek constitutional amendments permitting prayer in public schools and banning abortions.[43] The connection seems reasonably clear: Soviet power and influence must be combated, not simply because they represent a threat to the United States but because they are the embodiment—the symbol—of those trends toward government control and relaxed social conventions that conservatives deplore. Reagan and his principal advisers have little energy to focus on local realities abroad. Their attention is largely fixed on challenges to their values from leftists around the world. The exaggerated Soviet threat—a Moscow pushing its "evil" purposes in every corner of the globe—is the product of the conservatives' obsession with defeating unsettling current trends and bolstering their own self-esteem.

By Reagan's third year in office his actions in both domestic and foreign affairs had produced considerable skepticism about his capacity to effectively govern the United States. As *New York Times* columnist Anthony Lewis phrased it in February 1983, "The United States is conducting a remarkable experiment in modern government. It is testing the effects on a great democracy of a vacuum at the center: of a Chief Executive who is scarcely informed on the substance of issues and shows no interest in being informed . . . At the point of decision-making there . . . is a President with a seven-minute attention span, a President interested not in reality but in appearance, in slogans . . . None of this seems to affect Mr. Reagan's political appeal." Lewis concluded, "Indeed, a good part of that appeal may be the way he comes on as a bewildered ordinary guy, vulnerable, blundering at times, but aw shucks." The following week the syndicated columnist Joseph Kraft made a similar point: "With Ronald Reagan, the blithe spirit entered the White House. He exudes charm, geniality and good feeling. Even the massive inattention to the substance of policy has, with him, a positive side. He walks away from failure—changes policies in the middle of the debacle—in seeming innocence that anything much has happened." Reagan's response in the summer of 1983 to the charges that the Republicans stole Carter's debate papers in the 1980 campaign told Kraft something about the president's "true character." Reagan's replies to journalists' questions confirmed what many people sensed—namely "that the President is a front man, lacking the diligence, experience and analytic capacity to understand complex public business."

Although Kraft was not sure that the country could "do much better in this time of macro-confusion," one has to hope otherwise.[44] Despite the fact that effective presidents have been more the exception than the rule in our history, it is difficult to believe that a nation of 226 million people cannot find a more rational, thoughtful, and energetic leader with greater self-awareness and a better grip on national and international realities. Indeed, it is a tribute to the country's intrinsic strength that it has managed to sustain itself effectively with a government so intent upon doing very little in everything except defense, where it wants to do too much. Reagan's policies at home and abroad speak not to the difficult problems that defy easy solution but to the inner personal grievances that Reagan and his fellow conservatives have turned into public concerns. If Reagan and the 28 percent of the eligible voters who elected him are made to feel better by the administration's reduced social programs and increased anti-Sovietism, they are making the rest of the country and much of the world pay a heavy price in added economic problems and heightened international tensions. For people everywhere the American experiment in symbolic politics has not been a happy event.

NOTES
INDEX

Notes

1. ORIGINS

1. Ronald Reagan with Richard G. Hubler, *Where's the Rest of Me?* (New York: Duell, Sloan and Pearce, 1965), pp. 3, 11, 13, 17–18.
2. Paul A. Carter, *Another Part of the Twenties* (New York: Columbia University Press, 1977), pp. 2–5.
3. Reagan, *Where's the Rest,* pp. 10, 22–24, 26, 32, 34. The survey is in Robert S. Lynd and Helen M. Lynd, *Middletown: A Study in American Culture,* 2nd ed. (New York: Harcourt, Brace, 1956), pp. 200–201, 220.
4. William E. Leuchtenburg, *The Perils of Prosperity, 1914–1932* (Chicago: University of Chicago Press, 1958), p. 95. Paul A. Carter, *The Twenties in America,* 2nd ed. (Arlington Heights, Ill.: AHM Publishing, 1975), pp. 38–39, 43. Carter, *Another Part,* pp. 145–146.
5. Reagan, *Where's the Rest,* p. 303. *Los Angeles Times,* Mar. 27, 1982, p. 9.
6. Frank Van Der Linden, *The Real Reagan* (New York: William Morrow, 1981), pp. 25–26.
7. Carter, *Twenties,* pp. 28–30. David Riesman, *The Lonely Crowd: A Study of the Changing American Character* (New Haven, Conn.: Yale University Press, 1950).
8. Van Der Linden, *Real Reagan,* pp. 34, 41, 46–47. Reagan, *Where's the Rest,* pp. 17–18, 37–38, 43–52.
9. Reagan, *Where's the Rest,* pp. 56–59. Carter, *Twenties,* pp. 30–31.
10. Reagan, *Where's the Rest,* pp. 69–76.

11. Van Der Linden, *Real Reagan,* pp. 55–59. Reagan, *Where's the Rest,* chap. 6, and pp. 90–95, 4–6.
12. Reagan, *Where's the Rest,* p. 79. Robert Lindsey, "California Rehearsal," in Hedrick Smith *et al., Reagan the Man, the President* (New York: Macmillan, 1980), p. 48. Tom Shales of the *Washington Post,* quoted in the *Los Angeles Times,* Mar. 26, 1982, VI, 17. Also see Mark Crispin Miller, "On Television: Virtu, Inc.," *The New Republic,* Apr. 7, 1982, pp. 28–32.
13. Morton Kondracke, "Reagan's I.Q.," *The New Republic,* Mar. 24, 1982, pp. 9–12. *Los Angeles Times,* Aug. 15, 1982, p. 1.
14. Reagan, *Where's the Rest,* pp. 7–10, 54. Van Der Linden, *Real Reagan,* pp. 29–30, 33, 39.
15. Van Der Linden, *Real Reagan,* pp. 29–32, 73–74.
16. Ibid., pp. 33–35. Reagan, *Where's the Rest,* pp. 17, 7–8.
17. Reagan, *Where's the Rest,* pp. 20–21, 97–99.
18. Ibid., pp. 26–30.
19. Bill Boyarsky, *The Rise of Ronald Reagan* (New York: Random House, 1968), pp. 59–60.
20. Reagan, *Where's the Rest,* pp. 76–77, 82, 90–94. Lou Cannon, *Reagan* (New York: G. P. Putnam's Sons, 1982), pp. 51, 69. Van Der Linden, *Real Reagan,* pp. 56–57. Boyarsky, *Rise of Reagan,* pp. 65–66.
21. Reagan, *Where's the Rest,* pp. 104–105, 215–216, 79. Van Der Linden, *Real Reagan,* pp. 66–67.
22. Van Der Linden, *Real Reagan,* pp. 63–65. Reagan, *Where's the Rest,* pp. 42, 52–54, 138–142, 173–174. Boyarsky, *Rise of Reagan,* pp. 83–91.
23. Boyarsky, *Rise of Reagan,* pp. 76–82. Reagan, *Where's the Rest,* pp. 132–133, 174.
24. Reagan, *Where's the Rest,* pp. 157–171.
25. Van Der Linden, *Real Reagan,* pp. 65–66. Boyarsky, *Rise of Reagan,* pp. 91–92. Cannon, *Reagan,* pp. 62–64. There is a parallel here to Reagan's earlier engagement to his high school and college sweetheart, Margaret Cleaver. After college, the engagement fell apart when Reagan put everything aside to pursue his radio career. "She wanted to be a homebody; he was going for the bright lights," one reporter summed up the forces driving them apart. Cannon, *Reagan,* pp. 43–44.
26. Van Der Linden, *Real Reagan,* pp. 67–69. Boyarsky, *Rise of Reagan,* p. 96.
27. Boyarsky, *Rise of Reagan,* pp. 96–99. Van Der Linden, *Real Reagan,* pp. 69–70.

28. Reagan, *Where's the Rest,* pp. 257–259, 265–267, 296–297, 299. Boyarsky, *Rise of Reagan,* pp. 100–101.

29. Cannon, *Reagan,* pp. 32, 94–97, 99–100. William E. Leuchtenburg, "Ronald Reagan," chapter in an unpublished manuscript, *In the Shadow of FDR,* is a penetrating account of Reagan's contradictory ties to the New Deal and FDR. For some of this material, see Leuchtenburg, "Ronald Reagan's Liberal Past," *The New Republic,* May 23, 1983, pp. 18–25, from which I have quoted.

30. Van Der Linden, *Real Reagan,* pp. 77–78. Reagan, *Where's the Rest,* pp. 301–312.

2. The Ideologue as Politician

1. Richard Hofstadter, *The Paranoid Style in American Politics and Other Essays* (New York: Alfred A. Knopf, 1965), pp. 77–80.

2. David O. Sears and Jack Citrin, *Tax Revolt: Something for Nothing in California* (Cambridge, Mass.: Harvard University Press, 1982), pp. 9–10. Also see Bill Boyarsky, *The Rise of Reagan* (New York: Random House, 1968), pp. 7–9, 22–26, 39–41, who describes the attitudes of these Californians.

3. See Hofstadter, *Paranoid Style,* pp. 56–62, who relies on Theodore W. Adorno et al., *The Authoritarian Personality* (New York: Harper and Row, 1950).

4. Frank Van Der Linden, *The Real Reagan* (New York: William Morrow, 1981), pp. 82–83.

5. Boyarsky, *Rise of Reagan,* pp. 104–111; Lou Cannon, *Reagan* (New York: G. P. Putnam's Sons, 1982), pp. 101–106.

6. Boyarsky, *Rise of Reagan,* pp. 145–150; Cannon, *Reagan,* pp. 107–112.

7. Boyarsky, *Rise of Reagan,* pp. 121–122, 132–137; Cannon, *Reagan,* pp. 110, 113. For more recent work on the tensions between symbolic politics and interest politics, see James Q. Wilson, "Reaganism," *Commentary* (October 1980); D. O. Sears, R. R. Lau, T. R. Tyler, and H. M. Allen, Jr., "Self-Interest vs. Symbolic Politics in Policy Attitudes and Presidential Voting," *American Political Science Review* 74 (1980), 670–684; Sears and Citrin, *Tax Revolt,* especially chaps. 8 and 10.

8. Boyarsky, *Rise of Reagan,* pp. 137–140, 142–145, 150–155; Cannon, *Reagan,* pp. 108–118.

9. On conservative difficulties with developing a positive program, see Hofstadter, *Paranoid Style,* pp. 87–88. On Reagan's lack of plans, see

Cannon, *Reagan,* pp. 119–121; Boyarsky, *Rise of Reagan,* pp. 158–159; Hedrick Smith et al., *Reagan the Man, the President* (New York: Macmillan, 1980), p. 41.

10. Cannon, *Reagan,* pp. 121–122.

11. Boyarsky, *Rise of Reagan,* pp. 165–176; Cannon, *Reagan,* pp. 122–128, 140.

12. Boyarsky, *Rise of Reagan,* pp. 178–187; Cannon, *Reagan,* pp. 154–157.

13. Boyarsky, *Rise of Reagan,* pp. 188–192; Cannon, *Reagan,* pp. 128–132.

14. Boyarsky, *Rise of Reagan,* chap. 14; Cannon, *Reagan,* pp. 148–154.

15. Boyarsky, *Rise of Reagan,* pp. 193–201, 211.

16. Cannon, *Reagan,* pp. 132–138.

17. Ibid., pp. 166–176.

18. Ibid., pp. 176–184.

19. Ibid., pp. 184–185.

20. Ibid., pp. 191–192, 200–201; Elizabeth Drew, *Portrait of an Election: The 1980 Presidential Campaign* (New York: Simon and Schuster, 1981), p. 111.

21. Rowland Evans and Robert Novak, *The Reagan Revolution* (New York: E. P. Dutton, 1981), p. 40, for the quote.

22. Ibid., pp. 39–40; Cannon, *Reagan,* pp. 157–165.

23. Cannon describes the 1976 campaign in great detail in *Reagan,* pp. 192–226. Evans and Novak describe the campaign in chap. 3 of *The Reagan Revolution.*

24. On the 1980 nomination, see Cannon, *Reagan,* chaps. 16 and 17; Drew, *Portrait of an Election,* chaps. 5 and 9, and pp. 171–179; and Theodore H. White, America in Search of Itself: The Making of the President, 1956–1980 (New York: Harper and Row, 1982), chaps. 8, 10, and 11.

25. Cannon, *Reagan,* pp. 233–234, 267–268; White, *America in Search of Itself,* pp. 327–328, 381–382; Drew, *Portrait of an Election,* pp. 217–220.

26. Cannon, *Reagan,* pp. 269–274; White, *America in Search of Itself,* pp. 384–386.

27. The White quote is in White, *America in Search of Itself,* p. 419.

28. Drew, *Portrait of an Election,* pp. 269–270; Cannon, *Reagan,* pp. 274–279.

29. Cannon, *Reagan,* pp. 280–285, 295–298.

30. White, *America in Search of Itself,* pp. 412–416. On voter alienation, see Walter Dean Burnham, *The Current Crisis in American Politics* (New York: Oxford University Press, 1983).

3. Symbolic Victories

1. *Time,* Jan. 19, 1981, pp. 60–63; *New York Times,* Jan. 21, 1981, p. A1.
2. On symbolic politics, see Richard Hofstadter, *The Paranoid Style in American Politics* (New York: Alfred A. Knopf, 1965), pp. 86–87.
3. *New York Times,* Feb. 6, 1981, p. A12.
4. Ibid., Feb. 19, 1981, p. B8.
5. *Time,* Mar. 9, 1981, pp. 13–14, which cites the poll showing 66 percent support. For the rest see *Time,* Apr. 20, 1981, pp. 16–18; *Newsweek,* May 11, 1981, pp. 22–24.
6. *Newsweek,* May 18, 1981, pp. 38–40; *Time,* July 6, 1981, pp. 6–7.
7. *Newsweek,* May 25, 1981, pp. 41–42; June 15, 1981, pp. 26–27; *Time,* July 20, 1981, p. 23.
8. *Time,* Aug. 10, 1981, pp. 12–16; Lou Cannon, *Reagan* (New York: G. P. Putnam's Sons, 1982), p. 335.
9. See the *New York Times* forecast on Feb. 19, 1981, pp. B6–7. Galbraith's comment is in Cannon, *Reagan,* p. 338.
10. *Time,* July 13, 1981, pp. 8–10; Aug. 10, 1981, p. 15; Cannon, *Reagan,* pp. 335–336; *Los Angeles Times,* May 9, 1982, p. 1; May 25, II, 5.
11. *Time,* July 11, 1981, p. 13.
12. Ibid.
13. *Los Angeles Times,* Sept. 28, 1981, p. 1.
14. *New Republic,* Mar. 24, 1982, pp. 9–10.
15. James Fallows, "Entitlements," *Atlantic,* Nov. 1982, pp. 51–59. *Newsweek,* May 25, 1981, pp. 40–41; June 1, 1981, pp. 22–23.
16. Cannon, *Reagan,* pp. 336–337.
17. Ronald Brownstein and Nina Easton, *Reagan's Ruling Class: Portraits of the President's Top 100 Officials* (Washington, D.C.: The Presidential Accountability Group, 1982), pp. vii–xvii.
18. Ibid., pp. 643–647, 663–664. Cannon, *Reagan,* pp. 381, 306–307.
19. Brownstein and Easton, *Reagan's Ruling Class,* pp. 650–653. Cannon, *Reagan,* pp. 376–379, 372, 394, 239.
20. Brownstein and Easton, *Reagan's Ruling Class,* pp. 647–650, 666. Cannon, *Reagan,* pp. 307, 322, 332, 345–347, 379–382.
21. Cannon, *Reagan,* p. 310. Brownstein and Easton, *Reagan's Ruling Class,* pp. 349–355.
22. Brownstein and Easton, *Reagan's Ruling Class,* pp. 369–370, 660–662. *Los Angeles Times,* May 25, 1983, p. 1.

23. Samuel Eliot Morison, Henry Steele Commager, William E. Leuchten-
    burg, *A Concise History of the American Republic* (New York: Oxford
    University Press, 1977), p. 734. Cannon, *Reagan,* p. 379. Brownstein
    and Easton, *Reagan's Ruling Class,* pp. 357–358. *Los Angeles Times,* June
    8, 1983, p. 1; June 15, 1983, p. 1; July 13, 1983, p. 15.

24. *Time,* July 20, 1981, pp. 18–19; Sept. 21, 1981, p. 12. Cannon, *Reagan,*
    pp. 313–316. *Los Angeles Times,* June 16, 1983, p. 1.

25. *Time,* Aug. 23, 1982, pp. 26–27. Cannon, *Reagan,* p. 358. Brownstein
    and Easton, *Reagan's Ruling Class,* pp. 107–110.

26. Cannon, *Reagan,* pp. 359–370. *Time,* Aug. 23, 1982, p. 27. *Los Angeles
    Times,* Mar. 29, 1983, p. 1.

27. Brownstein and Easton, *Reagan's Ruling Class,* pp. 205–216. *Los Angeles
    Times,* Mar. 10, 1983, p. 1; Mar. 11, 1983, p. 1; Mar. 22, 1983, p. 1.

28. Brownstein and Easton, *Reagan's Ruling Class,* pp. 270–275. *Los Angeles
    Times,* June 10, 1983, p. 6; June 11, 1983, p. 3.

29. Brownstein and Easton, *Reagan's Ruling Class,* pp. 247–254. American
    Hospital Association, "Health Care: What Happens to People When
    Government Cuts Back," October 1982, pp. i–ii, iv, xiii. *Los Angeles
    Times,* June 8, 1983, p. 1.

30. John L. Palmer and Isabel V. Sawhill, eds., *The Reagan Experiment: An
    Examination of Economic and Social Policies under the Reagan Administra-
    tion* (Washington, D.C.: Urban Institute Press, 1982), pp. 142–144.
    Brownstein and Easton, *Reagan's Ruling Class,* pp. 292, 294–295.

31. *Time,* Aug. 17, 1981, pp. 14–20. Brownstein and Easton, *Reagan's Rul-
    ing Class,* pp. 292–293.

32. Brownstein and Easton, *Reagan's Ruling Class,* pp. 144–149, 225–230,
    236–242. Palmer and Sawhill, *Reagan Experiment,* pp. 152–153.

4. Real Defeats

1. *Los Angeles Times,* Dec. 14, 1982, II, 11.

2. John L. Palmer and Isabel V. Sawhill, eds., *The Reagan Experiment: An
   Examination of Economic and Social Policies under the Reagan Administration* (Washington, D.C.: Urban Institute Press, 1982), pp. 31–32,
   34–42.

3. Ibid., pp. 496, n. 18, 42–46. *Time,* Sept. 7, 1981, pp. 52–53.

4. William Greider, *The Education of David Stockman and Other Americans*
   (New York: E. P. Dutton, 1982), pp. ix–x, xvi, 14–27, 33–41, 47–51.
   The book is an expansion of Greider's article in *The Atlantic,* Novem-
   ber 1981.

5. Greider, *Education of David Stockman,* pp. 87–92, 139–159. Ronald Brownstein and Nina Easton, *Reagan's Ruling Class: Portraits of the President's Top 100 Officials* (Washington, D.C.: Presidential Accountability Group, 1982), pp. 53–55.

6. Robert Lekachman, *Greed Is Not Enough: Reaganomics* (New York: Pantheon Books, 1982), pp. 46–47.

7. *Los Angeles Times,* Jan. 21, 1982, p. 2.

8. *The New Republic,* Jan. 6 and 13, 1982, pp. 7–8; Jan. 20, 1982, pp. 10–13; Feb. 10. 1982, pp. 4–7; Feb. 24, 1982, pp. 13–14. *Time,* Mar. 8, 1982, pp. 17, 74–83.

9. Emma Rothschild, "The Philosophy of Reaganism," *New York Review of Books,* Apr. 15, 1982, pp. 19–26. *Los Angeles Times,* Mar. 14, 1982, IV, 2.

10. *New York Times,* Mar. 13, 1982, p. 11. *Los Angeles Times,* Mar. 18, 1982, II, 11; Apr. 4, 1982, p. 7.

11. *Los Angeles Times,* Mar. 18, 1982, p. 7; Apr. 4, 1982, p. 6.

12. Ibid., Mar. 14, 1982, IV, 1–2. Rothschild, "Philosophy of Reaganism," p. 25. James Tobin, "Sleight of Mind," *The New Republic,* Mar. 21, 1982, pp. 13–16. *Los Angeles Times,* Mar. 25, 1983, p. 1.

13. *Los Angeles Times,* June 5, 1982, p. 1; June 13, 1982, p. 1; July 6, 1982, IV, 3; July 14, 1982, p. 1; July 16, 1982, p. 1. *The Nation's Health: The Official Newspaper of the American Public Health Association,* July 1982, p. 1.

14. *Los Angeles Times,* Apr. 11, 1982, V, 3; Apr. 21, 1982, p. 1; Apr. 22, 1982, p. 4; Apr. 25, 1982, V, 1; Apr. 29, 1982, p. 1; Apr. 30, 1982, p. 1; May 17, 1982, II, 5.

15. Ibid., May 11, 1982, p. 1.

16. Ibid., May 26, 1982, p. 1; June 18, 1982, p. 1; June 24, 1982, p. 1.

17. Ibid., July 1, 1982, p. 1; July 19, 1982, p. 1; July 20, 1982, p. 1.

18. Ibid., July 20, 1982, p. 1; July 26, 1982, p. 1; July 27, 1982, II, 5.

19. Ibid., July 29, 1982, p. 1; Aug. 7, 1982, p. 1; Aug. 8, 1982, p. 1.

20. Ibid., Aug. 6, 1982, p. 1; Aug. 12, 1982, p. 1; Aug. 14, 1982, p. 1; Aug. 17, 1982, p. 1; Aug. 20, 1982, p. 1; Aug. 23, 1982, II, 7. On the issue of constitutionality, see *Los Angeles Times,* July 29, 1982, p. 1.

21. Ibid., July 31, 1982, p. 1; Aug. 14, 1982, p. 1; Aug. 27, 1982, p. 1.

22. Ibid., Sept. 5, 1982, p. 1; Sept. 10, 1982, p. 1; Sept. 11, 1982, p. 1.

23. Ibid., Sept. 6, 1982, p. 1; Sept. 16, 1982, p. 1; Sept. 22, 1982, p. 1; Oct. 1, 1982, p. 1; Oct. 9, 1982, p. 1; Oct. 15, 1982, p. 4; Oct. 21, 1982, p. 1;

Oct. 27, 1982, p. 1; Oct. 29, 1982, p. 8. Also see *Time,* Sept. 27, 1982, pp. 44–46.

24. *Los Angeles Times,* Oct. 1, 1982, p. 1; Oct. 28, 1982, p. 7. Lester Thurow, "Reagan's Self-Defeat," *New York Review of Books,* p. 8.

25. *Los Angeles Times,* Sept. 29, 1982, p. 1; Sept. 30, 1982, p. 11; Oct. 5, 1982, p. 16; Oct. 8, 1982, p. 1.

26. Ibid., Oct. 10, 1982, IV, 4; Oct. 14, 1982, p. 1; Oct. 17, 1982, IV, 3.

27. Ibid., Nov. 3, 1982, p. 1; Nov. 4, 1982, pp. 1 and 15; Nov. 4, 1982, II, 11; Nov. 5, 1982, p. 1. Also see *Time,* Oct. 25, 1982, pp. 18–19; Nov. 15, 1982, pp. 22–24, 29–32.

28. *Los Angeles Times,* Nov. 6, 1982, p. 1; Dec. 4, 1982, p. 1; Dec. 16, 1982, p. 4; Dec. 26, 1982, p. 1; Jan. 8, 1982, p. 1. *International Herald Tribune,* Dec. 16, 1982, p. 2.

29. *Los Angeles Times,* Nov. 9, 1982, p. 1; Nov. 22, 1982, p. 1; Jan. 5, 1983, p. 1; Nov. 17, 1982, p. 1; Jan. 2, 1983, V, 1–2; Jan. 7, 1983, p. 1, Jan. 15, 1983, p. 1. *International Herald Tribune,* Dec. 7, 1982, p. 7; Dec. 16, 1982, p. 11; Dec. 18–19, 1982, p. 7.

30. *Los Angeles Times,* Nov. 12, 1982, p. 20; Nov. 17, 1982, p. 15; Dec. 15, 1982, p. 1; Dec. 20, 1982, p. 1; Dec. 30, 1982, p. 6.

31. Ibid., Nov. 17, 1982, p. 14; Nov. 25, 1982, p. 1; Nov. 28, 1982, p. 18; Nov. 30, 1982, p. 1; Dec. 21, 1982, p. 1; Dec. 23, 1982, p. 1.

32. *Time,* Dec. 13, 1982, pp. 6–11. Also see a similar account in *Los Angeles Times,* Jan. 9, 1983, p. 1. For the jobs bill, see *Los Angeles Times,* Mar. 25, 1983, p. 1.

33. *Los Angeles Times,* Mar. 3, 1983, p. 1; Mar. 5, 1983, p. 1; Mar. 26, 1983, p. 1; Apr. 23, 1983, p. 1; Apr. 30, 1983, p. 1; May 7, 1983, p. 1; May 14, 1983, p. 1; May 25, 1983, p. 1; June 21, 1983, p. 1; June 22, 1983, p. 1; June 23, 1983, IV, 1.

34. Ibid., Mar. 11, 1983, IV, 1; May 18, 1983, II, 7; June 14, 1983, IV, 3; June 18, 1983, IV, 1; June 25, 1983, IV, 1, Aug. 6, 1983, p. 1. *Newsweek,* May 30, 1983, pp. 22–23, 25. Robert Lekachman, "A Keynes for All Seasons," *The New Republic,* June 20, 1983, pp. 21–25.

35. *Washington Post,* Feb. 17, 1982, p. A1; July 13, 1982, p. A2. *Los Angeles Times,* May 19, 1982, p. 23.

36. *Los Angeles Times,* July 1, 1982, p. 5; Aug. 8, 1982, p. 1; Dec. 16, 1982, p. 12; Jan. 15, 1983, p. 14.

37. Ibid., Nov. 30, 1982, p. 1; June 12, 1983, p. 7; June 13, 1983, p. 4; June 14, 1983, p. 4; June 7, 1983, IV, 1; June 23, 1983, p. 6.

38. Ibid., Aug. 4, 1982, p. 10.

39. Ibid., Sept. 10, 1982, p. 11.

40. Ibid., Sept. 24, 1982, p. 4. *Time,* Dec. 13, 1982, p. 10.

5. COLD WAR CERTAINTIES

1. *New York Times,* May 18, 1981, II, 7. *Los Angeles Times,* Dec. 6, 1982, II, 9.

2. The quotes are in Robert Scheer, *With Enough Shovels: Reagan, Bush and Nuclear War* (New York: Random House, 1982), pp. 42, 148–149; and *New York Times,* Jan. 30, 1981, p. A10.

3. *New York Times,* May 18, 1981, II, 7; May 28, 1981, IV, 20.

4. Ibid., June 18, 1982, p. A16.

5. Scheer, *With Enough Shovels,* p. 260.

6. *New York Times,* May 28, 1981, IV, 20.

7. Hofstadter, *The Paranoid Style in American Politics* (New York: Alfred A. Knopf, 1965), pp. 42–92, in general, and 58–61, 68–82, in particular. For the inaugural speech, see *New York Times,* Jan. 21, 1981, p. A1. On the point about renewed deference from other nations, see Ronald Steel, "Cold War, Cold Comfort," *The New Republic,* Apr. 11, 1981, p. 17.

8. Ronald Brownstein and Nina Easton, *Reagan's Ruling Class: Portraits of the President's Top 100 Officials* (Washington, D.C.: Presidential Accountability Group, 1982), pp. 433–438. *Time,* Apr. 27, 1981, p. 28.

9. Brownstein and Easton, *Reagan's Ruling Class,* pp. 439–449, 484–504. *Time,* Mar. 16, 1981, p. 32. Scheer, *With Enough Shovels,* pp. 5, 13–14, 37–40, 95–97, 129.

10. *Time,* Mar. 16, 1981, pp. 12–25. Brownstein and Easton, *Reagan's Ruling Class,* pp. 539–546.

11. *Time,* July 5, 1982, pp. 8–18. Scheer, *With Enough Shovels,* pp. 36, 40, 144–147. *Los Angeles Times,* June 26, 1982, p. 1.

12. Brownstein and Easton, *Reagan's Ruling Class,* pp. 725–726. *Time,* Apr. 6, 1981, pp. 8–11. Lou Cannon, *Reagan* (New York: G. P. Putnam's Sons, 1982), pp. 397–400.

13. Brownstein and Easton, *Reagan's Ruling Class,* pp. 654–657. Cannon, *Reagan,* pp. 396–401. *Los Angeles Times,* June 27, 1983, p. 12.

14. Brownstein and Easton, *Reagan's Ruling Class,* pp. 598–606.

15. *The New Republic,* Apr. 11, 1981, p. 15. *Time,* Mar. 16, 1981, p. 26. Also see *Los Angeles Times,* Mar. 27, 1983, p. 1.

16. *Time,* Mar. 16, 1981, pp. 26 and 31; July 6, 1981, p. 8.

17. Ibid., July 27, 1981, pp. 6–11. Compare James Fallows, "The Great Defense Deception," *New York Review of Books,* May 28, 1981, pp. 15–19.

18. Lester Thurow, "How to Wreck the Economy," *New York Review of Books,* May 14, 1981, pp. 3, 6, 8. Compare Charles L. Schultze, "Economic Effects of the Defense Budget," *The Brookings Bulletin,* Fall 1981, pp. 1–5.

19. *New York Times,* Aug. 14, 1981, p. A1.

20. *Time,* Aug. 24, 1981, pp. 30–31.

21. Ibid., August 31, 1981, p. 16; Oct. 12, 1981, pp. 18–19. Scheer, *With Enough Shovels,* pp. 6, 131. Also see Theodore White, "Weinberger on the Ramparts," *New York Times Magazine,* Feb. 6, 1983, pp. 17–18.

22. Scheer, *With Enough Shovels,* p. 18.

23. Ibid., pp. 19–26.

24. *Time,* Aug. 17, 1982, p. 15.

25. George Kennan, "A Modest Proposal," *New York Review of Books,* July 16, 1981, pp. 14, 16.

26. Hans A. Bethe, "The Inferiority Complex," *New York Review of Books,* June 10, 1982, p. 3. Also see *Los Angeles Times,* Apr. 11, 1982, V, 1.

27. *Los Angeles Times,* Apr. 11, 1982, V, 1; Oct. 25, 1982, II, 5.

28. George Kennan, "On Nuclear War," *New York Review of Books,* Jan. 21, 1982, pp. 8, 10, 12. "Advice from Admiral Rickover," *New York Review of Books,* Mar. 18, 1982, p. 14.

29. *Los Angeles Times,* Mar. 21, 1982, p. 1; June 13, 1982, p. 1. *Time,* Apr. 12, 1982, pp. 12–14. Kennan, "On Nuclear War," p. 8.

30. *Los Angeles Times,* Mar. 21, 1982, p. 21; Apr. 18, 1982, IV, 1.

31. See U.S. Dept. of State, Bureau of Public Affairs, "Current Policy No. 346," for the president's speech. *Los Angeles Times,* Apr. 1, 1982, p. 1; Apr. 18, 1982, p. 1.

32. See U.S. Dept. of State, Bureau of Public Affairs, "Current Policy No. 387," for the president's speech. Also see *Los Angeles Times,* May 10, 1982, p. 1; May 19, 1982, p. 1.

33. See U.S. Dept. of State, Bureau of Public Affairs, "Current Policy No. 399" and "No. 400" for the president's speeches. Also see *Los Angeles Times,* June 10, 1982, p. 1; June 12, 1982, p. 1.

34. *Los Angeles Times,* June 4, 1982, p. 5. Weinberger's letter is in *New York Review of Books,* Nov. 4, 1982, p. 27.

35. The quotes, except for the one from General Jones, which is in Scheer, *With Enough Shovels,* p. 9, are all in *New York Times,* May 30, 1982, p. A1; June 10, 1982, pp. A30–31; July 22, 1982, p. A6.

36. Theodore Draper, "Dear Mr. Weinberger: An Open Reply to an Open Letter," *New York Review of Books,* Nov. 4, 1982, pp. 26–31.

37. *Los Angeles Times,* Aug. 4, 1982, p. 1; Sept. 22, 1982, p. 20; Mar. 20, 1983, p. 1. Emma Rothschild, "The Delusions of Deterrence," *New York Review of Books,* Apr. 14, 1983, p. 40.

38. *Los Angeles Times,* Oct. 3, 1982, p. 10; Oct. 28, 1982, p. 1; Oct. 29, 1982, p. 1; Nov. 12, 1982, p. 20; Oct. 31, 1982, IV, 5.

39. Ibid., Nov. 23, 1982, p. 1; Dec. 7, 1982, p. 1; Dec. 11, 1982, p. 1. White, *New York Times Magazine,* Feb. 6, 1983, p. 24. *Los Angeles Times,* Jan. 18, 1983, p. 5; Jan. 31, 1983, p. 1; Feb. 2, 1983, p. 1; Feb. 9, 1983, p. 6; Apr. 9, 1983, p. 1; June 24, 1983, p. 1.

40. *Los Angeles Times,* Jan. 13, 1983, p. 1; Jan. 14, 1983, pp. 1, 10–11. *Time,* Jan. 24, 1983, pp. 16–18. *The New Republic,* Feb. 7, 1983, pp. 7–8. Adelman's appointment was confirmed after a sharp debate in the U.S. Senate: see *Los Angeles Times,* Apr. 15, 1983.

41. *Los Angeles Times,* Mar. 31, 1983, p. 1; Apr. 3, 1983, p. 1.

42. *New York Times,* Mar. 24, 1983, p. 1; *Los Angeles Times,* Mar. 25, 1983, p. 1. Also see *Time,* Apr. 18, 1983, pp. 16–29.

43. *Los Angeles Times,* Apr. 12, 1983, p. 1; Apr. 20, 1983, p. 1; May 4, 1983, p. 1; May 26, 1983, p. 1; June 2, 1983, p. 1; June 9, 1983, p. 1; II, 7; June 10, 1983, p. 12. *The New Republic,* May 9, 1983, pp. 7–10.

6. Cold War Confusions

1. Stanley Hoffmann, "The New Orthodoxy," *New York Review of Books,* Apr. 16, 1981, p. 22. *Los Angeles Times,* Oct. 3, 1982, IV, 5. *Time,* Dec. 13, 1982, p. 12.

2. Hoffmann, "New Orthodoxy," p. 22. Ronald Steel, "Cold War, Cold Comfort," *The New Republic,* Apr. 11, 1981, pp. 15–17.

3. Paul E. Sigmund, "Latin America: Change or Continuity?" *Foreign Affairs: America and the World, 1981,* pp. 632–633. Ronald Steel, "Salvadoran Quagmire," *The New Republic,* Mar. 14, 1981, pp. 15–17. Tom J. Farer, "Reagan's Latin America," *New York Review of Books,* Mar. 19, 1981, pp. 10, 12.

4. *Time,* Mar. 2, 1981, p. 30; Mar. 16, 1981, pp. 14–15.

5. Sigmund, "Latin America," p. 633. *Newsweek,* June 22, 1981, p. 55.

6. Sigmund, "Latin America," pp. 634–635.

7. Ibid., p. 637. Steel, "Salvadoran Quagmire," p. 17.

8. Sigmund, "Latin America," pp. 636–637. *Time,* Apr. 27, 1981, p. 27.

9. *Time,* Mar. 9, 1981, pp. 8, 25; Mar. 16, 1981, p. 14. William G. Hyland, "U.S.-Soviet Relations: The Long Road Back," *Foreign Affairs: America and the World, 1981,* pp. 527–528.

10. Hyland, "U.S.-Soviet Relations," pp. 529, 542–543, 548.

11. Flora Lewis, "Alarm Bells in the West," *Foreign Affairs: America and the World, 1981,* pp. 551–552, 556–557.

12. John C. Campbell, "The Middle East: A House of Containment Built on Shifting Sands," *Foreign Affairs: America and the World, 1981,* pp. 596–598, 623–625.

13. *Time,* Apr. 20, 1981, pp. 18–19.

14. *Newsweek,* May 4, 1981, p. 22; June 22, 1981, pp. 26–29.

15. *Time,* July 6, 1981, pp. 8–9; Aug. 17, 1981, pp. 25–26; Sept. 7, 1981, pp. 10–11; Oct. 19, 1981, p. 34.

16. Ibid., Oct. 19, 1981, p. 41; Oct. 26, 1981, p. 21. Campbell, "Middle East," pp. 608–610.

17. Campbell, "Middle East," pp. 611–619.

18. *New York Times,* Jan. 22, 1982, pp. A1, A8. Hoffmann is quoted in Alan Gartner, Colin Greer, and Frank Reissman, eds., *What Reagan Is Doing to Us* (New York: Harper & Row, 1982), p. 261.

19. Richard H. Solomon, "East Asia and the Great Power Coalitions," *Foreign Affairs: America and the World, 1981,* pp. 687, 694–695.

20. *Time,* Mar. 16, 1981, p. 15; July 6, 1981, p. 8. *Newsweek,* June 29, 1981, pp. 18–19. Solomon, "East Asia," pp. 695–701.

21. *Los Angeles Times,* May 30, 1982, p. 1.

22. For the president's speech, see U.S. Dept. of State, Bureau of Public Affairs, "Current Policy No. 370," Feb. 24, 1982. Alan Riding, "The Central American Quagmire," *Foreign Affairs: America and the World, 1982,* pp. 641–643, 655–656.

23. U.S. Dept. of State, Bureau of Public Affairs, "Current Policy No. 370," Feb. 24, 1982. Also see *Time,* Mar. 8, 1982, pp. 14–16.

24. *Los Angeles Times,* Mar. 7, 1982, V, 5; Mar. 15, 1982, II, 9; Mar. 1, 1983, pp. 1, 6. Riding, "Central American Quagmire," pp. 656–657.

25. *Los Angeles Times,* Feb. 28, 1983, II, 4, Apr. 21, 1983, p. 1; Apr. 27, 1983, p. 1; Apr. 28, 1983, p. 1. Riding, "Central American Quagmire," pp. 658–659.

26. *Los Angeles Times,* Apr. 29, 1983, p. 1; Apr. 30, 1983, p. 1; May 28, 1983, p. 1; May 30, 1983, II, 4; June 2, 1983, II, 7; June 3, 1983, p. 1; June 5, 1983, IV, 1; June 10, 1983, II, 7; June 12, 1983, IV, 1; June 22, 1983, II, 5; July 24, 1983, IV, 1.

27. Susan Kaufman Purcell, "War and Debt in South America," *Foreign Affairs: America and the World, 1982,* pp. 660–667.

28. *Los Angeles Times,* Oct. 26, 1982, p. 1; Dec. 1, 1982, p. 1; Dec. 2, 1982, pp. 1, 14.

29. Ibid., Dec. 4, 1982, p. 1; Dec. 5, 1982, p. 1; Dec. 6, 1982, p. 1; Dec. 7, 1982, II, 4. *New York Times,* Dec. 6, 1982, pp. A1, A23. Purcell, "War and Debt in South America," pp. 673–674.

30. Seweryn Bialer and Joan Afferica, "Reagan and Russia," *Foreign Affairs* 61 (Winter 1982–83), p. 249. *Los Angeles Times,* Jan. 19, 1982, pp. 1, 8.

31. Josef Joffe, "Europe and America: The Politics of Resentment," *Foreign Affairs: America and the World, 1982,* pp. 570–572, 577.

32. *Los Angeles Times,* June 6, 1982, p. 1; June 7, 1982, p. 1; June 19, 1982, p. 1. Joffe, "Europe and America," pp. 573–574.

33. *Los Angeles Times,* July 23, 1982, p. 1; Aug. 2, 1982, II, 5. *Time,* Aug. 9, 1982, p. 9. Michel Tatu, "U.S.-Soviet Relations: A Turning Point?" *Foreign Affairs: America and the World, 1982,* pp. 598–602.

34. *Los Angeles Times,* Nov. 14, 1982, p. 1; Nov. 16, 1982, p. 1; May 31, 1983, p. 1. Joffe, "Europe and America," pp. 574–575.

35. See Philip Geyelin's column, *Los Angeles Times,* Jan. 20, 1983, II, 11.

36. Joseph J. Sisco, "Middle East: Progress or Lost Opportunity?" *Foreign Affairs: America and the World, 1982,* pp. 617–618, 636–637, 640.

37. Ibid., pp. 618, 620–623. *Los Angeles Times,* June 13, 1982, V, 1–2.

38. For Kissinger's viewpoint, see *Los Angeles Times,* June 18, 1982, II, 7. For the rest, see *Washington Post,* Sept. 2, 1982, pp. A1, A8, A16, A18.

39. *Los Angeles Times,* Sept. 3, 1982, p. 1; Sept. 12, 1982, IV, 1; Sept. 15, 1982, p. 1; Feb. 10, 1983, p. 14; Apr. 11, 1983, p. 1; Apr. 12, 1983, p. 1; Apr. 23, 1983, p. 1; Apr. 26, 1983, p. 1; May 1, 1983, IV, 1; May 7, 1983, p. 1; May 14, 1983, p. 1; May 18, 1983, p. 1. Sisco, "Middle East," pp. 624–625, 628–636.

40. Robert A. Manning, "Shanghai II," *The New Republic,* Sept. 13, 1982, pp. 15–18. Michel Oksenberg, "A Decade of Sino-American Relations," *Foreign Affairs* 61 (Fall 1982), pp. 191–194.

41. *Los Angeles Times,* Sept. 24, 1982, p. 12; Jan. 27, 1983, p. 1; Feb. 7, 1983, p. 1; Feb. 20, 1983, IV, 2; Feb. 26, 1983, p. 5; Feb. 27, 1983, p. 11.

42. Oksenberg, "Decade of Sino-American Relations," p. 193. *Los Angeles Times,* Sept. 5, 1982, p. 1; Oct. 5, 1982, p. 6; Oct. 23, 1982, p. 9; Mar. 27, 1983, IV, 1; Apr. 8, 1983, p. 1; May 3, 1983, p. 8; May 23, 1983, p. 1.

43. *Los Angeles Times,* Mar. 9, 1983, p. 6; Mar. 10, 1983, p. 7.

44. *New York Times,* Feb. 20, 1983, IV, 19. *Los Angeles Times,* Feb. 28, 1983, II, 5; July 4, 1983, II, 5.

Index